THE BLUE
AND
BROWN BOOKS

hARPER TORCHBOOKS

A reference-list of Harper Torchbooks, classified
by subjects, is printed at the end of this volume.

PRELIMINARY STUDIES FOR
THE "PHILOSOPHICAL INVESTIGATIONS"

Generally known as

THE BLUE AND BROWN BOOKS

By

LUDWIG WITTGENSTEIN

HARPER TORCHBOOKS ❧ The Academy Library
Harper & Row, Publishers, New York

THE BLUE AND BROWN BOOKS

Note on the Second Edition (1960): There are a few alterations, taken from a text of the Blue Book in the possession of Mr. P. Sraffa. With the exception of changes on pp. 1 and 17 they make no difference to the sense, being mostly improvements in punctuation or grammar. We rejected such changes as were no improvements.

CONTENTS

PREFACE   vii

THE BLUE BOOK   1

THE BROWN BOOK   75

PREFACE

Wittgenstein dictated the "Blue Book" (though he did not call it that) to his class in Cambridge during the session 1933–34, and he had stencilled copies made. He dictated the "Brown Book" to two of his pupils (Francis Skinner and Alice Ambrose) during 1934–35. He had only three typed copies made of this, and he showed them only to very close friends and pupils. But people who borrowed them made their own copies, and there was a trade in them. If Wittgenstein had named these dictations, he might have called them "Philosophical Remarks" or "Philosophical Investigations". But the first lot was bound in blue wrappers and the second in brown, and they were always spoken of that way.

He sent a copy of the Blue Book to Lord Russell later on, with a covering note.

Dear Russell,

Two years ago, or so, I promised to send you a manuscript of mine. Now the one I am sending you to-day isn't *that* manuscript. I'm still pottering about with it, and God knows whether I will ever publish it, or any of it. But two years ago I held some lectures in Cambridge and dictated some notes to my pupils so that they might have something to carry home with them, in their hands if not in their brains. And I had these notes duplicated. I have just been correcting misprints and other mistakes in some of the copies and the idea came into my mind whether you might not like to have a copy. So I'm sending you one. I don't wish to suggest that you should read the lectures; but *if* you should have nothing better to do and *if* you should get some mild enjoyment out of them I should be very pleased indeed. (I think it's very difficult to understand them, as so many points are just hinted at. They are meant only for the people who heard the lectures.) As I say, if you don't read them *it doesn't matter at all.*

Yours ever,
Ludwig Wittgenstein.

That was all the Blue Book was, though: a set of notes. The Brown Book was rather different, and for a time he thought of it as a draft of something he might publish. He started more than once to make revisions of a German version of it. The last was in August, 1936. He brought this, with some minor changes and insertions, to the beginning of the discussion of voluntary action—about page 154 in

vii

our text. Then he wrote, in heavy strokes, "Dieser ganze 'Versuch einer Umarbeitung' vom (Anfang) bis hierher ist *nichts wert*". ("This whole attempt at a revision, from the start right up to this point, is *worthless*.") That was when he began what we now have (with minor revisions) as the first part of the *Philosophical Investigations*.

I doubt if he would have published the Brown Book in English, whatever happened. And anyone who can read his German will see why. His English style is often clumsy and full of Germanisms. But we have left it that way, except in a very few cases where it marred the sense and the correction was obvious. What we are printing here are notes he gave to his pupils, and a draft for his own use; that is all.

Philosophy was a method of investigation, for Wittgenstein, but his conception of the method was changing. We can see this in the way he uses the notion of "language games", for instance. He used to introduce them in order to shake off the idea of a necessary form of language. At least that was one use he made of them, and one of the earliest. It is often useful to imagine different language games. At first he would sometimes write "different forms of language"—as though that were the same thing; though he corrected it in later versions, sometimes. In the Blue Book he speaks sometimes of imagining different language games, and sometimes of imagining different *notations*—as though that were what it amounted to. And it looks as though he had not distinguished clearly between being able to speak and understanding a notation.

He speaks of coming to understand what people mean by having someone explain the meanings of the words, for instance. As though "understanding" and "explaining" were somehow correlative. But in the Brown Book he emphasizes that learning a language game is something prior to that. And what is needed is not explanation but *training*—comparable with the training you would give an animal. This goes with the point he emphasizes in the *Investigations*, that being able to speak and understand what is said—knowing what it means—does not mean that you can *say* what it means; nor is that what you have learned. He says there too (*Investigations*, par. 32) that "Augustine describes the learning of human language as if the child came into a strange country and did not understand the language of the country; that is, as if it already had a language, only not this one". You might see whether the child knows French by asking him what the expressions mean. But that is not how you tell whether a child can speak. And it is not what he learns when he learns to speak.

When the Brown Book speaks of different language games as "systems of communication" (Systeme menschlicher Verständigung), these are not just different notations. And this introduces a notion of understanding, and of the relation of understanding and language, which does not come to the front in the Blue Book at all. In the Brown Book he is insisting, for example, that "understanding" is not one thing; it is as various as the language games themselves are. Which would be one reason for saying that when we do imagine different language games, we are not imagining parts or possible parts of any general system of language.

The Blue Book is less clear about that. On page 17 he says that "the study of language games is the study of primitive forms of language or primitive languages". But then he goes on, "If we want to study the problems of truth and falsehood, of the agreement and disagreement of propositions with reality, of the nature of assertion, assumption and question, we shall with great advantage look at primitive forms of language in which these forms of thinking appear without the confusing background of highly complicated processes of thought. When we look at such simple forms of language, the mental mist which seems to enshroud our ordinary use of language disappears. We see activities, reactions, which are clear-cut and transparent. On the other hand we recognize in these simple processes forms of language not separated by a break from our more complicated ones. We see that we can build up the complicated forms from the primitive ones by gradually adding new forms."

That almost makes it look as though we were trying to give something like an analysis of our ordinary language. As though we wanted to discover something that goes on in our language as we speak it, but which we cannot see until we take this method of getting through the mist that enshrouds it. And as if "the nature of assertion, assumption and question" were the same there; we have just found a way of making it transparent. Whereas the Brown Book is denying that. That is why he insists in the Brown Book (p. 81) that he is "not regarding the language games which we describe as incomplete parts of a language, but as languages complete in themselves". So that, for instance, certain grammatical functions in one language would not have any counterpart in another at all. And "agreement or disagreement with reality" would be something different in the different languages—so that the study of it in that language might not show you much about what it is in this one. That is why he asks in the

Brown Book whether "Brick" means the same in the primitive language as it does in ours; this goes with his contention that the simpler
language is not an incomplete form of the more complicated one.
That discussion of whether we have to do here with an elliptical
sentence is an important part of his account of what different language
games are. But there is not even an anticipation of it in the Blue Book.

In one of Wittgenstein's note-books there is a remark about language
games, which he must have written at the beginning of 1934. I suspect
it is later than the one I have quoted from page 17; anyway, it is
different. "Wenn ich bestimmte einfache Sprachspiele beschreibe, so
geschieht es nicht, um mit ihnen nach und nach die Vorgänge der
ausgebildeten Sprache — oder des Denkens — aufzubauen, was nur
zu Ungerechtigkeiten führt (Nicod und Russell), — sondern ich stelle
die Spiele als solche hin, und lasse sie ihre aufklärende Wirkung auf
die besonderen Probleme ausstrahlen." ("When I describe certain
simple language games, this is not in order to construct from them
gradually the processes of our developed language—or of thinking—
which only leads to injustices (Nicod and Russell). I simply set forth
the games as what they are, and let them shed their light on the particular problems.")

I think that would be a good description of the method in the first
part of the Brown Book. But it also points to the big difference
between the Brown Book and the *Investigations*.

In the Brown Book the account of the different language games is
not directly a discussion of particular philosophical problems, although
it is intended to throw light on them. It throws light on various
aspects of language, especially—aspects to which we are often blinded
just by the tendencies that find their sharpest expression in the problems of philosophy. And in this way the discussion does suggest
where it is that the difficulties arise which give birth to those problems.

For instance, in what he says about "can", and the connection
between this and "seeing what is common", he is raising the question
of what it is that you learn when you learn the language; or of what
you know when you know what something means. But he is also
raising the question of what it would mean to ask how the language
can be developed—"Is that still something that has sense? Are you
still speaking now, or is it gibberish?" And this may lead on to the
question of "What can be said", or again of "How we should know
it was a proposition"; or what a proposition is, or what language is.
The way in which he describes the language games here is intended

to show that one *need* not be led into asking those questions, and that
it would be a misunderstanding if one were. But the trouble is that
we are left wondering why people constantly *are*. And in this the
Investigations is different.

The language games there (in the *Investigations*) are not stages in the
exposition of a more complicated language, any more than they are in
the Brown Book; less so, if anything. But they are stages in a discussion
leading up to the "big question" of what language is (in par. 65).

He brings them in—in the *Investigations* and in the Brown Book
too—to throw light on the question about the relation of words and
what they stand for. But in the *Investigations* he is concerned with "the
philosophical conception of meaning" which we find in Augustine,
and he shows that this is the expression of a tendency which comes out
most plainly in that theory of logically proper names which holds that
the only *real* names are the demonstratives *this* and *that*. He calls this
"a tendency to sublime the logic of our language" (die Logik unserer
Sprache zu sublimieren) (par. 38)—partly because, in comparison
with the logically proper names, "anything else we might call a name
was one only in an inexact, approximate sense". It is this tendency
which leads people to talk about the ultimate nature of language, or
the logically correct grammar. But why should people fall into it?
There is no simple answer, but Wittgenstein begins an answer here
by going on to discuss the notions of "simple" and "complex" and
the idea of logical analysis. (He does not do this in the Brown Book
at all; and if all he wanted were to throw light on the functioning of
language, there would be no need to.)

The whole idea of a logical analysis of language, or the logical
analysis of propositions, is a queer and confused one. And in setting
forth his language games Wittgenstein was not trying to give any
analysis at all. If we call them "more primitive" or "simpler" languages,
that does not mean that they reveal anything like the elements which
a more complicated language must have. (Cf. *Investigations*, par. 64.)
They are different languages—not elements or aspects of "Language".
But then we may want to ask what there is about them that makes us
say that they *are* all languages. What makes anything a language,
anyway? And that is the "big question" (par. 65) about the nature
of language or the nature of the proposition, which has lain behind
the whole discussion up to this point.

We might even say that the discussion up to this point in the *Investigations* has been an attempt to bring out the sense of treating philosophical

problems by reference to language games at all. Or perhaps better: to show how the use of language games can make clear what a philosophical problem is.

In the Brown Book, on the other hand, he passes from examples of different sorts of naming to a discussion of various ways of "comparing with reality". This is still a discussion of the relations of words and what they stand for, no doubt. But he is not trying here to bring out the tendency behind that way of looking at words which has given trouble in philosophy.

In the *Investigations* he goes on then to a discussion of the relations of logic and language, but he does not do that in the Brown Book—although it is closely connected with what he says there. I mean especially what he says there about "can", and the connection of that with the idea of what can be said. ("When do we say that this is still language? When do we say it is a proposition?") For the temptation then is to think of a calculus, and of what can be said in it. But Wittgenstein would call that a misunderstanding of what a rule of language is, and of what using language is. When we speak as we generally do, we are not using precisely definable concepts, nor precise rules either. And the intelligibility is something different from intelligibility in a calculus.

It was because people thought of "what can be said" as "what is allowed in a calculus" ("For what other sense of 'allowed' is there?")—it was for that reason that logic was supposed to govern the *unity* of language: what belongs to language and what does not; what is intelligible and what is not; what is a proposition and what is not. In the Brown Book Wittgenstein is insisting that language does not have *that* kind of unity. Nor that kind of intelligibility. But he does not really discuss why people have wanted to suppose that it has.

You might think he had done that earlier, in the Blue Book, but I do not think he did. I do not think he sees the question about logic and language there which the Brown Book is certainly bringing out, even if it does not make quite clear what kind of difficulty it is. On page 25 of the Blue Book he says that "in general we don't use language according to strict rules—it hasn't been taught us by means of strict rules, either. *We*, in our discussions on the other hand, constantly compare language with a calculus proceeding according to exact rules." When he asks (at the bottom of the page) *why* we do this, he replies simply, "The answer is that the puzzles which we try to remove always spring from just this attitude towards language". And

you might wonder whether that *is* an answer. His point, as he puts it
on page 27, for instance, is that "the man who is philosophically
puzzled sees a law in the way a word is used, and, trying to apply this
law consistently, comes up against .... paradoxical results". And at
first that looks something like what he said later, in the *Investigations*,
about a tendency to sublime the logic of our language. But here in the
Blue Book he does not bring out what there is about the use of language
or the understanding of language that *leads* people to think of words in
that way. Suppose we say that it is because philosophers look on
language metaphysically. All right; but when we ask what makes
them do *that*, Wittgenstein answers in the Blue Book that it is because
of a craving for generality, and because "philosophers constantly see
the method of science before their eyes, and are irresistibly tempted
to ask and answer questions in the way science does" (p. 18). In
other words, he does not find the source of metaphysics in anything
specially connected with language. That is one very important point
here, and it means that he was not anything like as clear about the
character of philosophical puzzlement as he was when he wrote the
Investigations. But in any case, it is not that tendency—to ask and
answer questions in the way science does—or it is not primarily that,
which leads philosophers to think of an ideal language or of a logically
correct grammar when they are puzzled about language or about
understanding. That comes in a different way.

Wittgenstein is quite clear in the Blue Book that we do not use
language according to strict rules, and that we do not use words
according to laws like the laws that science speaks of. But he is not
quite clear about the notions of "knowing the meaning" or of "understanding"; and that means that he is still unclear about a great deal in
the notion of "following a rule" too. And for that reason he does not
altogether recognize the kind of confusions that there may be when
people say that knowing the language is knowing what *can* be said.

"What does the *possibility* of the meanings of our words depend on?"
That is what is behind the idea of meaning that we find in the theory
of logically proper names and of logical analysis. And it goes with
a question of what you learn when you learn the language; or of what
learning the language is. Wittgenstein makes it plain in the Blue
Book that words have the meanings we give them, and that it would
be a confusion to think of an investigation into their *real* meanings.
But he has not yet seen clearly the difference between learning a

language game and learning a notation. And for that reason he cannot
quite make out the character of the confusion he is opposing.

In other words, in the Blue Book Wittgenstein had not seen clearly
what the question about the requirements of language or the intelligibility of language is. That is why he can say, on page 28, that "ordinary
language is all right". Which is like saying "it is a language, all right".
And that seems to mean that it satisfies the requirements. But when
he speaks like that, he is himself in the sort of confusion that he later
brought out. And it seems to me to obscure the point of ideal languages—to obscure what those who spoke of them were trying to do—
if one speaks, as Wittgenstein does here, as though "making up ideal
languages" were what he was doing when he made up language games.
He would not have spoken that way later.

It may be this same unclarity, or something akin to it, that leads
Wittgenstein to speak more than once in the Blue Book of "the
calculus of language" (e.g. p. 42, top paragraph; or, better, p. 65, middle
paragraph and last line)—although he has also said that it is only in
very rare cases that we use language as a calculus. If you have not
distinguished between a language and a notation, you may hardly see
any difference between following a language and following a notation.
But in that case you may well be unclear about the difficulties in
connection with the relation between language and logic.

Those difficulties become much clearer in the Brown Book, even
though he does not explicitly refer to them there. We might say that
they are the principal theme of the *Investigations*.

For that is the theme that underlies the discussions of "seeing
something as something" as well as the earlier parts. And once again
we find that Wittgenstein in the *Investigations* is making these discussions
into an exposition of the philosophical difficulties, in a way that he
has not done in the Brown Book.

At one time Wittgenstein was interested in the question of what it
is to "recognize it as a proposition" (even though it may be entirely
unfamiliar), or to recognize something as language—to recognize that
that is something written there, for instance—independently of your
recognition of what it says. The second part of the Brown Book
bears on this. And it shows that when such "recognitions" are rightly
seen, they should not lead to the kinds of questions that philosophers
have asked. The analogies that he draws between understanding a
sentence and understanding a musical theme, for instance; or between
wanting to say that this sentence means something and wanting to

say that this colour pattern says something—show clearly that it is
not as though you were recognizing any *general* character (of intelligibility, perhaps) and that you ought to be able to tell us what that is,
any more than it would make sense for you to ask me what the colour
pattern does say.

But why *have* people wanted to speak of "meta-logic" in this connection, for instance? The Brown Book does something to explain that,
and hints at more. But there is something about the way in which we
use language, and in the connection of language and thinking—the
force of an argument, and the force of expressions generally—which
makes it seem as though recognizing it as a language were very
different even from recognizing it as a move in a game. (As though
understanding were something outside the signs; and as though to be
a language it needs something that does not appear in the system of
signs themselves.) And in the last sections of the *Investigations* he is
trying to take account of this.

He had spoken of "operating with signs". And someone might
say, "You make it look just like operating a mechanism; like any other
mechanism. And if that is all there is to it—just the mechanism—then
it is not a language." Well, there is no short answer to that. But it is
an important question. So is the question of what we mean by "thinking *with* signs", for instance. What is that? And is the reference to
making pencil strokes on paper really helpful?

Much of all this can be answered by emphasizing that speaking and
writing belong to intercourse with other people. The signs get their
life there, and that is why the language is not just a mechanism.

But the objection is that someone might do all that, make the signs
correctly in the "game" with other people and get along all right, even
if he were "meaning-blind". Wittgenstein used that expression in
analogy with "colour-blind" and "tone-deaf". If I say an ambiguous
word to you, like "board", for instance, I may ask you what meaning
you think of when you hear it, and you may say that you think of a
committee like the Coal Board, or perhaps you do not but think of
a plank. Well, could we not imagine someone who could make no
sense of such a question? If you just said a word to him like that, it
gave him no meaning. And yet he could "react with words" to the
sentences and other utterances he encountered, and to situations too,
and react correctly. Or can we *not* imagine that? Wittgenstein was
not sure, I think. If a man were "meaning-blind", would that make

any difference to his use of language? Or does the perception of
meaning fall outside the use of language?

There is something wrong about that last question; something
wrong about *asking* it. But it seems to show that there is still something unclear in our notion of "the use of language".

Or again, if we simply emphasize that signs belong to intercourse
with people, what are we going to say about the role of "insight" in
connection with mathematics and the discovery of proofs, for instance?

So long as there are such difficulties, people will still think that
there must be something like an interpretation. They will still think
that if it is language then it must mean something to *me*. And so on.
And for this reason—in order to try to understand the kinds of difficulties these are—it was necessary for Wittgenstein to go into the
whole complicated matter of "seeing something as something" in the
way he was doing.

And the method has to be somewhat different there. One cannot do
so much with language games.

Rush Rhees

March, 1958

THE BLUE BOOK

THE BLUE BOOK

WHAT is the meaning of a word?

Let us attack this question by asking, first, what is an explanation of the meaning of a word; what does the explanation of a word look like?

The way this question helps us is analogous to the way the question "how do we measure a length?" helps us to understand the problem "what is length?"

The questions "What is length?", "What is meaning?", "What is the number one?" etc., produce in us a mental cramp. We feel that we can't point to anything in reply to them and yet ought to point to something. (We are up against one of the great sources of philosophical bewilderment : a substantive makes us look for a thing that corresponds to it.)

Asking first "What's an explanation of meaning?" has two advantages. You in a sense bring the question "what is meaning?" down to earth. For, surely, to understand the meaning of "meaning" you ought also to understand the meaning of "explanation of meaning". Roughly: "let's ask what the explanation of meaning is, for whatever that explains will be the meaning." Studying the grammar of the expression "explanation of meaning" will teach you something about the grammar of the word "meaning" and will cure you of the temptation to look about you for some object which you might call "the meaning".

What one generally calls "explanations of the meaning of a word" can, *very roughly*, be divided into verbal and ostensive definitions. It will be seen later in what sense this division is only rough and provisional (and that it is, is an important point). The verbal definition, as it takes us from one verbal expression to another, in a sense gets us no further. In the ostensive definition however we seem to make a much more real step towards learning the meaning.

One difficulty which strikes us is that for many words in our language there do not seem to be ostensive definitions; e.g. for such words as "one", "number", "not", etc.

Question: Need the ostensive definition itself be understood?—Can't the ostensive definition be misunderstood?

If the definition explains the meaning of a word, surely it can't be essential that you should have heard the word before. It is the ostensive definition's business to *give* it a meaning. Let us then explain the word "tove" by pointing to a pencil and saying "this is tove". (Instead of "this is tove" I could here have said "this is called 'tove' ". I point this out to remove, once and for all, the idea that the words of the ostensive definition predicate something of the defined; the confusion between the sentence "this is red", attributing the colour red to something, and the ostensive definition "this is called 'red' ".) Now the ostensive definition "this is tove" can be interpreted in all sorts of ways. I will give a few such interpretations and use English words with well established usage. The definition then can be interpreted to mean:

> "This is a pencil",
> "This is round",
> "This is wood",
> "This is one",
> "This is hard", etc. etc.

One might object to this argument that all these interpretations presuppose another word-language. And this objection is significant if by "interpretation" we only mean "translation into a word-language".— Let me give some hints which might make this clearer. Let us ask ourselves what is our criterion when we say that someone has interpreted the ostensive definition in a particular way. Suppose I give to an Englishman the ostensive definition "this is what the Germans call 'Buch' ". Then, in the great majority of cases at any rate, the English word "book" will come into the Englishman's mind. We may say he has interpreted "Buch" to mean "book". The case will be different if e.g. we point to a thing which he has never seen before and say: "This is a banjo". Possibly the word "guitar" will then come into his mind, possibly no word at all but the image of a similar instrument, possibly nothing at all. Supposing then I give him the order "now pick a banjo from amongst these things." If he picks what we call a "banjo" we might say "he has given the word 'banjo' the correct interpretation"; if he picks some other instrument—"he has interpreted 'banjo' to mean 'string instrument' ".

We say "he has given the word 'banjo' this or that interpretation", and are inclined to assume a definite act of interpretation besides the act of choosing.

Our problem is analogous to the following:

If I give someone the order "fetch me a red flower from that meadow", how is he to know what sort of flower to bring, as I have only given him a *word*?

Now the answer one might suggest first is that he went to look for a red flower carrying a red image in his mind, and comparing it with the flowers to see which of them had the colour of the image. Now there is such a way of searching, and it is not at all essential that the image we use should be a mental one. In fact the process may be this: I carry a chart co-ordinating names and coloured squares. When I hear the order "fetch me etc." I draw my finger across the chart from the word "red" to a certain square, and I go and look for a flower which has the same colour as the square. But this is not the only way of searching and it isn't the usual way. We go, look about us, walk up to a flower and pick it, without comparing it to anything. To see that the process of obeying the order can be of this kind, consider the order "*imagine* a red patch". You are not tempted in this case to think that *before* obeying you must have imagined a red patch to serve you as a pattern for the red patch which you were ordered to imagine.

Now you might ask: do we *interpret* the words before we obey the order? And in some cases you will find that you do something which might be called interpreting before obeying, in some cases not.

It seems that there are *certain definite* mental processes bound up with the working of language, processes through which alone language can function. I mean the processes of understanding and meaning. The signs of our language seem dead without these mental processes; and it might seem that the only function of the signs is to induce such processes, and that these are the things we ought really to be interested in. Thus, if you are asked what is the relation between a name and the thing it names, you will be inclined to answer that the relation is a psychological one, and perhaps when you say this you think in particular of the mechanism of association.—We are tempted to think that the action of language consists of two parts; an inorganic part, the handling of signs, and an organic part, which we may call understanding these signs, meaning them, interpreting them, thinking. These latter activities seem to take place in a queer kind of medium, the mind; and the mechanism of the mind, the nature of which, it seems, we don't quite understand, can bring about effects which no material mechanism could. Thus e.g. a thought (which is such a mental process) can agree or disagree with reality; I am able to think of a man who isn't present; I am able to imagine him, 'mean him' in a remark which I make about him, even if he is thousands of miles away or dead. "What a queer mechanism," one might say, "the mechanism of wishing must be if I can wish that which will never happen".

There is one way of avoiding at least partly the occult appearance of the processes of thinking, and it is, to replace in these processes any working of the imagination by acts of looking at real objects. Thus it may seem essential that, at least in certain cases, when I hear the word "red" with understanding, a red image should be before my mind's eye. But why should I not substitute seeing a red bit of paper for imagining a red patch? The visual image will only be the more vivid. Imagine a man always carrying a sheet of paper in his pocket on which the names of colours are co-ordinated with coloured patches. You may say that it would be a nuisance to carry such a table of samples about with you, and that the mechanism of association is what we always use instead of it. But this is irrelevant; and in many cases it is not even true. If, for instance, you were ordered to paint a particular shade of blue called "Prussian Blue", you might have to use a table to lead you from the word "Prussian Blue" to a sample of the colour, which would serve you as your copy.

We could perfectly well, for our purposes, replace every process of imagining by a process of looking at an object or by painting, drawing or modelling; and every process of speaking to oneself by speaking aloud or by writing.

Frege ridiculed the formalist conception of mathematics by saying that the formalists confused the unimportant thing, the sign, with the important, the meaning. Surely, one wishes to say, mathematics does not treat of dashes on a bit of paper. Frege's idea could be expressed thus: the propositions of mathematics, if they were just complexes of dashes, would be dead and utterly uninteresting, whereas they obviously have a kind of life. And the same, of course, could be said of any proposition: Without a sense, or without the thought, a proposition would be an utterly dead and trivial thing. And further it seems clear that no adding of inorganic signs can make the proposition live. And the conclusion which one draws from this is that what must be added to the dead signs in order to make a live proposition is something immaterial, with properties different from all mere signs.

But if we had to name anything which is the life of the sign, we should have to say that it was its *use*.

If the meaning of the sign (roughly, that which is of importance about the sign) is an image built up in our minds when we see or hear the sign, then first let us adopt the method we just described of replacing this mental image by some outward object seen, e.g. a painted or modelled image. Then why should the written sign plus this painted image be alive if the written sign alone was dead?—In fact, as soon as you think of replacing the mental image by, say, a painted one, and as soon as the image thereby loses its occult character, it ceases to seem to impart any life to the sentence at all. (It was in fact just the occult character of the mental process which you needed for your purposes.)

The mistake we are liable to make could be expressed thus: We are looking for the use of a sign, but we look for it as though it were an object *co-existing* with the sign. (One of the reasons for this mistake is again that we are looking for a "thing corresponding to a substantive.")

The sign (the sentence) gets its significance from the system of signs, from the language to which it belongs. Roughly: understanding a sentence means understanding a language.

As a part of the system of language, one may say, the sentence has life. But one is tempted to imagine that which gives the sentence life as something in an occult sphere, accompanying the sentence. But whatever accompanied it would for us just be another sign.

It seems at first sight that that which gives to thinking its peculiar character is that it is a train of mental states, and it seems that what is queer and difficult to understand about thinking is the processes which happen in the medium of the mind, processes possible only in this medium. The comparison which forces itself upon us is that of the mental medium with the protoplasm of a cell, say, of an amoeba. We observe certain actions of the amoeba, its taking food by extending arms, its splitting up into similar cells, each of which grows and behaves like the original one. We say "of what a queer nature the protoplasm must be to act in such a way", and perhaps we say that no physical mechanism could behave in this way, and that the mechanism of the amoeba must be of a totally different kind. In the same way we are tempted to say "the mechanism of the mind must be of a most peculiar kind to be able to do what the mind does". But here we are making two mistakes. For what struck *us* as being queer about thought and thinking was not at all that it had curious effects which we were not yet able to explain (causally). Our problem, in other words, was not a scientific one; but a muddle felt as a problem.

Supposing we tried to construct a mind-model as a result of psychological investigations, a model which, as we should say, would explain the action of the mind. This model would be part of a psychological theory in the way in which a mechanical model of the ether can be part of a theory of electricity. (Such a model, by the way, is always part of the *symbolism* of a theory. Its advantage may be that it can be taken in at a glance and easily held in the mind. It has been said that a model, in a sense, dresses up the pure theory; that the *naked* theory is sentences or equations. This must be examined more closely later on.)

We may find that such a mind-model would have to be very complicated and intricate in order to explain the observed mental activities; and on this ground we might call the mind a queer kind of medium. But this aspect of the mind does not interest us. The problems which it may set are psychological problems, and the method of their solution is that of natural science.

Now if it is not the causal connections which we are concerned with, then the activities of the mind lie open before us. And when we are worried about the nature of thinking, the puzzlement which we wrongly interpret to be one about the nature of a medium is a puzzlement caused by the mystifying use of our language. This kind of mistake recurs again and again in philosophy; e.g. when we are puzzled about the nature of time, when time seems to us a *queer thing*. We are most strongly tempted to think that here are things hidden, something we can see from the outside but which we can't look into. And yet nothing of the sort is the case. It is not new facts about time which we want to know. All the facts that concern us lie open before us. But it is the use of the substantive "time" which mystifies us. If we look into the grammar of that word, we shall feel that it is no less astounding that man should have conceived of a deity of time than it would be to conceive of a deity of negation or disjunction.

It is misleading then to talk of thinking as of a "mental activity". We may say that thinking is essentially the activity of operating with signs. This activity is performed by the hand, when we think by writing; by the mouth and larynx, when we think by speaking; and if we think by imagining signs or pictures, I can give you no agent that thinks. If then you say that in such cases the mind thinks, I would only draw your attention to the fact that you are using a metaphor, that here the mind is an agent in a different sense from that in which the hand can be said to be the agent in writing.

If again we talk about the locality where thinking takes place we have a right to say that this locality is the paper on which we write or the mouth which speaks. And if we talk of the head or the brain as the locality of thought, this is using the expression "locality of thinking" in a different sense. Let us examine what are the reasons for calling the head the place of thinking. It is not our intention to criticize this form of expression, or to show that it is not appropriate. What we must do is: understand its working, its grammar, e.g. see what relation this grammar has to that of the expression "we think with our mouth", or "we think with a pencil on a piece of paper".

Perhaps the main reason why we are so strongly inclined to talk of the head as the locality of our thoughts is this: the existence of the words "thinking" and "thought" alongside of the words denoting (bodily) activities, such as writing, speaking, etc., makes us look for an activity, different from these but analogous to them, corresponding to the word "thinking". When words in our ordinary language have prima facie analogous grammars we are inclined to try to interpret them analogously; i.e. we try to make the analogy hold throughout.— We say, "The thought is not the same as the sentence; for an English and a French sentence, which are utterly different, can express the same thought". And now, as the sentences are *somewhere*, we look for a place for the thought. (It is as though we looked for the place of the king of which the rules of chess treat, as opposed to the places of the various bits of wood, the kings of the various sets.)—We say, "surely the thought is *something*; it is not nothing"; and all one can answer to this is, that the word "thought" has its *use*, which is of a totally different kind from the use of the word "sentence".

Now does this mean that it is nonsensical to talk of a locality where thought takes place? Certainly not. This phrase has sense if we give it sense. Now if we say "thought takes place in our heads", what is the sense of this phrase soberly understood? I suppose it is that certain physiological processes correspond to our thoughts in such a way that if we know the correspondence we can, by observing these processes, find the thoughts. But in what sense can the physiological processes be said to correspond to thoughts, and in what sense can we be said to get the thoughts from the observation of the brain?

I suppose we imagine the correspondence to have been verified experimentally. Let us imagine such an experiment crudely. It consists in looking at the brain while the subject thinks. And now you may think that the reason why my explanation is going to go wrong is that of course the experimenter gets the thoughts of the subject only *indirectly* by being told them, the subject *expressing* them in some way or other. But I will remove this difficulty by assuming that the subject is at the same time the experimenter, who is looking at his own brain, say by means of a mirror. (The crudity of this description in no way reduces the force of the argument.)

Then I ask you, is the subject-experimenter observing one thing or two things? (Don't say that he is observing one thing both from the inside and from the outside; for this does not remove the difficulty. We will talk of inside and outside later.[1]) The subject-experimenter is observing a correlation of two phenomena. One of them he, perhaps, calls the *thought*. This may consist of a train of images, organic sensations, or on the other hand of a train of the various visual, tactual and muscular experiences which he has in writing or speaking a sentence.—The other experience is one of seeing his brain work. Both these phenomena could correctly be called "expressions of thought"; and the question "where is the thought itself?" had better, in order to prevent confusion, be rejected as nonsensical. If however we do use the expression "the thought takes place in the head", we have given this expression its meaning by describing the experience which would justify the *hypothesis* that the thought takes places in our heads, by describing the experience which we wish to call "observing thought in our brain".

We easily forget that the word "locality" is used in many different senses and that there are many different kinds of statements about a thing which in a particular case, in accordance with general usage, we may call specifications of the locality of the thing. Thus it has been said of visual space that its place is in our head; and I think one has been tempted to say this, partly, by a grammatical misunderstanding.

I can say: "in my visual field I see the image of the tree to the right of the image of the tower" or "I see the image of the tree in the middle of the visual field". And now we are inclined to ask "and where do you see the visual field?" Now if the "where" is meant to ask for a locality in the sense in which we have specified the locality of the image of the tree, then I would draw your attention to the fact that you have not yet given this question sense; that is, that you have been

[1] See pp. 16, 44ff.

proceeding by a grammatical analogy without having worked out the analogy in detail.

In saying that the idea of our visual field being located in our brain arose from a grammatical misunderstanding, I did not mean to say that we could not give sense to such a specification of locality. We could, e.g., easily imagine an experience which we should describe by such a statement. Imagine that we looked at a group of things in this room, and, while we looked, a probe was stuck into our brain and it was found that if the point of the probe reached a particular point in our brain, then a particular small part of our visual field was thereby obliterated. In this way we might co-ordinate points of our brain to points of the visual image, and this might make us say that the visual field was seated in such and such a place in our brain. And if now we asked the question "Where do you see the image of this book?" the answer could be (as above) "To the right of that pencil", or "In the left hand part of my visual field", or again: "Three inches behind my left eye".

But what if someone said "I can assure you I feel the visual image to be two inches behind the bridge of my nose";—what are we to answer him? Should we say that he is not speaking the truth, or that there cannot be such a feeling? What if he asks us "do you know all the feelings there are? How do you know there isn't such a feeling?"

What if the diviner tells us that when he holds the rod he *feels* that the water is five feet under the ground? or that he *feels* that a mixture of copper and gold is five feet under the ground? Suppose that to our doubts he answered: "You can estimate a length when you see it. Why shouldn't I have a different way of estimating it?"

If we understand the idea of such an estimation, we shall get clear about the nature of our doubts about the statements of the diviner, and of the man who said he felt the visual image behind the bridge of his nose.

There is the statement: "this pencil is five inches long", and the statement, "I feel that this pencil is five inches long", and we must get clear about the relation of the grammar of the first statement to the grammar of the second. To the statement "I feel in my hand that the water is three feet under the ground" we should like to answer: "I don't know what this *means*". But the diviner would say: "Surely you know what it means. You know what 'three feet under the ground' means, and you know what 'I feel' means!" But I should answer him: I know what a word means *in certain contexts*. Thus I understand the phrase, "three feet under the ground", say, in the connections "The measurement has shown that the water runs three feet under the ground", "If we dig three feet deep we are going to strike water", "The depth of the water is three feet by the eye". But the use of the expression "a feeling in my hands of water being three feet under the ground" has yet to be explained to me.

We could ask the diviner "how did you learn the meaning of the word 'three feet'? We suppose by being shown such lengths, by having measured them and such like. Were you also taught to talk of a feeling of water being three feet under the ground, a feeling, say, in your hands? For if not, what made you connect the word 'three feet' with a feeling in your hand?" Supposing we had been estimating lengths by the eye, but had never spanned a length. How could we estimate a length in inches by spanning it? I.e., how could we interpret the experience of spanning in inches? The question is: what connection is there between, say, a tactual sensation and the experience of measuring a thing by means of a yard rod? This connection will show us what it means to 'feel that a thing is six inches long'. Supposing the diviner said "I have never learnt to correlate depth of water under the ground with feelings in my hand, but when I have a certain feeling of tension in my hands, the words 'three feet' spring up in my mind." We should answer "This is a perfectly good explanation of what you mean by 'feeling the depth to be three feet', and the statement that you feel this will have neither more, nor less, meaning than your explanation has given it. And if experience shows that the actual depth of the water always agrees with the words 'n feet' which come into your mind, your experience will be very useful for determining the depth of water".—But you see that the meaning of the words "I feel the depth of the water to be n feet" had to be explained; it was not known when the meaning of the words "n feet" in the ordinary sense (i.e. in the ordinary contexts) was known.—We don't say that the man who tells us he feels the visual image two inches behind the bridge of his nose is telling a lie or talking nonsense. But we say that we don't understand the meaning of such a phrase. It combines well-known words, but combines them in a way we don't yet understand. The grammar of this phrase has yet to be explained to us.

The importance of investigating the diviner's answer lies in the fact that we often think we have given a meaning to a statement P if only we assert "I *feel* (or I believe) that P is the case." (We shall talk at a later occasion[1] of Prof. Hardy saying that Goldbach's theorem is a proposition because he can believe that it is true.) We have already said that by merely explaining the meaning of the words "three feet" in the usual way we have not yet explained the sense of the phrase "feeling that water is three feet etc." Now we should not have felt these difficulties had the diviner said that he had *learnt* to estimate the depth of the water, say, by digging for water whenever he had a particular feeling and in this way correlating such feelings with *measurements* of depth. Now we must examine the relation of the process of *learning to estimate* with the act of estimating. The importance of this examination lies in this, that it applies to the relation between learning the meaning of a word and making use of the word. Or, more generally, that it shows the different possible relations between a rule given and its application.

Let us consider the process of estimating a length by the eye: It is extremely important that you should realise that there are a great many different processes which we call "estimating by the eye".

Consider these cases:—

(1) Someone asks "How did you estimate the height of this building?" I answer: "It has four storeys; I suppose each storey is about fifteen feet high; so it must be about sixty feet."

(2) In another case: "I roughly know what a yard at that distance looks like; so it must be about four yards long."

(3) Or again: "I can imagine a tall man reaching to about this point; so it must be about six feet above the ground."

(4) Or: "I don't know; it just looks like a yard."

This last case is likely to puzzle us. If you ask "what happened in this case when the man estimated the length?" the correct answer may be: "he *looked* at the thing and *said* 'it looks one yard long'." This may be all that has happened.

We said before that we should not have been puzzled about the diviner's answer if he had told us that he had *learnt* how to estimate depth. Now learning to estimate may, broadly speaking, be seen in two different relations to the act of estimating; either as a cause of the phenomenon of estimating, or as supplying us with a rule (a table, a chart, or some such thing) which we make use of when we estimate.

Supposing I teach someone the use of the word "yellow" by repeatedly pointing to a yellow patch and pronouncing the word.

[1] This promise is not kept.—*Edd.*

On another occasion I make him apply what he has learnt by giving
him the order, "choose a yellow ball out of this bag". What was it
that happened when he obeyed my order? I say "possibly just this: he
heard my words and took a yellow ball from the bag". Now you may
be inclined to think that this couldn't possibly have been all; and the
kind of thing that you would suggest is that he imagined something
yellow when he *understood* the order, and then chose a ball according to
his image. To see that this is not *necessary* remember that I could have
given him the order, "Imagine a yellow patch". Would you still be
inclined to assume that he first imagines a yellow patch, just *understanding* my order, and then imagines a yellow patch to match the first?
(Now I don't say that this is not possible. Only, putting it in this way
immediately shows you that it need not happen. This, by the way,
illustrates the method of philosophy.)

If we are taught the meaning of the word "yellow" by being given
some sort of ostensive definition (a rule of the usage of the word) this
teaching can be looked at in two different ways.

A. The teaching is a drill. This drill causes us to associate a yellow
image, yellow things, with the word "yellow". Thus when I gave the
order "Choose a yellow ball from this bag" the word "yellow" might
have brought up a yellow image, or a feeling of recognition when the
person's eye fell on the yellow ball. The drill of teaching could in
this case be said to have built up a psychical mechanism. This, however, would only be a hypothesis or else a metaphor. We could
compare teaching with installing an electric connection between a
switch and a bulb. The parallel to the connection going wrong or
breaking down would then be what we call forgetting the explanation,
or the meaning, of the word. (We ought to talk further on about the
meaning of "forgetting the meaning of a word"[1]).

In so far as the teaching brings about the association, feeling of
recognition, etc. etc., it is the *cause* of the phenomena of understanding, obeying, etc.; and it is a hypothesis that the process of
teaching should be needed in order to bring about these effects. It is
conceivable, in this sense, that *all* the processes of understanding,
obeying, etc., should have happened without the person ever having
been taught the language. (This, just now, seems extremely paradoxical.)

B. The teaching may have supplied us with a rule which is itself
involved in the processes of understanding, obeying, etc.; "involved",

---

[1] This he never does.—*Edd*.

however, meaning that the expression of this rule forms part of these processes.

We must distinguish between what one might call "a process being *in accordance with* a rule", and, "a process involving a rule" (in the above sense).

Take an example. Some one teaches me to square cardinal numbers; he writes down the row

$$1 \quad 2 \quad 3 \quad 4,$$

and asks me to square them. (I will, in this case again, replace any processes happening 'in the mind' by processes of calculation on the paper.) Suppose, underneath the first row of numbers, I then write:

$$1 \quad 4 \quad 9 \quad 16.$$

What I wrote is in accordance with the general rule of squaring; but it obviously is also in accordance with any number of other rules; and amongst these it is not more in accordance with one than with another. In the sense in which before we talked about a rule being involved in a process, *no* rule was involved in this. Supposing that in order to get to my results I calculated 1×1, 2×2, 3×3, 4×4 (that is, in this case wrote down the calculations); these would again be in accordance with any number of rules. Supposing, on the other hand, in order to get to my results I had written down what you may call "the rule of squaring", say algebraically. In this case this rule was involved in a sense in which no other rule was.

We shall say that the rule is *involved* in the understanding, obeying, etc., if, as I should like to express it, the symbol of the rule forms part of the calculation. (As we are not interested in where the processes of thinking, calculating, take place, we can for our purpose imagine the calculations being done entirely on paper. We are not concerned with the difference: internal, external.)

A characteristic example of the case B would be one in which the teaching supplied us with a table which we actually make use of in understanding, obeying, etc. If we are taught to play chess, we may be taught rules. If then we play chess, these rules need not be involved in the act of playing. But they may be. Imagine, e.g., that the rules were expressed in the form of a table; in one column the shapes of the chessmen are drawn, and in a parallel column we find diagrams showing the 'freedom' (the legitimate moves) of the pieces. Suppose now that the way the game is played involves making the transition from the shape to the possible moves by running one's finger across the table, and then making one of these moves.

Teaching as the hypothetical history of our subsequent actions (understanding, obeying, estimating a length, etc.) drops out of our considerations. The rule which has been taught and is subsequently applied interests us only so far as it is involved in the application. A rule, so far as it interests us, does not act at a distance.

Suppose I pointed to a piece of paper and said to someone: "this colour I call 'red' ". Afterwards I give him the order: "now paint me a red patch". I then ask him: "why, in carrying out my order, did you paint just this colour?" His answer could then be: "This colour (pointing to the sample which I have given him) was called red; and the patch I have painted has, as you see, the colour of the sample". He has now given me a reason for carrying out the order in the way he did. Giving a reason for something one did or said means showing a *way* which leads to this action. In some cases it means telling the way which one has gone oneself; in others it means describing a way which leads there and is in accordance with certain accepted rules. Thus when asked, "why did you carry out my order by painting just this colour?" the person could have described the way he had actually taken to arrive at this particular shade of colour. This would have been so if, hearing the word "red", he had taken up the sample I had given him, labelled "red", and had *copied* that sample when painting the patch. On the other hand he might have painted it 'automatically' or from a memory image, but when asked to give the reason he might still point to the sample and show that it matched the patch he had painted. In this latter case the reason given would have been of the second kind; i.e. a justification *post hoc*.

Now if one thinks that there could be no understanding and obeying the order without a previous teaching, one thinks of the teaching as supplying a *reason* for doing what one did; as supplying the road one walks. Now there is the idea that if an order is understood and obeyed there must be a reason for our obeying it as we do; and, in fact, a chain of reasons reaching back to infinity. This is as if one said: "Wherever you are, you must have got there from somewhere else, and to that previous place from another place; and so on *ad infinitum*". (If, on the other hand, you had said, "wherever you are, you *could* have got there from another place ten yards away; and to that other place from a third, ten yards further away, and so on *ad infinitum*", if you had said this you would have stressed the infinite *possibility* of making a step.

Thus the idea of an infinite chain of reasons arises out of a confusion similar to this: that a line of a certain length consists of an infinite number of parts because it is indefinitely divisible; i.e., because there is no end to the possibility of dividing it.)

If on the other hand you realize that the chain of *actual* reasons has a beginning, you will no longer be revolted by the idea of a case in which there is *no* reason for the way you obey the order. At this point, however, another confusion sets in, that between reason and cause. One is led into this confusion by the ambiguous use of the word "why". Thus when the chain of reasons has come to an end and still the question "why?" is asked, one is inclined to give a cause instead of a reason. If, e.g., to the question, "why did you paint just this colour when I told you to paint a red patch?" you give the answer: "I have been shown a sample of this colour and the word 'red' was pronounced to me at the same time; and therefore this colour now always comes to my mind when I hear the word 'red' ", then you have given a cause for your action and not a reason.

The proposition that your action has such and such a cause, is a hypothesis. The hypothesis is well-founded if one has had a number of experiences which, roughly speaking, agree in showing that your action is the regular sequel of certain conditions which we then call causes of the action. In order to know the reason which you had for making a certain statement, for acting in a particular way, etc., no number of agreeing experiences is necessary, and the statement of your reason is not a hypothesis. The difference between the grammars of "reason" and "cause" is quite similar to that between the grammars of "motive" and "cause". Of the cause one can say that one can't *know* it but can only *conjecture* it. On the other hand one often says: "Surely *I* must know why I did it" talking of the *motive*. When I say: "we can only *conjecture* the cause but we *know* the motive" this statement will be seen later on to be a grammatical one. The "can" refers to a *logical* possibility.

The double use of the word "why", asking for the cause and asking for the motive, together with the idea that we can know, and not only conjecture, our motives, gives rise to the confusion that a motive is a cause of which we are immediately aware, a cause 'seen from the inside', or a cause experienced.—Giving a reason is like giving a calculation by which you have arrived at a certain result.

Let us go back to the statement that thinking essentially consists in operating with signs. My point was that it is liable to mislead us if we say 'thinking is a mental activity'. The question what kind of an activity thinking is is analogous to this: "Where does thinking take place?" We can answer: on paper, in our head, in the mind. None of these statements of locality gives *the* locality of thinking. The use of all these specifications is correct, but we must not be misled by the similarity of their linguistic form into a false conception of their grammar. As, e.g., when you say: "Surely, the *real* place of thought is in our head". The same applies to the idea of thinking as an activity. It is correct to say that thinking is an activity of our writing hand, of our larynx, of our head, and of our mind, so long as we understand the grammar of these statements. And it is, furthermore, extremely important to realize how, by misunderstanding the grammar of our expressions, we are led to think of one in particular of these statements as giving the *real* seat of the activity of thinking.

There is an objection to saying that thinking is some such thing as an activity of the hand. Thinking, one wants to say, is part of our 'private experience'. It is not material, but an event in private consciousness. This objection is expressed in the question: "Could a machine think?" I shall talk about this at a later point,[1] and now only refer you to an analogous question: "Can a machine have toothache?" You will certainly be inclined to say: "A machine can't have toothache". All I will do now is to draw your attention to the use which you have made of the word "can" and to ask you: "Did you mean to say that all our past experience has shown that a machine never had toothache?" The impossibility of which you speak is a logical one. The question is: What is the relation between thinking (or toothache) and the subject which thinks, has toothache, etc.? I shall say no more about this now.

If we say thinking is essentially operating with signs, the first question you might ask is: "What are signs?"—Instead of giving any kind of general answer to this question, I shall propose to you to look closely at particular cases which we should call "operating with signs". Let us look at a simple example of operating with words. I give someone the order: "fetch me six apples from the grocer", and I will describe a way of making use of such an order: The words "six apples" are written on a bit of paper, the paper is handed to the grocer, the grocer compares the word "apple" with labels on different shelves. He finds it to agree with one of the labels, counts from 1 to the number written on the slip of paper, and for every number counted

[1] See p. 47 for a few further remarks on this topic.—*Edd.*

takes a fruit off the shelf and puts it in a bag.—And here you have a case of the use of words. I shall in the future again and again draw your attention to what I shall call language games. These are ways of using signs simpler than those in which we use the signs of our highly complicated everyday language. Language games are the forms of language with which a child begins to make use of words. The study of language games is the study of primitive forms of language or primitive languages. If we want to study the problems of truth and falsehood, of the agreement and disagreement of propositions with reality, of the nature of assertion, assumption, and question, we shall with great advantage look at primitive forms of language in which these forms of thinking appear without the confusing background of highly complicated processes of thought. When we look at such simple forms of language the mental mist which seems to enshroud our ordinary use of language disappears. We see activities, reactions, which are clear-cut and transparent. On the other hand we recognize in these simple processes forms of language not separated by a break from our more complicated ones. We see that we can build up the complicated forms from the primitive ones by gradually adding new forms.

Now what makes it difficult for us to take this line of investigation is our craving for generality.

This craving for generality is the resultant of a number of tendencies connected with particular philosophical confusions. There is—

(a) The tendency to look for something in common to all the entities which we commonly subsume under a general term.—We are inclined to think that there must be something in common to all games, say, and that this common property is the justification for applying the general term "game" to the various games; whereas games form a *family* the members of which have family likenesses. Some of them have the same nose, others the same eyebrows and others again the same way of walking; and these likenesses overlap. The idea of a general concept being a common property of its particular instances connects up with other primitive, too simple, ideas of the structure of language. It is comparable to the idea that *properties* are *ingredients* of the things which have the properties; e.g. that beauty is an ingredient of all beautiful things as alcohol is of beer and wine, and that we therefore could have pure beauty, unadulterated by anything that is beautiful.

(b) There is a tendency rooted in our usual forms of expression, to think that the man who has learnt to understand a general term, say, the term "leaf", has thereby come to possess a kind of general picture of a leaf, as opposed to pictures of particular leaves. He was shown different leaves when he learnt the meaning of the word "leaf"; and showing him the particular leaves was only a means to the end of producing 'in him' an idea which we imagine to be some kind of general image. We say that he sees what is in common to all these leaves; and this is true if we mean that he can on being asked tell us certain features or properties which they have in common. But we are inclined to think that the general idea of a leaf is something like a visual image, but one which only contains what is common to all leaves. (Galtonian composite photograph.) This again is connected with the idea that the meaning of a word is an image, or a thing correlated to the word. (This roughly means, we are looking at words as though they all were proper names, and we then confuse the bearer of a name with the meaning of the name.)

(c) Again, the idea we have of what happens when we get hold of the general idea 'leaf', 'plant', etc. etc., is connected with the confusion between a mental state, meaning a state of a hypothetical mental mechanism, and a mental state meaning a state of consciousness (toothache, etc.).

(d) Our craving for generality has another main source: our pre-occupation with the method of science. I mean the method of reducing the explanation of natural phenomena to the smallest possible number of primitive natural laws; and, in mathematics, of unifying the treatment of different topics by using a generalization. Philosophers constantly see the method of science before their eyes, and are irresistibly tempted to ask and answer questions in the way science does. This tendency is the real source of metaphysics, and leads the philosopher into complete darkness. I want to say here that it can never be our job to reduce anything to anything, or to explain anything. Philosophy really *is* 'purely descriptive'. (Think of such questions as "Are there sense data?" and ask: What method is there of determining this? Introspection?)

Instead of "craving for generality" I could also have said "the contemptuous attitude towards the particular case". If, e.g., someone tries to explain the concept of number and tells us that such and such a definition will not do or is clumsy because it only applies to, say, finite cardinals I should answer that the mere fact that he could have given such a limited definition makes this definition extremely important to us. (Elegance is *not* what we are trying for.) For why should what finite and transfinite numbers have in common be more interesting to us than what distinguishes them? Or rather, I should not have said "why should it be more interesting to us?"—it *isn't*; and this characterizes our way of thinking.

The attitude towards the more general and the more special in logic is connected with the usage of the word "kind" which is liable to cause confusion. We talk of kinds of numbers, kinds of propositions, kinds of proofs; and, also, of kinds of apples, kinds of paper, etc. In one sense what defines the kind are properties, like sweetness, hardness, etc. In the other the different kinds are different grammatical structures. A treatise on pomology may be called incomplete if there exist kinds of apples which it doesn't mention. Here we have a standard of completeness in nature. Supposing on the other hand there was a game resembling that of chess but simpler, no pawns being used in it. Should we call this game incomplete? Or should we call a game more complete than chess if it in some way contained chess but added new elements? The contempt for what seems the less general case in logic springs from the idea that it is incomplete. It is in fact confusing to talk of cardinal arithmetic as something special as opposed to something more general. Cardinal arithmetic bears no mark of incompleteness; nor does an arithmetic which is cardinal and finite. (There are no subtle distinctions between logical forms as there are between the tastes of different kinds of apples.)

If we study the grammar, say, of the words "wishing", "thinking", "understanding", "meaning", we shall not be dissatisfied when we have described various cases of wishing, thinking, etc. If someone said, "surely this is not all that one calls 'wishing'", we should answer, "certainly not, but you can build up more complicated cases if you like." And after all, there is not one definite class of features which characterize all cases of wishing (at least not as the word is commonly used). If on the other hand you wish to give a definition of wishing, i.e., to draw a sharp boundary, then you are free to draw it as you like; and this boundary will never entirely coincide with the actual usage, as this usage has no sharp boundary.

The idea that in order to get clear about the meaning of a general term one had to find the common element in all its applications has shackled philosophical investigation; for it has not only led to no result, but also made the philosopher dismiss as irrelevant the concrete cases, which alone could have helped him to understand the usage of the general term. When Socrates asks the question, "what is know-ledge?" he does not even regard it as a *preliminary* answer to enumerate cases of knowledge.[1] If I wished to find out what sort of thing arith-metic is, I should be very content indeed to have investigated the case of a finite cardinal arithmetic. For

(*a*) this would lead me on to all the more complicated cases,

(*b*) a finite cardinal arithmetic is not incomplete, it has no gaps which are then filled in by the rest of arithmetic.

What happens if from 4 till 4.30 A expects B to come to his room? In one sense in which the phrase "to expect something from 4 to 4.30" is used it certainly does not refer to one process or state of mind going on throughout that interval, but to a great many different activities and states of mind. If for instance I expect B to come to tea, what happens *may* be this: At four o'clock I look at my diary and see the name "B" against to-day's date; I prepare tea for two; I think for a moment "does B smoke?" and put out cigarettes; towards 4.30 I begin to feel impatient; I imagine B as he will look when he comes into my room. All this is called "expecting B from 4 to 4.30". And there are endless variations to this process which we all describe by the same expression. If one asks what the different processes of expecting someone to tea have in common, the answer is that there is no single feature in common to all of them, though there are many common features overlapping. These cases of expectation form a family; they have family likenesses which are not clearly defined.

There is a totally different use of the word "expectation" if we use it to mean a particular sensation. This use of the words like "wish", "expectation", etc., readily suggests itself. There is an obvious connection between this use and the one described above. There is no doubt that in many cases if we expect some one, in the first sense, some, or all, of the activities described are accompanied by a peculiar feeling, a tension; and it is natural to use the word "expectation" to mean this experience of tension.

There arises now the question: is this sensation to be called "the sensation of expectation", or "the sensation of expectation that B will come"? If the first case to say that you are in a state of expecta-tion admittedly does not fully describe the situation of expecting that so-and-so will happen. The second case is often rashly suggested as an explanation of the use of the phrase "expecting that so-and-so will happen", and you may even think that with this explanation you are

[1] *Theaetetus* 146D-7C.

on safe ground, as every further question is dealt with by saying that the sensation of expectation is indefinable.

Now there is no objection to calling a particular sensation "the expectation that B will come". There may even be good practical reasons for using such an expression. Only mark:—if we have explained the meaning of the phrase "expecting that B will come" in this way no phrase which is derived from this by substituting a different name for "B" is thereby explained. One might say that the phrase "expecting that B will come" is not a value of a function "expecting that x will come". To understand this compare our case with that of the function "I eat x". We understand the proposition "I eat a chair" although we weren't specifically taught the meaning of the expression "eating a chair".

The role which in our present case the name "B" plays in the expression "I expect B" can be compared with that which the name "Bright" plays in the expression "Bright's disease".[1] Compare the grammar of this word, when it denotes a particular kind of disease, with that of the expression "Bright's disease" when it means the disease which Bright has. I will characterize the difference by saying that the word "Bright" in the first case is an index in the complex *name* "Bright's disease"; in the second case I shall call it an argument of the function "x's disease". One may say that an index *alludes* to something, and such an allusion may be justified in all sorts of ways. Thus calling a sensation "the expectation that B will come" is giving it a complex name and "B" possibly alludes to the man whose coming had regularly been preceded by the sensation.

Again we may use the phrase "expectation that B will come" not as a name but as a characteristic of certain sensations. We might, e.g., explain that a certain tension is said to be an expectation that B will come if it is relieved by B's coming. If this is how we use the phrase then it is true to say that we don't know what we expect until our expectation has been fulfilled (cf. Russell). But no one can believe that this is the only way or even the most common way of using the word "expect". If I ask someone "whom do you expect?" and after receiving the answer ask again "Are you sure that you don't expect someone else?" then, in most cases, this question would be regarded as absurd, and the answer will be something like "Surely, I must know whom I expect".

One may characterize the meaning which Russell gives to the word

[1] See *Tractatus* 5.02.

"wishing" by saying that it means to him a kind of hunger.—It is a hypothesis that a particular feeling of hunger will be relieved by eating a particular thing. In Russell's way of using the word "wishing" it makes no sense to say "I wished for an apple but a pear has satisfied me".[1] But we do sometimes say this, using the word "wishing" in a way different from Russell's. In this sense we can say that the tension of wishing was relieved without the wish being fulfilled; and also that the wish was fulfilled without the tension being relieved. That is, I may, in this sense, become satisfied without my wish having been satisfied.

Now one might be tempted to say that the difference which we are talking about simply comes to this, that in some cases we know what we wish and in others we don't. There are certainly cases in which we say, "I feel a longing, though I don't know what I'm longing for" or, "I feel a fear, but I don't know what I'm afraid of", or again: "I feel fear, but I'm not afraid of anything in particular".

Now we may describe these cases by saying that we have certain sensations not referring to objects. The phrase "not referring to objects" introduces a grammatical distinction. If in characterizing such sensations we use verbs like "fearing", "longing", etc., these verbs will be intransitive; "I fear" will be analogous to "I cry". We may cry about something, but what we cry about is not a constituent of the process of crying; that is to say, we could describe all that happens when we cry without mentioning what we are crying about.

Suppose now that I suggested we should use the expression "I feel fear", and similar ones, in a transitive way only. Whenever before we said "I have a sensation of fear" (intransitively) we will now say "I am afraid of something, but I don't know of what". Is there an objection to this terminology?

We may say: "There isn't, except that we are then using the word 'to know' in a queer way". Consider this case:—we have a general undirected feeling of fear. Later on, we have an experience which makes us say, "Now I know what I was afraid of. I was afraid of so-and-so happening". Is it correct to describe my first feeling by an intransitive verb, or should I say that my fear had an object although I did not know that it had one? Both these forms of description can be used. To understand this examine the following example:— It might be found practical to call a certain state of decay in a tooth, not accompanied by what we commonly call toothache, "unconscious

---

[1] Cf. Russell, *Analysis of Mind*, III.

toothache" and to use in such a case the expression that we have toothache, but don't know it. It is in just this sense that psycho-analysis talks of unconscious thoughts, acts of volition, etc. Now is it wrong in this sense to say that I have toothache but don't know it? There is nothing wrong about it, as it is just a new terminology and can at any time be retranslated into ordinary language. On the other hand it obviously makes use of the word "to know" in a new way. If you wish to examine how this expression is used it is helpful to ask yourself "what in this case is the process of getting to know like?" "What do we call 'getting to know' or, 'finding out'?"

It isn't wrong, according to our new convention, to say "I have unconscious toothache". For what more can you ask of your notation than that it should distinguish between a bad tooth which doesn't give you toothache and one which does? But the new expression misleads us by calling up pictures and analogies which make it difficult for us to go through with our convention. And it is extremely difficult to discard these pictures unless we are constantly watchful; particularly difficult when, in philosophizing, we contemplate what we *say* about things. Thus, by the expression "unconscious toothache" you may either be misled into thinking that a stupendous discovery has been made, a discovery which in a sense altogether bewilders our under-standing; or else you may be extremely puzzled by the expression (the puzzlement of philosophy) and perhaps ask such a question as "How is unconscious toothache possible?" You may then be tempted to deny the possibility of unconscious toothache; but the scientist will tell you that it is a proved fact that there is such a thing, and he will say it like a man who is destroying a common prejudice. He will say: "Surely it's quite simple; there are other things which you don't know of, and there can also be toothache which you don't know of. It is just a new discovery". You won't be satisfied, but you won't know what to answer. This situation constantly arises between the scientist and the philosopher.

In such a case we may clear the matter up by saying: "Let's see how the word 'unconscious', 'to know', etc. etc., is used in *this* case, and how it's used in others". *How far does the analogy between these uses go?* We shall also try to construct new notations, in order to break the spell of those which we are accustomed to.

We said that it was a way of examining the grammar (the use) of the word "to know", to ask ourselves what, in the particular case we are examining, we should call "getting to know". There is a temptation to think that this question is only vaguely relevant, if relevant at all, to the question: "what is the meaning of the word 'to know'?" We seem to be on a side-track when we ask the question "What is it like in this case 'to get to know'?" But this question really is a question concerning the grammar of the word "to know", and this becomes clearer if we put it in the form: "What do we *call* 'getting to know'?" It is part of the grammar of the word "chair" that *this* is what we call "to sit on a chair", and it is part of the grammar of the word "meaning" that *this* is what we call "explanation of a meaning"; in the same way to explain my criterion for another person's having toothache is to give a grammatical explanation about the word "toothache" and, in this sense, an explanation concerning the meaning of the word "toothache".

When we learnt the use of the phrase "so-and-so has toothache" we were pointed out certain kinds of behaviour of those who were said to have toothache. As an instance of these kinds of behaviour let us take holding your cheek. Suppose that by observation I found that in certain cases whenever these first criteria told me a person had toothache, a red patch appeared on the person's cheek. Supposing I now said to someone "I see A has toothache, he's got a red patch on his cheek". He may ask me "How do you know A has toothache when you see a red patch?" I should then point out that certain phenomena had always coincided with the appearance of the red patch.

Now one may go on and ask: "How do you know that he has got toothache when he holds his cheek?" The answer to this might be, "I say, *he* has toothache when he holds his cheek because I hold my cheek when I have toothache". But what if we went on asking:— "And why do you suppose that toothache corresponds to his holding his cheek just because your toothache corresponds to your holding your cheek?" You will be at a loss to answer this question, and find that here we strike rock bottom, that is we have come down to conventions. (If you suggest as an answer to the last question that, whenever we've seen people holding their cheeks and asked them what's the matter, they have answered, "I have toothache",—remember that this experience only co-ordinates holding your cheek with saying certain words.)

Let us introduce two antithetical terms in order to avoid certain elementary confusions: To the question "How do you know that so-and-so is the case?", we sometimes answer by giving '*criteria*' and sometimes by giving '*symptoms*'. If medical science calls angina an inflammation caused by a particular bacillus, and we ask in a particular case "why do you say this man has got angina?" then the answer "I have found the bacillus so-and-so in his blood" gives us the criterion, or what we may call the defining criterion of angina. If on the other hand the answer was, "His throat is inflamed", this might give us a symptom of angina. I call "symptom" a phenomenon of which experience has taught us that it coincided, in some way or other, with the phenomenon which is our defining criterion. Then to say "A man has angina if this bacillus is found in him" is a tautology or it is a loose way of stating the definition of "angina". But to say, "A man has angina whenever he has an inflamed throat" is to make a hypothesis.

In practice, if you were asked which phenomenon is the defining criterion and which is a symptom, you would in most cases be unable to answer this question except by making an arbitrary decision *ad hoc*. It may be practical to define a word by taking one phenomenon as the defining criterion, but we shall easily be persuaded to define the word by means of what, according to our first use, was a symptom. Doctors will use names of diseases without ever deciding which phenomena are to be taken as criteria and which as symptoms; and this need not be a deplorable lack of clarity. For remember that in general we don't use language according to strict rules—it hasn't been taught us by means of strict rules, either. *We*, in our discussions on the other hand, constantly compare language with a calculus proceeding according to exact rules.

This is a very one-sided way of looking at language. In practice we very rarely use language as such a calculus. For not only do we not think of the rules of usage—of definitions, etc.—while using language, but when we are asked to give such rules, in most cases we aren't able to do so. We are unable clearly to circumscribe the concepts we use; not because we don't know their real definition, but because there is no real 'definition' to them. To suppose that there *must* be would be like supposing that whenever children play with a ball they play a game according to strict rules.

When we talk of language as a symbolism used in an exact calculus, that which is in our mind can be found in the sciences and in mathematics. Our ordinary use of language conforms to this standard of exactness only in rare cases. Why then do we in philosophizing constantly compare our use of words with one following exact rules?

The answer is that the puzzles which we try to remove always spring from just this attitude towards language.

Consider as an example the question "What is time?" as Saint Augustine and others have asked it. At first sight what this question asks for is a definition, but then immediately the question arises: "What should we gain by a definition, as it can only lead us to other undefined terms?" And why should one be puzzled just by the lack of a definition of time, and not by the lack of a definition of "chair"? Why shouldn't we be puzzled in all cases where we haven't got a definition? Now a definition often clears up the *grammar* of a word. And in fact it is the grammar of the word "time" which puzzles us. We are only expressing this puzzlement by asking a slightly misleading question, the question: "What is . . .?" This question is an utterance of unclarity, of mental discomfort, and it is comparable with the question "Why?" as children so often ask it. This too is an expression of a mental discomfort, and doesn't necessarily ask for either a cause or a reason. (Hertz, *Principles of Mechanics*.) Now the puzzlement about the grammar of the word "time" arises from what one might call apparent contradictions in that grammar.

It was such a "contradiction" which puzzled Saint Augustine when he argued: How is it possible that one should measure time? For the past can't be measured, as it is gone by; and the future can't be measured because it has not yet come. And the present can't be measured for it has no extension.

The contradiction which here seems to arise could be called a conflict between two different usages of a word, in this case the word "measure". Augustine, we might say, thinks of the process of measuring a *length*: say, the distance between two marks on a travelling band which passes us, and of which we can only see a tiny bit (the present) in front of us. Solving this puzzle will consist in comparing what we mean by "measurement" (the grammar of the word "measurement") when applied to a distance on a travelling band with the grammar of that word when applied to time. The problem may seem simple, but its extreme difficulty is due to the fascination which the analogy between two similar structures in our language can exert on us. (It is helpful here to remember that it is sometimes almost impossible for a child to believe that one word can have two meanings.)

Now it is clear that this problem about the concept of time asks for an answer given in the form of strict rules. The puzzle is about rules.—Take another example: Socrates' question "What is knowledge?" Here the case is even clearer, as the discussion begins with the pupil giving an example of an exact definition, and then analogous to this a definition of the word "knowledge" is asked for. As the problem is put, it seems that there is something wrong with the ordinary use of the word "knowledge". It appears we don't know what it means, and that therefore, perhaps, we have no right to use it. We should reply: "There is no one exact usage of the word 'knowledge'; but we can make up several such usages, which will more or less agree with the ways the word is actually used".

The man who is philosophically puzzled sees a law in the way a word is used, and, trying to apply this law consistently, comes up against cases where it leads to paradoxical results. Very often the way the discussion of such a puzzle runs is this: First the question is asked "What is time?" This question makes it appear that what we want is a definition. We mistakenly think that a definition is what will remove the trouble (as in certain states of indigestion we feel a kind of hunger which cannot be removed by eating). The question is then answered by a wrong definition; say: "Time is the motion of the celestial bodies". The next step is to see that this definition is unsatisfactory. But this only means that we don't use the word "time" synonymously with "motion of the celestial bodies". However in saying that the first definition is wrong, we are now tempted to think that we must replace it by a different one, the correct one.

Compare with this the case of the definition of number. Here the explanation that a number is the same thing as a numeral satisfies that first craving for a definition. And it is very difficult not to ask: "Well, if it isn't the numeral, *what is* it?"

Philosophy, as we use the word, is a fight against the fascination which forms of expression exert upon us.

I want you to remember that words have those meanings which we have given them; and we give them meanings by explanations. I may have given a definition of a word and used the word accordingly, or those who taught me the use of the word may have given me the explanation. Or else we might, by the explanation of a word, mean the explanation which, on being asked, we are ready to give. That is, if we *are* ready to give any explanation; in most cases we aren't. Many words in this sense then don't have a strict meaning. But this is not a defect. To think it is would be like saying that the light of my reading lamp is no real light at all because it has no sharp boundary.

Philosophers very often talk about investigating, analysing, the

meaning of words. But let's not forget that a word hasn't got a meaning given to it, as it were, by a power independent of us, so that there
could be a kind of scientific investigation into what the word *really*
means. A word has the meaning someone has given to it.

There are words with several clearly defined meanings. It is easy to
tabulate these meanings. And there are words of which one might say:
They are used in a thousand different ways which gradually merge into
one another. No wonder that we can't tabulate strict rules for their
use.

It is wrong to say that in philosophy we consider an ideal language
as opposed to our ordinary one. For this makes it appear as though
we thought we could improve on ordinary language. But ordinary
language is all right. Whenever we make up 'ideal languages' it is not
in order to replace our ordinary language by them; but just to remove
some trouble caused in someone's mind by thinking that he has got
hold of the exact use of a common word. That is also why our method
is not merely to enumerate actual usages of words, but rather deliberately to invent new ones, some of them because of their absurd
appearance.

When we say that by our method we try to counteract the misleading effect of certain analogies, it is important that you should
understand that the idea of an analogy being misleading is nothing
sharply defined. No sharp boundary can be drawn round the cases
in which we should say that a man was misled by an analogy. The use
of expressions constructed on analogical patterns stresses analogies
between cases often far apart. And by doing this these expressions
may be extremely useful. It is, in most cases, impossible to show an
exact point where an analogy begins to mislead us. Every particular
notation stresses some particular point of view. If, e.g., we call our
investigations "philosophy", this title, on the one hand, seems
appropriate, on the other hand it certainly has misled people. (One
might say that the subject we are dealing with is one of the heirs of the
subject which used to be called "philosophy".) The cases in which
particularly we wish to say that someone is misled by a form of expression are those in which we would say: "he wouldn't talk as he does
if he were aware of this difference in the grammar of such-and-such
words, of if he were aware of this other possibility of expression"
and so on. Thus we may say of some philosophizing mathematicians
that they are obviously not aware of the difference between the many
different usages of the word "proof"; and that they are not clear about

the difference between the uses of the word "kind", when they talk
of kinds of numbers, kinds of proofs, as though the word "kind" here
meant the same thing as in the context "kinds of apples". Or, we may
say, they are not aware of the different *meanings* of the word "discovery",
when in one case we talk of the discovery of the construction of the
pentagon and in the other case of the discovery of the South Pole.

Now when we distinguished a transitive and an intransitive use of
such words as "longing", "fearing", "expecting", etc., we said that
some one might try to smooth over our difficulties by saying: "The
difference between the two cases is simply that in one case we know
what we are longing for and in the other we don't". Now who says
this, I think, obviously doesn't see that the difference which he tried
to explain away reappears when we carefully consider the use of the
word "to know" in the two cases. The expression "the difference is
simply . . ." makes it appear as though we had analysed the case and
found a simple analysis; as when we point out that two substances
with very different names hardly differ in composition.

We said in this case that we might use both expressions: "we feel
a longing" (where "longing" is used intransitively) and "we feel a
longing and don't know what we are longing for". It may seem queer
to say that we may correctly use either of two forms of expression which
seem to contradict each other; but such cases are very frequent.

Let us use the following example to clear this up. We say that the
equation $x^2 = -1$ has the solution $\pm\sqrt{-1}$. There was a time when
one said that this equation had no solution. Now this statement,
whether agreeing or disagreeing with the one which told us the solu-
tions, certainly hasn't its multiplicity. But we can easily give it that
multiplicity by saying that an equation $x^2 + ax + b = 0$ hasn't got
a solution but comes a near to the nearest solution which is β. Analogously we can say either "A straight line always intersects a circle;
sometimes in real, sometimes in complex points", or, "A straight line
either intersects a circle, or it doesn't and is a far from doing so".
These two statements mean exactly the same. They will be more
or less satisfactory according to the way a man wishes to look at it.
He may wish to make the difference between intersecting and not
intersecting as inconspicuous as possible. Or on the other hand he
may wish to stress it; and either tendency may be justified, say, by his
particular practical purposes. But this may not be the reason at all
why he prefers one form of expression to the other. Which form he

prefers, and whether he has a preference at all, often depends on general, deeply rooted, tendencies of his thinking.

(Should we say that there are cases when a man despises another man and doesn't know it; or should we describe such cases by saying that he doesn't despise him but unintentionally behaves towards him in a way—speaks to him in a tone of voice, etc.—which in general would go together with despising him? Either form of expression is correct; but they may betray different tendencies of the mind.)

Let us revert to examining the grammar of the expressions "to wish", "to expect", "to long for", etc., and consider that most important case in which the expression, "I wish so and so to happen" is the direct description of a conscious process. That is to say, the case in which we should be inclined to answer the question "Are you sure that it is this you wish?" by saying: "Surely I must know what I wish". Now compare this answer to the one which most of us would give to the question: "Do you know the ABC?" Has the emphatic assertion that you know it a sense analogous to that of the former assertion? Both assertions in a way brush aside the question. But the former doesn't wish to say "Surely I know such a simple thing as this" but rather: "The question which you asked me makes no sense". We might say: We adopt in this case a wrong method of brushing aside the question. "Of course I know" could here be replaced by "Of course, there is no doubt" and this interpreted to mean "It makes, in this case, no sense of talk of a doubt". In this way the answer "Of course I know what I wish" can be interpreted to be a grammatical statement.

It is similar when we ask, "Has this room a length?", and someone answers: "Of course it has". He might have answered, "Don't ask nonsense". On the other hand "The room has length" can be used as a grammatical statement. It then says that a sentence of the form "The room is —— feet long" makes sense.

A great many philosophical difficulties are connected with that sense of the expressions "to wish", "to think", etc., which we are now considering. These can all be summed up in the question: "How can one think what is not the case?"

This is a beautiful example of a philosophical question. It asks "How can one . . .?" and while this puzzles us we must admit that nothing is easier than to think what is not the case. I mean, this shows us again that the difficulty which we are in does not arise through our inability to imagine how thinking something is done; just as the philosophical difficulty about the measurement of time did not arise through our inability to imagine how time was actually measured. I say this because sometimes it almost seems as though our difficulty were one of remembering exactly what happened when we thought something, a difficulty of introspection, or something of the sort; whereas in fact it arises when we look at the facts through the medium of a misleading form of expression.

"How can one think what is not the case? If I think that King's College is on fire when it is not on fire, the fact of its being on fire does not exist. Then how can I think it? How can we hang a thief who doesn't exist?" Our answer could be put in this form: "I can't hang him when he doesn't exist; but I can look for him when he doesn't exist".

We are here misled by the substantives "object of thought" and "fact", and by the different meanings of the word "exist".

Talking of the fact as a "complex of objects" springs from this confusion (cf. *Tractatus Logico-philosophicus*). Supposing we asked: "How can one *imagine* what does not exist?" The answer seems to be: "If we do, we imagine non-existent combinations of existing elements". A centaur doesn't exist, but a man's head and torso and arms and a horse's legs do exist. "But can't we imagine an object utterly different from any one which exists?"—We should be inclined to answer: "No; the elements, individuals, must exist. If redness, roundness and sweetness did not exist, we could not imagine them".

But what do you mean by "redness exists"? My watch exists, if it hasn't been pulled to pieces, if it hasn't been *destroyed*. What would we call "destroying redness"? We might of course mean destroying all red objects; but would this make it impossible to imagine a red object? Supposing to this one answered: "But surely, red objects must have existed and you must have seen them if you are able to imagine them"?—But how do you know that this is so? Suppose I said "Exerting a pressure on your eye-ball produces a red image". Couldn't the way by which you first became acquainted with red have been this? And why shouldn't it have been just imagining a red patch? (The difficulty which you may feel here will have to be discussed at a later occasion.[1])

We may now be inclined to say: "As the fact which would make our thought true if it existed does not always exist, it is not the *fact* which we think". But this just depends upon how I wish to use the word

[1] He does not do this.—*Edd.*

"fact". Why shouldn't I say: "I believe the fact that the college is on fire"? It is just a clumsy expression for saying: "I believe that the college is on fire". To say "It is not the fact which we believe", is itself the result of a confusion. We think we are saying something like: "It isn't the sugar-cane which we eat but the sugar", "It isn't Mr. Smith who hangs in the gallery, but his picture".

The next step we are inclined to take is to think that as the object of our thought isn't the fact it is a shadow of the fact. There are different names for this shadow, e.g. "proposition", "sense of the sentence".

But this doesn't remove our difficulty. For the question now is: "How can something be the shadow of a fact which doesn't exist?"

I can express our trouble in a different form by saying: "How can we know what the shadow is a shadow of?"—The shadow would be some sort of portrait; and therefore I can restate our problem by asking: "What makes a portrait a portrait of Mr. N?" The answer which might first suggest itself is: "The similarity between the portrait and Mr. N". This answer in fact shows what we had in mind when we talked of the shadow of a fact. It is quite clear, however, that similarity does not constitute our idea of a portrait; for it is in the essence of this idea that it should make sense to talk of a good or a bad portrait. In other words, it is essential that the shadow should be capable of representing things as in fact they are not.

An obvious, and correct, answer to the question "What makes a portrait the portrait of so-and-so?" is that it is the *intention*. But if we wish to know what it means "intending this to be a portrait of so-and-so" let's see what actually happens when we intend this. Remember the occasion when we talked of what happened when we expect some one from four to four-thirty. To intend a picture to be the portrait of so-and-so (on the part of the painter, e.g.) is neither a particular state of mind nor a particular mental process. But there are a great many combinations of actions and states of mind which we should call "intending . . ." It might have been that he was told to paint a portrait of N, and sat down before N, going through certain actions which we call "copying N's face". One might object to this by saying that the essence of copying is the intention to copy. I should answer that there are a great many different processes which we call "copying something". Take an instance. I draw an ellipse on a sheet of paper and ask you to copy it. What characterizes the process of copying? For it is clear that it isn't the fact that you draw a similar ellipse. You might have tried to copy it and not succeeded; or you might have drawn an ellipse with a totally different intention, and it happened to be like the one you should have copied. So what do you do when you try to copy the ellipse? Well, you look at it, draw something on a piece of paper, perhaps measure what you have drawn, perhaps you curse if you find it doesn't agree with the model; or perhaps you say "I am going to copy this ellipse" and just draw an ellipse like it. There are an endless variety of actions and words, having a family likeness to each other, which we call "trying to copy".

Suppose we said "that a picture is a portrait of a particular object consists in its being derived from that object in a particular way". Now it is easy to describe what we should call processes of deriving a picture from an object (roughly speaking, processes of projection). But there is a peculiar difficulty about admitting that any such process is what we call "intentional representation". For describe whatever process (activity) of projection we may, there is a way of reinterpreting this projection. Therefore—one is tempted to say—such a process can never be the intention itself. For we could always have intended the opposite by reinterpreting the process of projection. Imagine this case: We give someone an order to walk in a certain direction by pointing or by drawing an arrow which points in the direction. Suppose drawing arrows is the language in which generally we give such an order. Couldn't such an order be interpreted to mean that the man who gets it is to walk in the direction opposite to that of the arrow? This could obviously be done by adding to our arrow some symbols which we might call "an *interpretation*". It is easy to imagine a case in which, say to deceive someone, we might make an arrangement that an order should be carried out in the sense opposite to its normal one. The symbol which adds the interpretation to our original arrow could, for instance, be another arrow. Whenever we interpret a symbol in one way or another, the interpretation is a new symbol added to the old one.

Now we might say that whenever we give someone an order by showing him an arrow, and don't do it 'mechanically' (without thinking), we *mean* the arrow in one way or another. And this process of meaning, of whatever kind it may be, can be represented by another arrow (pointing in the same or the opposite sense to the first). In this picture which we make of 'meaning and saying' it is essential that we should imagine the processes of saying and meaning to take place in two different spheres.

Is it then correct to say that no arrow could be the meaning, as every arrow could be meant the opposite way?—Suppose we write down the scheme of saying and meaning by a column of arrows one below the other.

Then if this scheme is to serve our purpose at all, it must show us which of the three levels is the level of meaning. I can, e.g., make a scheme with three levels, the bottom level always being the level of meaning. But adopt whatever model or scheme you may, it will have a bottom level, and there will be no such thing as an interpretation of that. To say in this case that every arrow can still be interpreted would only mean that I *could* always make a different model of saying and meaning which had one more level than the one I am using.

Let us put it in this way:—What one wishes to say is: "Every sign is capable of interpretation; but the *meaning* mustn't be capable of interpretation. It is the last interpretation." Now I assume that you take the meaning to be a process accompanying the saying, and that it is translatable into, and so far equivalent to, a further sign. You have therefore further to tell me what you take to be the distinguishing mark between *a sign* and *the meaning*. If you do so, e.g., by saying that the meaning is the arrow which you *imagine* as opposed to any which you may draw or produce in any other way, you thereby say that you will call no further arrow an interpretation of the one which you have imagined.

All this will become clearer if we consider what it is that really happens when we say a thing and mean what we say.—Let us ask ourselves: If we say to someone "I should be delighted to see you" and mean it, does a conscious process run alongside these words, a process which could itself be translated into spoken words? This will hardly ever be the case.

But let us imagine an instance in which it does happen. Supposing I had a habit of accompanying every English sentence which I said aloud by a German sentence spoken to myself inwardly. If then, for some reason or other, you call the silent sentence the meaning of the one spoken aloud, the process of meaning accompanying the process of saying would be one which could itself be translated into outward signs. Or, *before* any sentence which we say aloud we say its meaning (whatever it may be) to ourselves in a kind of aside. An example at least similar to the case we want would be saying one thing and at the same time seeing a picture before our mind's eye which is the meaning and agrees or disagrees with what we say. Such cases and similar ones exist, but they are not at all what happens as a rule when we say something and mean it, or mean something else. There are, of course, real cases in which what we call meaning is a definite conscious process accompanying, preceding, or following the verbal expression and itself a verbal expression of some sort or translatable into one. A typical example of this is the 'aside' on the stage.

But what tempts us to think of the meaning of what we say as a process essentially of the kind which we have described is the analogy between the forms of expression:

"to say something"
"to mean something",

which seem to refer to two parallel processes.

A process accompanying our words which one might call the "process of meaning them" is the modulation of the voice in which we speak the words; or one of the processes similar to this, like the play of facial expression. These accompany the spoken words not in the way a German sentence might accompany an English sentence, or writing a sentence accompany speaking a sentence; but in the sense in which the tune of a song accompanies its words. This tune corresponds to the 'feeling' with which we say the sentence. And I wish to point out that this feeling is the expression with which the sentence is said, or something similar to this expression.

Let us revert to our question: "What is the object of a thought?" (e.g. when we say, "I think that King's College is on fire").

The question as we put it is already the expression of several confusions. This is shown by the mere fact that it almost sounds like a question of physics; like asking: "What are the ultimate constituents of matter?" (It is a typically metaphysical question; the characteristic of a metaphysical question being that we express an unclarity about the grammar of words in the *form* of a scientific question.)

One of the origins of our question is the two-fold use of the propositional function "I think x". We say, "I think that so-and-so will happen" or "that so-and-so is the case", and also "I think just the same *thing* as he"; and we say "I expect him", and also "I expect that he will come". Compare "I expect him" and "I shoot him". We can't shoot him if he isn't there. This is how the question arises: "How can we expect something that is not the case?", "How can we expect a fact which does not exist?"

The way out of this difficulty seems to be: what we expect is not the fact, but a shadow of the fact; as it were, the next thing to the fact. We have said that this is only pushing the question one step further back. There are several origins to this idea of a shadow. One of them is this: we say "Surely two sentences of different languages can have the same sense"; and we argue, "therefore the sense is not the same as the sentence", and ask the question "What is the sense?" And we make of 'it' a shadowy being, one of the many which we create when we wish to give meaning to substantives to which no material objects correspond.

Another source of the idea of a shadow being the object of our thought is this: We imagine the shadow to be a picture the intention of which *cannot be questioned*, that is, a picture which we don't interpret in order to understand it, but which we understand without interpreting it. Now there are pictures of which we should say that we interpret them, that is, translate them into a different kind of picture, in order to understand them; and pictures of which we should say that we understand them immediately, without any further interpretation. If you see a telegram written in cipher, and you know the key to this cipher, you will, in general, not say that you understand the telegram before you have translated it into ordinary language. Of course you have only replaced one kind of symbols by another; and yet if now you read the telegram in your language no further process of interpretation will take place.—Or rather, you may now, in certain cases, again translate this telegram, say into a picture; but then too you have only replaced one set of symbols by another.

The shadow, as we think of it, is some sort of a picture; in fact, something very much like an image which comes before our mind's eye; and this again is something not unlike a painted representation in the ordinary sense. A source of the idea of the shadow certainly is the fact that in some cases saying, hearing, or reading a sentence brings images before our mind's eye, images which more or less strictly correspond to the sentence, and which are therefore, in a sense, translations of this sentence into a pictorial language.— But it is absolutely essential for the picture which we imagine the shadow to be that it is what I shall call a "picture by similarity". I don't mean by this that it is a picture similar to what it is intended to represent, but that it is a picture which is correct only when it is similar to what it represents. One might use for this kind of picture the word "copy". Roughly speaking, copies are good pictures when they can easily be mistaken for what they represent.

A plane projection of one hemisphere of our terrestrial globe is not a picture by similarity or a copy in this sense. It would be conceivable that I portrayed some one's face by projecting it in some queer way, though correctly according to the adopted rule of projection, on a piece of paper, in such a way that no one would normally call the projection "a good portrait of so-and-so" because it would not look a bit like him.

If we keep in mind the possibility of a picture which, though correct, has no similarity with its object, the interpolation of a shadow between the sentence and reality loses all point. For now the sentence itself can serve as such a shadow. The sentence is just such a picture, which hasn't the slightest similarity with what it represents. If we were doubtful about how the sentence "King's College is on fire" can be a picture of King's College on fire, we need only ask ourselves: "How should we explain what the sentence means?" Such an explanation might consist of ostensive definitions. We should say, e.g., "this is King's College" (pointing to the building), "this is a fire" (pointing to a fire). This shews you the way in which words and things may be connected.

The idea that that which we wish to happen must be present as a shadow in our wish is deeply rooted in our forms of expression. But, in fact, we might say that it is only the next best absurdity to the one which we should really like to say. If it weren't too absurd we should say that the fact which we wish for must be present in our wish. For how can we wish *just this* to happen if just this isn't present in our wish? It is quite true to say: The mere shadow won't do; for it stops short before the object; and we want the wish to contain the object itself.—We want that the wish that Mr. Smith should come into this room should wish that just *Mr. Smith*, and no substitute, should do the *coming*, and no substitute for that, *into my room*, and no substitute for that. But this is exactly what we said.

Our confusion could be described in this way: Quite in accordance with our usual form of expression we think of the fact which we wish for as a thing which is not yet here, and to which, therefore, we cannot point. Now in order to understand the grammar of our expression "object of our wish" let's just consider the answer which we give to the question: "What is the object of your wish?" The answer to this question of course is "I wish that so-and-so should happen". Now what would the answer be if we went on asking: "And what is the object of this wish?" It could only consist in a repetition of our previous expression of the wish, or else in a translation into some other form of expression. We might, e.g., state what we wished in other words or illustrate it by a picture, etc., etc. Now when we are under the impression that what we call the object of our wish is, as it were, a man who has not yet entered our room, and therefore can't yet be seen, we imagine that any explanation of what it is we wish is only the next best thing to the explanation which would show *the actual fact*—which, we are afraid, can't yet be shown as it has not yet entered.—It is as though I said to some one "I am expecting Mr. Smith", and he asked me "Who is Mr. Smith?", and I answered, "I can't show him to you now, as he isn't there. All I can show you is a picture of him". It then seems as though I could never entirely explain what I wished until it had actually happened. But of course this is a delusion. The truth is that I needn't be able to give a better explanation of what I wished after the wish was fulfilled than before; for I might perfectly well have shown Mr. Smith to my friend, and have shown him what "coming in" means, and have shown him what my room is, before Mr. Smith came into my room.

Our difficulty could be put this way: We think about things,—but how do these things enter into our thoughts? We think about Mr. Smith; but Mr. Smith need not be present. A picture of him won't do; for how are we to know whom it represents? In fact no substitute for him will do. Then how can he himself be an object of our thoughts? (I am here using the expression "object of our thought" in a way different from that in which I have used it before. I mean now a thing I am thinking *about*, not 'that which I am thinking'.)

We said the connection between our thinking, or speaking, about a man and the man himself was made when, in order to explain the meaning of the word "Mr. Smith" we pointed to him, saying "this is Mr. Smith". And there is nothing mysterious about this connection. I mean, there is no queer mental act which somehow conjures up Mr. Smith in our minds when he really isn't here. What makes it difficult to see that this is the connection is a peculiar form of expression of ordinary language, which makes it appear that the connection between our thought (or the expression of our thought) and the thing we think about must have subsisted *during* the act of thinking.

"Isn't it queer that in Europe we should be able to mean someone who is in America?"—If someone had said "Napoleon was crowned in 1804", and we asked him "Did you mean the man who won the battle of Austerlitz?" he might say "Yes, I meant him". And the use of the past tense "meant" might make it appear as though the idea of Napoleon having won the battle of Austerlitz must have been present in the man's mind when he said that Napoleon was crowned in 1804.

Someone says, "Mr. N. will come to see me this afternoon"; I ask "Do you mean him?" pointing to someone present, and he answers "Yes". In this conversation a connection was established between the word "Mr. N." and Mr. N. But we are tempted to think that while my friend said, "Mr. N. will come to see me", and meant what he said, his mind must have made the connection.

This is partly what makes us think of meaning or thinking as a peculiar *mental activity*; the word "mental" indicating that we mustn't expect to understand how these things work.

What we said of thinking can also be applied to imagining. Someone says, he imagines King's College on fire. We ask him: "How do you know that it's *King's College* you imagine on fire? Couldn't it be a different building, very much like it? In fact, is your imagination so absolutely exact that there might not be a dozen buildings whose representation your image could be?"—And still you say: "There's no doubt I imagine King's College and no other building". But can't saying this be making the very connection we want? For saying it is like writing the words "Portrait of Mr. So-and-so" under a picture. It might have been that *while* you imagined King's College on fire you said the words "King's College is on fire". But in very many cases you certainly don't speak explanatory words in your mind while you have the image. And consider, even if you do, you are not going the whole way from your image to King's College, but only to the words "King's College". The connection between these words and King's College was, perhaps, made at another time.

The fault which in all our reasoning about these matters we are inclined to make is to think that images and experiences of all sorts, which are in some sense closely connected with each other, must be present in our mind at the same time. If we sing a tune we know by heart, or say the alphabet, the notes or letters seem to hang together, and each seems to draw the next after it, as though they were a string of pearls in a box, and by pulling out one pearl I pulled out the one following it.

Now there is no doubt that, having the visual image of a string of beads being pulled out of a box through a hole in the lid, we should be inclined to say: "These beads must all have been together in the box before". But it is easy to see that this is making a hypothesis. I should have had the same image if the beads had gradually come into existence in the hole of the lid. We easily overlook the distinction between stating a conscious mental event, and making a hypothesis about what one might call the mechanism of the mind. All the more as such hypotheses or pictures of the working of our mind are embodied in many of the forms of expression of our everyday language. The past tense "meant" in the sentence "I meant the man who won the battle of Austerlitz" is part of such a picture, the mind being conceived as a place in which what we remember is kept, stored, before we express it. If I whistle a tune I know well and am interrupted in the middle, if then someone asks me "did you know how to go on?" I should answer "yes, I did". What sort of process is this *knowing how to go on*? It might appear as though the whole continuation of the tune had to be present while I knew how to go on.

Ask yourself such a question as: "How long does it take to know how to go on?" Or is it an instantaneous process? Aren't we making a mistake like mixing up the existence of a gramophone record of a tune with the existence of the tune? And aren't we assuming that whenever a tune passes through existence there must be some sort of a gramophone record of it from which it is played?

Consider the following example: A gun is fired in my presence and I say: "This crash wasn't as loud as I had expected". Someone asks me: "How is this possible? Was there a crash, louder than that of a gun, in your imagination?" I must confess that there was nothing of the sort. Now he says: "Then you didn't really expect a louder crash—but perhaps the shadow of one.—And how did you know that it was the shadow of a louder crash?"—Let's see what, in such a case, might really have happened. Perhaps in waiting for the report I opened my mouth, held on to something to steady myself, and perhaps I said: "This is going to be terrible". Then, when the explosion was over: "It wasn't so loud after all".—Certain tensions in my body relax. But what is the connection between these tensions, opening my mouth, etc., and a real louder crash? Perhaps this connection was made by having heard such a crash and having had the experiences mentioned.

Examine expressions like "having an idea in one's mind", "analysing the idea before one's mind". In order not to be misled by them see what really happens when, say, in writing a letter you are looking for the words which correctly express the idea which is "before your mind". To say that we are trying to express the idea which is before our mind is to use a metaphor, one which very naturally suggests itself; and which is all right so long as it doesn't mislead us when we are philosophizing. For when we recall what really happens in such cases we find a great variety of processes more or less akin to each other.—We might be inclined to say that in all such cases, at any rate, we are *guided* by something before our mind. But then the words "guided" and "thing before our mind" are used in as many senses as the words "idea" and "expression of an idea".

The phrase "to express an idea which is before our mind" suggests that what we are trying to express in words is already expressed, only in a different language; that this expression is before our mind's eye; and that what we do is to translate from the mental into the verbal language. In most cases which we call "expressing an idea, etc." something very different happens. Imagine what it is that happens in cases such as this: I am groping for a word. Several words are suggested and I reject them. Finally one is proposed and I say: "That is what I meant!"

(We should be inclined to say that the proof of the impossibility of trisecting the angle with ruler and compasses analyses our idea of the trisection of an angle. But the proof gives us a new idea of tri-section, one which we didn't have before the proof constructed it. The proof led us a road *which we were inclined to go*; but it led us away from where we were, and didn't just show us clearly the place where we had been all the time.)

Let us now revert to the point where we said that we gained nothing by assuming that a shadow must intervene between the expression of our thought and the reality with which our thought is concerned. We said that if we wanted a picture of reality the sentence itself *is* such a picture (though not a picture by similarity).

I have been trying in all this to remove the temptation to think that there '*must*' be' what is called a mental process of thinking, hoping, wishing, believing, etc., independent of the process of expressing a thought, a hope, a wish, etc. And I want to give you the following rule of thumb: If you are puzzled about the nature of thought, belief, knowledge, and the like, substitute for the thought the expression of the thought, etc. The difficulty which lies in this substitution, and at the same time the whole point of it, is this: the expression of belief, thought, etc., is just a sentence;—and the sentence has sense only as a member of a system of language; as one expression within a calculus. Now we are tempted to imagine this calculus, as it were, as a permanent background to every sentence which we say, and to think that, although the sentence as written on a piece of paper or spoken stands isolated, in the mental act of thinking the calculus is there—all in a lump. The mental act seems to perform in a miraculous way what could not be performed by any act of manipulating symbols. Now when the temptation to think that in some sense the whole calculus must be present at the same time vanishes, there is no more point in *postulating* the existence of a peculiar kind of mental act alongside of our expression. This, of course, doesn't mean that we have shown that peculiar acts of consciousness do not accompany the expressions of our thoughts! Only we no longer say that they *must* accompany them.

"But the expression of our thoughts can always lie, for we may say one thing and mean another". Imagine the many different things which happen when we say one thing and mean another!—Make the following experiment: say the sentence "It is hot in this room", and mean: "it is cold". Observe closely what you are doing.

We could easily imagine beings who do their private thinking by means of 'asides' and who manage their lies by saying one thing aloud, following it up by an aside which says the opposite.

"But meaning, thinking, etc., are private experiences. They are not activities like writing, speaking, etc."—But why shouldn't they be the specific private experiences of writing—the muscular, visual, tactile sensations of writing or speaking?

Make the following experiment: say and mean a sentence, e.g.: "It will probably rain tomorrow". Now think the same thought again, mean what you just meant, but without saying anything (either aloud or to yourself). If thinking that it will rain tomorrow accompanied saying that it will rain tomorrow, then just do the first activity and leave out the second.—If thinking and speaking stood in the relation of the words and the melody of a song, we could leave out the speaking and do the thinking just as we can sing the tune without the words.

But can't one at any rate speak **and** leave out the thinking? Certainly—but observe what sort of thing you are doing if you speak without thinking. Observe first of all that the process which we might call "speaking and meaning what you speak" is not necessarily distinguished from that of speaking thoughtlessly by what happens *at the time when you speak*. What distinguishes the two may very well be what happens before or after you speak.

Suppose I tried, deliberately, to speak without thinking;—what in fact would I do? I might read out a sentence from a book, trying to read it automatically, that is, trying to prevent myself from following the sentence with images and sensations which otherwise it would produce. A way of doing this would be to concentrate my attention on something else while I was speaking the sentence, e.g., by pinching my skin hard while I was speaking.—Put it this way: Speaking a sentence without thinking consists in switching on speech and switching off certain accompaniments of speech. Now ask yourself: Does thinking the sentence without speaking it consist in turning over the switch (switching on what we previously switched off and vice versa); that is: does thinking the sentence without speaking it now simply consist in keeping on what accompanied the words but leaving out the words? Try to think the thoughts of a sentence without the sentence and see whether this is what happens.

Let us sum up: If we scrutinize the usages which we make of such words as "thinking", "meaning", "wishing", etc., going through this process rids us of the temptation to look for a peculiar act of thinking, independent of the act of expressing our thoughts, and stowed away in some peculiar medium. We are no longer prevented by the established forms of expression from recognizing that the experience of thinking *may* be just the experience of saying, or may consist of this experience plus others which accompany it. (It is useful also to examine the following case: Suppose a multiplication is part of a sentence; ask yourself what it is like to say the multiplication $7 \times 5 = 35$, thinking it, and, on the other hand, saying it without thinking.) The scrutiny of the grammar of a word weakens the position of certain fixed standards of our expression which had prevented us from seeing facts with unbiassed eyes. Our investigation tried to remove this bias, which forces us to think that the facts *must* conform to certain pictures embedded in our language.

"Meaning" is one of the words of which one may say that they have odd jobs in our language. It is these words which cause most philosophical troubles. Imagine some institution: most of its members have certain regular functions, functions which can easily be described, say, in the statutes of the institution. There are, on the other hand, some members who are employed for odd jobs, which nevertheless may be extremely important.—What causes most trouble in philosophy is that we are tempted to describe the use of important 'odd-job' words as though they were words with regular functions.

The reason I postponed talking about personal experience was that thinking about this topic raises a host of philosophical difficulties which threaten to break up all our commonsense notions about what we should commonly call the objects of our experience. And if we were struck by these problems it might seem to us that all we have said about signs and about the various objects we mentioned in our examples may have to go into the melting-pot.

The situation in a way is typical in the study of philosophy; and one sometimes has described it by saying that no philosophical problem can be solved until all philosophical problems are solved; which means that as long as they aren't all solved every new difficulty renders all our previous results questionable. To this statement we can only give a rough answer if we are to speak about philosophy in such general terms. It is, that every new problem which arises may put in question the *position* which our previous partial results are to occupy in the final picture. One then speaks of having to reinterpret these previous results; and we should say: they have to be placed in a different surrounding.

Imagine we had to arrange the books of a library. When we begin the books lie higgledy-piggledy on the floor. Now there would be many ways of sorting them and putting them in their places. One would be to take the books one by one and put each on the shelf in its right place. On the other hand we might take up several books from the floor and put them in a row on a shelf, merely in order to indicate that these books ought to go together in this order. In the course of arranging the library this whole row of books will have to change its place. But it would be wrong to say that therefore putting them together on a shelf was no step towards the final result. In this case, in fact, it is pretty obvious that having put together books which belong together was a definite achievement, even though the whole row of them had to be shifted. But some of the greatest achievements in philosophy could only be compared with taking up some books which seemed to belong together, and putting them on different shelves; nothing more being final about their positions than that they no longer lie side by side. The onlooker who doesn't know the difficulty of the task might well think in such a case that nothing at all had been achieved.—The difficulty in philosophy is to say no more than we know. E.g., to see that when we have put two books together in their right order we have not thereby put them in their final places.

When we think about the relation of the objects surrounding us to our personal experiences of them, we are sometimes tempted to say that these personal experiences are the material of which reality consists. How this temptation arises will become clearer later on.

When we think in this way we seem to lose our firm hold on the objects surrounding us. And instead we are left with a lot of separate personal experiences of different individuals. These personal experiences again seem vague and seem to be in constant flux. Our language seems not to have been made to describe them. We are tempted to think that in order to clear up such matters philosophically our ordinary language is too coarse, that we need a more subtle one.

We seem to have made a discovery—which I could describe by saying that the ground on which we stood and which appeared to be firm and reliable was found to be boggy and unsafe.—That is, this happens when we philosophize; for as soon as we revert to the standpoint of common sense this *general* uncertainty disappears.

This queer situation can be cleared up somewhat by looking at an example; in fact a kind of parable illustrating the difficulty we are in, and also showing the way out of this sort of difficulty: We have been told by popular scientists that the floor on which we stand is not solid, as it appears to common sense, as it has been discovered that the wood consists of particles filling space so thinly that it can almost be called empty. This is liable to perplex us, for in a way of course we know that the floor is solid, or that, if it isn't solid, this may be due to the wood being rotten but not to its being composed of electrons. To say, on this latter ground, that the floor is not solid is to misuse language. For even if the particles were as big as grains of sand, and as close together as these are in a sandheap, the floor would not be solid if it were composed of them in the sense in which a sandheap is composed of grains. Our perplexity was based on a misunderstanding; the picture of the thinly filled space had been wrongly *applied*. For this picture of the structure of matter was meant to explain the very phenomenon of solidity.

As in this example the word "solidity" was used wrongly and it seemed that we had shown that nothing really was solid, just in this way, in stating our puzzles about the *general vagueness* of sense-experience, and about the flux of all phenomena, we are using the words "flux" and "vagueness" wrongly, in a typically metaphysical way, namely without an antithesis; whereas in their correct and every-day use vagueness is opposed to clearness, flux to stability, inaccuracy to accuracy, and *problem* to *solution*. The very word "problem", one might say, is misapplied when used for our philosophical troubles. These difficulties, as long as they are seen as problems, are tantalizing, and appear insoluble.

There is a temptation for me to say that only my own experience is real: "I know that *I* see, hear, feel pains, etc., but not that anyone else does. I can't know this, because I am I and they are they."

On the other hand I feel ashamed to say to anyone that my experience is the only real one; and I know that he will reply that he could say exactly the same thing about his experience. This seems to lead to a silly quibble. Also I am told: "If you pity someone for having pains, surely you must at least *believe* that he has pains". But how can I even *believe* this? How can these words make sense to me? How could I even have come by the idea of another's experience if there is no possibility of any evidence for it?

But wasn't this a queer question to ask? *Can't* I believe that someone else has pains? Is it not quite easy to believe this?—Is it an answer to say that things are as they appear to common sense?—Again, needless to say, we don't feel these difficulties in ordinary life. Nor is it true to say that we feel them when we scrutinize our experiences by intro-spection, or make scientific investigations about them. But somehow, when we look at them in a certain way, our expression is liable to get into a tangle. It seems to us as though we had either the wrong pieces, or not enough of them, to put together our jig-saw puzzle. But they are all there, only all mixed up; and there is a further analogy between the jig-saw puzzle and our case: It's no use trying to apply force in fitting pieces together. All we should do is to look at them *carefully* and arrange them.

There are propositions of which we may say that they describe facts in the material world (external world). Roughly speaking, they treat of physical objects: bodies, fluids, etc. I am not thinking in particular of the laws of the natural sciences, but of any such proposi-tion as "the tulips in our garden are in full bloom", or "Smith will come in any moment". There are on the other hand propositions describing personal experiences, as when the subject in a psychological experiment describes his sense-experiences; say his visual experience, independent of what bodies are actually before his eyes and, *n.b.*, independent also of any processes which might be observed to take place in his retina, his nerves, his brain, or other parts of his body. (That is, independent of both physical and physiological facts.)

At first sight it may appear (but why it should can only become clear later) that here we have two kinds of worlds, worlds built of different materials; a mental world and a physical world. The mental world in fact is liable to be imagined as gaseous, or rather, aethereal. But let me remind you here of the queer role which the gaseous and the aethereal play in philosophy,—when we perceive that a substantive is not used as what in general we should call the name of an object, and when therefore we can't help saying to ourselves that it is the name of an aethereal object. I mean, we already know the idea of 'aethereal objects' as a subterfuge, when we are embarrassed about the grammar of certain words, and when all we know is that they are not used as names for material objects. This is a hint as to how the problem of the two materials, *mind* and *matter*, is going to dissolve.

It seems to us sometimes as though the phenomena of personal experience were in a way phenomena in the upper strata of the atmosphere as opposed to the material phenomena which happen on the ground. There are views according to which these phenomena in the upper strata arise when the material phenomena reach a certain degree of complexity. E.g., that the mental phenomena, sense experience, volition, etc., emerge when a type of animal body of a certain complexity has been evolved. There seems to be some obvious truth in this, for the amoeba certainly doesn't speak or write or discuss, whereas we do. On the other hand the problem here arises which could be expressed by the question: "Is it possible for a machine to think?" (whether the action of this machine can be described and predicted by the laws of physics or, possibly, only by laws of a different kind applying to the behaviour of organisms). And the trouble which is expressed in this question is not really that we don't yet know a machine which could do the job. The question is not analogous to that which someone might have asked a hundred years ago: "Can a machine liquefy a gas?" The trouble is rather that the sentence, "A machine thinks (perceives, wishes)": seems somehow nonsensical. It is as though we had asked "Has the number 3 a colour?" ("What colour could it be, as it obviously has none of the colours known to us?") For in one aspect of the matter, personal experience, far from being the *product* of physical, chemical, physiological processes, seems to be the very *basis* of all that we say with any sense about such processes. Looking at it in this way we are inclined to use our idea of a building-material in yet another misleading way, and to say that the whole world, mental and physical, is made of one material only.

When we look at everything that we know and can say about the world as resting upon personal experience, then what we know seems to lose a good deal of its value, reliability, and solidity. We are then inclined to say that it is all "subjective"; and "subjective" is used derogatorily, as when we say that an opinion is *merely* subjective, a matter of taste. Now, that this aspect should seem to shake the authority of experience and knowledge points to the fact that here our language is tempting us to draw some misleading analogy. This should remind us of the case when the popular scientist appeared to have shown us that the floor which we stand on is not really solid because it is made up of electrons.

We are up against trouble caused by our way of expression.

Another such trouble, closely akin, is expressed in the sentence: "I can only know that *I* have personal experiences, not that anyone else has".—Shall we then call it an unnecessary hypothesis that anyone else has personal experiences?—But is it an hypothesis at all? For how can I even make the hypothesis if it transcends all possible experience? How could such a hypothesis be backed by meaning? (Is it not like paper money, not backed by gold?)—It doesn't help if anyone tells us that, though we don't know whether the other person has pains, we certainly believe it when, for instance, we pity him. Certainly we shouldn't pity him if we didn't believe that he had pains; but is this a philosophical, a metaphysical belief? Does a realist pity me more than an idealist or a solipsist?—In fact the solipsist asks: "How *can* we believe that the other has pain; what does it mean to believe this? How can the expression of such a supposition make sense?"

Now the answer of the common-sense philosopher—and that, *n.b.*, is not the common-sense man, who is as far from realism as from idealism—the answer of the common-sense philosopher is that surely there is no difficulty in the idea of supposing, thinking, imagining that someone else has what I have. But the trouble with the realist is always that he does not solve but skip the difficulties which his adversaries see, though they too don't succeed in solving them. The

realist answer, for us, just brings out the difficulty; for who argues
like this overlooks the difference between different usages of the words
"to have", "to imagine". "A has a gold tooth" means that the tooth is
in A's mouth. This may account for the fact that I am not able to see it.
Now the case of his toothache, of which I say that I am not able
to feel it because it is in his mouth, is not analogous to the case
of the gold tooth. It is the apparent analogy, and again the lack of
analogy, between these cases which causes our trouble. And it is this
troublesome feature in our grammar which the realist does not notice.
It is conceivable that I feel pain in a tooth in another man's mouth;
and the man who says that he cannot feel the other's toothache is
not denying *this*. The grammatical difficulty which we are in we shall
only see clearly if we get familiar with the idea of feeling pain in
another person's body. For otherwise, in puzzling about this problem,
we shall be liable to confuse our metaphysical proposition "I can't feel
his pain" with the experiential proposition, "We can't have (haven't
as a rule) pains in another person's tooth". In this proposition the
word "can't" is used in the same way as in the proposition "An iron
nail can't scratch glass". (We could write this in the form "experience
teaches that an iron nail *doesn't* scratch glass", thus doing away with
the "can't".) In order to see that it is conceivable that one person
should have pain in another person's body, one must examine what
sort of facts we call criteria for a pain being in a certain place. It is
easy to imagine the following case: When I see my hands I am not
always aware of their connection with the rest of my body. That is
to say, I often see my hand moving but don't see the arm which
connects it to my torso. Nor do I necessarily, at the time, check up
on the arm's existence in any other way. Therefore the hand may,
for all I know, be connected to the body of a man standing beside me
(or, of course, not to a human body at all). Suppose I feel a pain
which on the evidence of the pain alone, e.g., with closed eyes, I
should call a pain in my left hand. Someone asks me to touch the
painful spot with my right hand. I do so and looking round perceive
that I am touching my neighbour's hand (meaning the hand connected
to my neighbour's torso).

Ask yourself: How do we know where to point to when we are asked
to point to the painful spot? Can this sort of pointing be compared
with pointing to a black spot on a sheet of paper when someone
says: "Point to the black spot on this sheet"? Suppose someone said
"You point to this spot because you know before you point that the

pains are there"; ask yourself "What does it mean to *know* that the
pains are there?" The word "there" refers to a locality;—but in
what space, i.e., a 'locality' in what sense? Do we know the place of
pain in Euclidean space, so that when we know where we have pains
we know how far away from two of the walls of this room, and from
the floor? When I have pain in the tip of my finger and touch my tooth
with it, is my pain now both a toothache and a pain in my finger?
Certainly, in one sense the pain can be said to be located on the tooth.
Is the reason why in this case it is wrong to say I have toothache,
that in order to be in the tooth the pain should be one sixteenth of an
inch away from the tip of my finger? Remember that the word "where"
can refer to localities in many different senses. (Many different grammatical games, resembling each other *more* or *less*, are played with this
word. Think of the different uses of the numeral "1".) I may know
where a thing is and then point to it by virtue of that knowledge.
The knowledge tells me where to point to. We here conceived this
knowledge as the condition for deliberately pointing to the object.
Thus one can say: "I can point to the spot you mean because I see it",
"I can direct you to the place because I know where it is; first turning
to the right, etc." Now one is inclined to say "I must know where a
thing is before I can point to it". Perhaps you will feel less happy
about saying: "I must know where a thing is before I can look at it".
Sometimes of course it is correct to say this. But we are tempted to
think that there is one particular psychical state or event, the knowledge of the place, which must precede every deliberate act of pointing,
moving towards, etc. Think of the analogous case: "One can only
obey an order after having understood it".

If I point to the painful spot on my arm, in what sense can I be said
to have known where the pain was before I pointed to the place?
Before I pointed I could have said "The pain is in my left arm".
Supposing my arm had been covered with a meshwork of lines
numbered in such a way that I could refer to any place on its surface.
Was it necessary that I should have been able to describe the painful
spot by means of these co-ordinates before I could point to it? What
I wish to say is that the act of pointing *determines* a place of pain. This
act of pointing, by the way, is not to be confused with that of finding
the painful spot by probing. In fact the two may lead to different
results.

An innumerable variety of cases can be thought of in which we
should say that someone has pains in another person's body; or, say,

in a piece of furniture, or in any empty spot. Of course we mustn't forget that a pain in a particular part of our body, e.g., in an upper tooth, has a peculiar tactile and kinaesthetic neighbourhood. Moving our hand upward a little distance we touch our eye; and the word "little distance" here refers to tactile distance or kinaesthetic distance, or both. (It is easy to imagine tactile and kinaesthetic distances correlated in ways different from the usual. The distance from our mouth to our eye might seem very great 'to the muscles of our arm' when we move our finger from the mouth to the eye. Think how large you imagine the cavity in your tooth when the dentist is drilling and probing it.)

When I said that if we moved our hand upward a little, we touch our eye, I was referring to tactile evidence only. That is, the criterion for my finger touching my eye was to be only that I had the particular feeling which would have made me say that I was touching my eye, even if I had no visual evidence for it, and even if, on looking into a mirror, I saw my finger not touching my eye, but, say, my forehead. Just as the 'little distance' I referred to was a tactile or kinaesthetic one, so also the places of which I said, "they lie a little distance apart" were tactile places. To say that my finger in tactile and kinaesthetic space moves from my tooth to my eye then means that I have those tactile and kinaesthetic experiences which we normally have when we say "my finger moves from my tooth to my eye". But what we regard as evidence for this latter proposition is, as we all know, by no means only tactile and kinaesthetic. In fact if I had the tactile and kinaesthetic sensations referred to, I might still deny the proposition "my finger moves etc. . . ." because of what I saw. That proposition is a proposition about physical objects. (And now don't think that the expression "physical objects" is meant to distinguish one kind of object from another.) The grammar of propositions which we call propositions about physical objects admits of a variety of evidences for every such proposition. It characterizes the grammar of the proposition "my finger moves, etc." that I regard the propositions "I see it move", "I feel it move", "He sees it move", "He tells me that it moves", etc. as evidences for it. Now if I say "I see my hand move", this at first sight seems to presuppose that I agree with the proposition "my hand moves". But if I regard the proposition "I see my hand move" as one of the evidences for the proposition "my hand moves", the truth of the latter is, of course, not presupposed in the truth of the former. One might therefore suggest the expression "It looks as though my hand were moving" instead of "I see my hand moving". But this expression, although it indicates that my hand may appear to be moving without really moving, might still suggest that after all there must be a hand in order that it should appear to be moving; whereas we could easily imagine cases in which the proposition describing the visual evidence is true and at the same time other evidences make us say that I have no hand. Our ordinary way of expression obscures this. We are handicapped in ordinary language by having to describe, say, a tactile sensation by means of terms for physical objects such as the word "eye", "finger", etc., when what we want to say does not entail the existence of an eye or finger, etc.. We have to use a roundabout description of our sensations. This of course does not mean that ordinary language is insufficient for our special purposes, but that it is slightly cumbrous and sometimes misleading. The reason for this peculiarity of our language is of course the regular coincidence of certain sense experiences. Thus when I feel my arm moving I mostly also can see it moving. And if I touch it with my hand, also that hand feels the motion, etc. (The man whose foot has been amputated will describe a particular pain as pain in his foot.) We feel in such cases a strong need for such an expression as: "a sensation travels from my tactual cheek to my tactual eye". I said all this because, if you are aware of the tactual and kinaesthetic environment of a pain, you may find a difficulty in imagining that one could have toothache anywhere else than in one's own teeth. But if we imagine such a case, this simply means that we imagine a correlation between visual, tactual, kinaesthetic, etc., experiences different from the ordinary correlation. Thus we can imagine a person having the sensation of toothache plus those tactual and kinaesthetic experiences which are normally bound up with seeing his hand travelling from his tooth to his nose, to his eyes, etc., but correlated to the visual experience of his hand moving to those places in another person's face. Or again, we can imagine a person having the kinaesthetic sensation of moving his hand, and the tactual sensation, in his fingers and face, of his fingers moving over his face, whereas his kinaesthetic and visual sensations should have to be described as those of his fingers moving over his knee. If we had a sensation of toothache plus certain tactual and kinaesthetic sensations usually characteristic of touching the painful tooth and neighbouring parts of our face, and if these sensations were accompanied by seeing my hand touch, and move about on, the edge of my table, we should feel doubtful whether to call this experience an experience of toothache in the table or not. If, on the other hand, the tactual and kinaesthetic sensations described were correlated to the visual experience of seeing my hand touch a tooth and other parts of the face of another person, there is no doubt that I would call this experience "toothache in another person's tooth".

I said that the man who contended that it was impossible to feel the other person's pain did not thereby wish to deny that one person could feel pain in another person's body. In fact, he would have said: "I may have toothache in another man's tooth, but not *his* toothache".

Thus the propositions "A has a gold tooth" and "A has toothache" are not used analogously. They differ in their grammar where at first sight they might not seem to differ.

As to the use of the word "imagine"—one might say: "Surely there is quite a definite act of imagining the other person to have pain". Of course we don't deny this, or any other statement about facts. But let us see: If we make an image of the other person's pain, do we apply it in the same way in which we apply the image, say, of a black eye, when we imagine the other person having one? Let us again replace imagining, in the ordinary sense, by making a painted image. (This could quite well be *the* way certain beings did their imagining.) Then let a man imagine in this way that A has a black eye. A very important application of this picture will be comparing it with the real eye to see if the picture is correct. When we vividly imagine that some-one suffers pain, there often enters in our image what one might call a shadow of a pain felt in the locality corresponding to that in which we say his pain is felt. But the sense in which an image is an image is determined by the way in which it is compared with reality. This we might call the method of projection. Now think of comparing an image of A's toothache with his toothache. How would you compare them? If you say, you compare them 'indirectly' via his bodily behaviour, I answer that this means you *don't* compare them as you compare the picture of his behaviour with his behaviour.

Again, when you say, "I grant you that you can't *know* when A has pain, you can only conjecture it", you don't see the difficulty which lies in the different uses of the words "conjecturing" and "knowing". What sort of impossibility were you referring to when you said you *couldn't* know? Weren't you thinking of a case analogous to that when one couldn't know whether the other man had a gold tooth in his mouth because he had his mouth shut? Here what you didn't know you could nevertheless imagine knowing; it made sense to say that you saw that tooth although you didn't see it; or rather, it makes sense to say that you don't see his tooth and therefore it also makes sense to say that you do. When on the other hand, you granted me that a man can't *know* whether the other person has pain, you do not wish to say that as a matter of fact people didn't know, but that it made no sense to say they knew (and therefore no sense to say they don't know). If therefore in this case you use the term "conjecture" or "believe", you don't use it as opposed to "know". That is, you did not state that knowing was a goal which you could not reach, and that you have to be contented with conjecturing; rather, there is no goal in this game. Just as when one says "You can't count through the whole series of cardinal numbers", one doesn't state a fact about human frailty but about a convention which we have made. Our statement is not comparable, though always falsely compared, with such a one as "it is impossible for a human being to swim across the Atlantic"; but it *is* analogous to a statement like "there is no goal in an endurance race". And this is one of the things which the person feels dimly who is not satisfied with the explanation that though you can't know . . . you can conjecture. . . .

If we are angry with someone for going out on a cold day with a cold in his head, we sometimes say: "I won't feel your cold". And this can mean: "I don't suffer when you catch a cold". This is a proposition taught by experience. For we could imagine a, so to speak, wireless connection between the two bodies which made one person feel pain in his head when the other had exposed his to the cold air. One might in this case argue that the pains are mine because they are felt in my head; but suppose I and someone else had a part of our bodies in common, say a hand. Imagine the nerves and tendons of my arm and A's connected to this hand by an operation. Now imagine the hand stung by a wasp. Both of us cry, contort our faces, give the same description of the pain, etc. Now are we to say we have the same pain or different ones? If in such a case you say: "We feel pain in the same place, in the same body, our descriptions tally, but still my pain can't be his", I suppose as a reason you will be inclined to say: "because my pain is my pain and his pain is his pain". And here you are making a grammatical statement about the use of such a phrase as "the same pain". You say that you don't wish to apply the phrase, "he has got my pain" or "we both have the same pain", and instead, perhaps, you will apply such a phrase as "his pain is exactly like mine". (It would be no argument to say that the two couldn't have the same pain because one might anaesthetize or kill one of them while the other still felt pain.) Of course, if we exclude the phrase "I have his toothache" from our language, we thereby also exclude "I have (or feel) *my* toothache". Another form of our metaphysical statement is this: "A man's sense data are private to himself". And this way of expressing it is even more misleading because it looks still more like an experiential proposition; the philosopher who says this may well think that he is expressing a kind of scientific truth.

We use the phrase "two books have the same colour", but we could perfectly well say: "They can't have the *same* colour, because, after all, this book has its own colour, and the other book has its own colour too". This also would be stating a grammatical rule—a rule, incidentally, not in accordance with our ordinary usage. The reason why one should think of these two different usages at all is this: We compare the case of sense data with that of physical bodies, in which case we make a distinction between: "this is the same chair that I saw an hour ago" and "this is not the same chair, but one exactly like the other". Here it makes sense to say, and it is an experiential proposition: "A and B couldn't have seen the same chair, for A was in London and B in Cambridge; they saw two chairs exactly alike". (Here it will be useful if you consider the different criteria for what we call the "identity of these objects". How do we apply the statements: "This is the same day . . .", "This is the same word . . .", "This is the same occasion . . .", etc.?)

What we did in these discussions was what we always do when we meet the word "can" in a metaphysical proposition. We show that this proposition hides a grammatical rule. That is to say, we destroy the outward similarity between a metaphysical proposition and an experiential one, and we try to find the form of expression which fulfils a certain craving of the metaphysician which our ordinary language does not fulfil and which, as long as it isn't fulfilled, produces the metaphysical puzzlement. Again, when in a metaphysical sense I say "I *must* always know when I have pain", this simply makes the word "know" redundant; and instead of "I know that I have pain", I can simply say "I have pain". The matter is different, of course, if we give the phrase "unconscious pain" sense by fixing experiential criteria for the case in which a man has pain and doesn't know it, and if then we say (rightly or wrongly) that as a matter of fact nobody has ever had pains which he didn't know of.

When we say "I can't feel his pain", the idea of an insurmountable barrier suggests itself to us. Let us think straight away of a similar case: "The colours green and blue can't be in the same place simultaneously". Here the picture of physical impossibility which suggests itself is, perhaps, not that of a barrier; rather we feel that the two colours are in each other's way. What is the origin of this idea?—We say three people can't sit side by side on this bench; they have no room. Now the case of the colours is not analogous to this; but it is somewhat analogous to saying: "3 × 18 inches won't go into 3 feet". This is a grammatical rule and states a logical impossibility. The proposition "three men can't sit side by side on a bench a yard long" states a physical impossibility; and this example shows clearly why the two impossibilities are confused. (Compare the proposition "He is 6 inches taller than I" with "6 foot is 6 inches longer than 5 foot 6". These propositions are of utterly different kinds, but look exactly alike.) The reason why in these cases the idea of physical impossibility suggests itself to us is that on the one hand we decide against using a particular form of expression, on the other hand we are strongly tempted to use it, since (*a*) it sounds English, or German, etc., all right, and (*b*) there are closely similar forms of expression used in other departments of our language. We have decided against using the phrase "They are in the same place"; on the other hand this phrase strongly recommends itself to us through the analogy with other phrases, so that, in a sense, we have to turn this form of expression out by force. And this is why we seem to ourselves to be rejecting a universally false proposition. We make a picture like that of the two colours being in each other's way, or that of a barrier which doesn't allow one person to come closer to another's experience than to the point of observing his behaviour; but on looking closer we find that we can't apply the picture which we have made.

Our wavering between logical and physical impossibility makes us make such statements as this: "If what I feel is always *my* pain only, what can the supposition mean that someone else has pain?" The thing to do in such cases is always to look how the words in question *are actually used in our language*. We are in all such cases thinking of a use different from that which our ordinary language makes of the words. Of a use, on the other hand, which just then for some reason strongly recommends itself to us. When something seems queer about the grammar of our words, it is because we are alternately tempted to use a word in several different ways. And it is particularly difficult to discover that an assertion which the metaphysician makes expresses discontentment with our grammar when the words of this assertion can also be used to state a fact of experience. Thus when he says "only my pain is real pain", this sentence might mean that the other people are only pretending. And when he says "this tree doesn't exist when nobody sees it", this might mean: "this tree vanishes when we turn our backs to it". The man who says "only my pain is real", doesn't mean to say that he has found out by the common criteria— the criteria, i.e., which give our words their common meanings— that the others who said they had pains were cheating. But what he rebels against is the use of *this* expression in connection with *these* criteria. That is, he objects to using this word in the particular way in which it is commonly used. On the other hand, he is not aware that he is objecting to a convention. He sees a way of dividing the country different from the one used on the ordinary map. He feels tempted, say, to use the name "Devonshire" not for the county with its conventional boundary, but for a region differently bounded. He could express this by saying: "Isn't it absurd to make *this* a county, to draw the boundaries *here*?" But what he says is: "The *real* Devonshire is this". We could answer: "What you want is only a new notation, and by a new notation no facts of geography are changed". It is true, however, that we may be irresistibly attracted or repelled by a notation. (We easily forget how much a notation, a form of expression, may mean to us, and that changing it isn't always as easy as it often is in mathematics or in the sciences. A change of clothes or of names may mean very little and it may mean a great deal.)

I shall try to elucidate the problem discussed by realists, idealists, and solipsists by showing you a problem closely related to it. It is this: "Can we have unconscious thoughts, unconscious feelings, etc.?" The idea of there being unconscious thoughts has revolted many people. Others again have said that these were wrong in supposing that there could only be conscious thoughts, and that psychoanalysis had discovered unconscious ones. The objectors to unconscious thought did not see that they were not objecting to the newly discovered psychological reactions, but to the way in which they were described. The psychoanalysts on the other hand were misled by their own way of expression into thinking that they had done more than discover new psychological reactions; that they had, in a sense, discovered conscious thoughts which were unconscious. The first could have stated their objection by saying "We don't wish to use the phrase 'unconscious thoughts'; we wish to reserve the word 'thought' for

what you call 'conscious thoughts' ". They state their case wrongly
when they say: "There can only be conscious thoughts and no unconscious ones". For if they don't wish to talk of "unconscious thought"
they should not use the phrase "conscious thought", either.

But is it not right to say that in any case the person who talks
both of conscious and unconscious thoughts thereby uses the word
"thoughts" in two different ways?—Do we use a hammer in two different
ways when we hit a nail with it and, on the other hand, drive a peg
into a hole? And do we use it in two different ways or in the same way
when we drive this peg into this hole and, on the other hand, another
peg into another hole? Or should we only call it different uses when
in one case we drive something into something and in the other, say,
we smash something? Or is this all using the hammer in one way
and is it to be called a different way only when we use the hammer as a
paper weight?—In which cases are we to say that a word is used in two
different ways and in which that it is used in one way? To say that a
word is used in two (or more) different ways does in itself not yet give
us any idea about its use. It only specifies a way of looking at this
usage by providing a schema for its description with two (or more)
subdivisions. It is all right to say: "I do *two* things with this hammer:
I drive a nail into this board and one into that board". But I could
also have said: "I am doing only one thing with this hammer; I am
driving a nail into this board and one into that board". There can be
two kinds of discussions as to whether a word is used in one way or
in two ways: (*a*) Two people may discuss whether the English word
"cleave" is only used for chopping up something or also for joining
things together. This is a discussion about the facts of a certain actual
usage. (*b*) They may discuss whether the word "altus", standing for
both "deep" and "high", is *thereby* used in two different ways. This
question is analogous to the question whether the word "thought"
is used in two ways or in one when we talk of conscious and unconscious thought. The man who says "surely, these are two different
usages" has already decided to use a two-way schema, and what he
said expressed this decision.

Now when the solipsist says that only his own experiences are real,
it is no use answering him: "Why do you tell us this if you don't
believe that we really hear it?" Or anyhow, if we give him this answer,
we mustn't believe that we have answered his difficulty. There is no
common sense answer to a philosophical problem. One can defend
common sense against the attacks of philosophers only by solving

their puzzles, i.e., by curing them of the temptation to attack common sense; not by restating the views of common sense. A philosopher is not a man out of his senses, a man who doesn't see what everybody sees; nor on the other hand is his disagreement with common sense that of the scientist disagreeing with the coarse views of the man in the street. That is, his disagreement is not founded on a more subtle knowledge of fact. We therefore have to look round for the *source* of his puzzlement. And we find that there is puzzlement and mental discomfort, not only when our curiosity about certain facts is not satisfied or when we can't find a law of nature fitting in with all our experience, but also when a notation dissatisfies us—perhaps because of various associations which it calls up. Our ordinary language, which of all possible notations is the one which pervades all our life, holds our mind rigidly in one position, as it were, and in this position sometimes it feels cramped, having a desire for other positions as well. Thus we sometimes wish for a notation which stresses a difference more strongly, makes it more obvious, than ordinary language does, or one which in a particular case uses more closely similar forms of expression than our ordinary language. Our mental cramp is loosened when we are shown the notations which fulfil these needs. These needs can be of the greatest variety.

Now the man whom we call a solipsist and who says that only his own experiences are real, does not thereby disagree with us about any practical question of fact, he does not say that we are simulating when we complain of pains, he pities us as much as anyone else, and at the same time he wishes to restrict the use of the epithet "real" to what we should call his experiences; and perhaps he doesn't want to call our experiences "experiences" at all (again without disagreeing with us about any question of fact). For he would say that it was *inconceivable* that experiences other than his own were real. He ought therefore to use a notation in which such a phrase as "A has real toothache" (where A is not he) is meaningless, a notation whose rules exclude this phrase as the rules of chess exclude a pawn's making a knight's move. The solipsist's suggestion comes to using such a phrase as "there is real toothache" instead of "Smith (the solipsist) has toothache". And why shouldn't we grant him this notation? I needn't say that in order to avoid confusion he had in this case better not use the word "real" as opposed to "simulated" at all; which just means that we shall have to provide for the distinction "real"/"simulated" in some other way. The solipsist who says "only I feel real pain", "only I really see (or hear)" is not stating an opinion; and that's why he is so sure of what he says. He is irresistibly tempted to use a certain form of expression; but we must yet find *why* he is.

The phrase "only I really see" is closely connected with the idea expressed in the assertion "we never know what the other man really sees when he looks at a thing" or this, "we can never know whether he calls the same thing 'blue' which we call 'blue' ". In fact we might argue: "I can never know what he sees or that he sees at all, for all I have is signs of various sorts which he gives me; therefore it is an unnecessary hypothesis altogether to say that he sees; what seeing is I only know from seeing myself; I have only learnt the word 'seeing' to mean what *I* do". Of course this is just not true, for I have definitely learned a different and much more complicated use of the word "to see" than I here profess. Let us make clear the tendency which guided me when I did so, by an example from a slightly different sphere: Consider this argument: "How can we wish that this paper were red if it isn't red? Doesn't this mean that I wish that which doesn't exist at all? Therefore my wish can only contain something *similar* to the paper's being red. Oughtn't we therefore to use a different word instead of 'red' when we talk of wishing that something were red? The imagery of the wish surely shows us something less definite, something hazier, than the reality of the paper being red. I should therefore say, instead of 'I wish this paper were red', something like 'I wish a pale red for this paper' ". But if in the usual way of speaking he had said, "I wish a pale red for this paper," we should, in order to fulfil his wish, have painted it a pale red—and this wasn't what he wished. On the other hand there is no objection to adopting the form of expression which he suggests as long as we know that he uses the phrase "I wish a pale *x* for this paper", always to mean what ordinarily we express by "I wish this paper had the colour *x*". What he said really recommended his notation, in the sense in which a notation can be recommended. But he did not tell us a new truth and did not show us that what we said before was false. (All this connects our present problem with the problem of negation. I will only give you a hint, by saying that a notation would be possible in which, to put it roughly, a quality had always two names, one for the case when something is said to have it, the other for the case when something is said not to have it. The negation of "This paper is red" could then be, say, "This paper is not rode". Such a notation would actually fulfil some of the

wishes which are denied us by our ordinary language and which sometimes produce a cramp of philosophical puzzlement about the idea of
negation.)

The difficulty which we express by saying "I can't know what he
sees when he (truthfully) says that he sees a blue patch" arises from the
idea that "knowing what he sees" means: "seeing that which he also
sees"; not, however, in the sense in which we do so when we both have
the same object before our eyes: but in the sense in which the object
seen would be an object, say, in his head, or in *him*. The idea is that the
same object may be before his eyes and mine, but that I can't stick my
head into his (or my mind into his, which comes to the same) so that
the *real* and *immediate* object of his vision becomes the real and immediate object of my vision too. By "I don't know what he sees" we
really mean "I don't know what he looks at", where 'what he looks at'
is hidden and he can't show it to me; it is *before his mind's eye*. Therefore,
in order to get rid of this puzzle, examine the grammatical difference
between the statements "I don't know what he sees" and "I don't
know what he looks at", as they are actually used in our language.

Sometimes the most satisfying expression of our solipsism seems to
be this: "When anything is seen (really *seen*), it is always I who see it".

What should strike us about this expression is the phrase "always
I". Always *who*?—For, queer enough, I don't mean: "always L. W."
This leads us to considering the criteria for the identity of a person.
Under what circumstances do we say: "This is the same person whom
I saw an hour ago"? Our actual use of the phrase "the same person"
and of the name of a person is based on the fact that many characteristics
which we use as the criteria for identity coincide in the vast majority of
cases. I am as a rule recognized by the appearance of my body. My
body changes its appearance only gradually and comparatively little,
and likewise my voice, characteristic habits, etc. only change slowly
and within a narrow range. We are inclined to use personal names in
the way we do, only as a consequence of these facts. This can best be
seen by imagining unreal cases which show us what different
'geometries' we would be inclined to use if facts were different.
Imagine, e.g., that all human bodies which exist looked alike, that on
the other hand, different sets of characteristics seemed, as it were,
to change their habitation among these bodies. Such a set of characteristics might be, say, mildness, together with a high pitched voice,
and slow movements, or a choleric temperament, a deep voice, and
jerky movements, and such like. Under such circumstances, although

it would be possible to give the bodies names, we should perhaps be as little inclined to do so as we are to give names to the chairs of our dining-room set. On the other hand, it might be useful to give names to the sets of characteristics, and the use of these names would now *roughly* correspond to the personal names in our present language.

Or imagine that it were usual for human beings to have two characters, in this way: People's shape, size and characteristics of behaviour periodically undergo a complete change. It is the usual thing for a man to have two such states, and he lapses suddenly from one into the other. It is very likely that in such a society we should be inclined to christen every man with two names, and perhaps to talk of the pair of persons in his body. Now were Dr. Jekyll and Mr. Hyde two persons or were they the same person who merely changed? We can say whichever we like. We are not forced to talk of a double personality.

There are many uses of the word "personality" which we may feel inclined to adopt, all more or less akin. The same applies when we define the identity of a person by means of his memories. Imagine a man whose memories on the even days of his life comprise the events of all these days, skipping entirely what happened on the odd days. On the other hand, he remembers on an odd day what happened on previous odd days, but his memory then skips the even days without a feeling of discontinuity. If we like we can also assume that he has alternating appearances and characteristics on odd and even days. Are we bound to say that here two persons are inhabiting the same body? That is, is it right to say that there are, and wrong to say that there aren't, or vice versa? Neither. For the *ordinary* use of the word "person" is what one might call a composite use suitable under the ordinary circumstances. If I assume, as I do, that these circumstances are changed, the application of the term "person" or "personality" has thereby changed; and if I wish to preserve this term and give it a use analogous to its former use, I am at liberty to choose between many uses, that is, between many different kinds of analogy. One might say in such a case that the term "personality" hasn't got one legitimate heir only. (This kind of consideration is of importance in the philosophy of mathematics. Consider the use of the words "proof", "formula", and others. Consider the question: "Why should what we do here be called 'philosophy'? Why should it be regarded as the only legitimate heir of the different activities which had this name in former times?")

Now let us ask ourselves what sort of identity of personality it is we are referring to when we say "when anything is seen, it is always I who see". What is it I want all these cases of seeing to have in common? As an answer I have to confess to myself that it is not my bodily appearance. I don't always see part of my body when I see. And it isn't essential that my body, if seen amongst the things I see, should always look the same. In fact I don't mind how much it changes. And I feel the same way about all the properties of my body, the characteristics of my behaviour, and even about my memories.— When I think about it a little longer I see that what I wished to say was: "Always when anything is seen, something is seen". I.e., that of which I said it continued during all the experiences of seeing was not any particular entity "I", but the experience of seeing itself. This may become clearer if we imagine the man who makes our solipsistic statement to point to his eyes while he says "I". (Perhaps because he wishes to be exact and wants to say expressly which eyes belong to the mouth which says "I" and to the hands pointing to his own body). But what is he pointing to? These particular eyes with the identity of physical objects? (To understand this sentence, you must remember that the grammar of words of which we say that they stand for physical objects is characterized by the way in which we use the phrase "the *same* so-and-so", or "the identical so-and-so", where "so-and-so" designates the physical object.) We said before that he did not wish to point to a particular physical object at all. The idea that he had made a significant statement arose from a confusion corresponding to the confusion between what we shall call "the geometrical eye" and "the physical eye". I will indicate the use of these terms: If a man tries to obey the order "Point to your eye", he may do many different things, and there are many different criteria which he will accept for having pointed to his eye. If these criteria, as they usually do, coincide, I may use them alternately and in different combinations to show me that I have touched my eye. If they don't coincide, I shall have to distinguish between different senses of the phrase "I touch my eye" or "I move my finger towards my eye". If, e.g., my eyes are shut, I can still have the characteristic kinaesthetic experience in my arm which I should call the kinaesthetic experience of raising my hand to my eye. That I had succeeded in doing so, I shall recognize by the peculiar tactile sensation of touching my eye. But if my eye were behind a glass plate fastened in such a way that it prevented me from exerting a pressure on my eye with my finger, there would still be a criterion of muscular sensation which would make me say that now my finger was in front of my eye. As to visual criteria, there are two I can adopt. There is the ordinary experience of seeing my hand rise and come towards my eye, and this experience, of course, is different from seeing two things meet, say, two finger tips. On the other hand, I can use as a criterion for my finger moving towards my eye, what I see when I look into a mirror and see my finger nearing my eye. If that place on my body which, we say, 'sees' is to be determined by moving my finger towards my eye, according to the second criterion, then it is conceivable that I may see with what according to other criteria is the tip of my nose, or places on my forehead; or I might in this way point to a place lying outside my body. If I wish a person to point to his eye (or his eyes) according to the second criterion *alone*, I shall express my wish by saying: "Point to your geometrical eye (or eyes)". The grammar of the word "geometrical eye" stands in the same relation to the grammar of the word "physical eye" as the grammar of the expression "the visual sense datum of a tree" to the grammar of the expression "the physical tree". In either case it confuses everything to say "the one is a *different kind* of object from the other"; for those who say that a sense datum is a different kind of object from a physical object misunderstand the grammar of the word "kind", just as those who say that a number is a different kind of object from a numeral. They think they are making such a statement as "A railway train, a railway station, and a railway car are different kinds of objects", whereas their statement is analogous to "A railway train, a railway accident, and a railway law are different kinds of objects".

What tempted me to say "it is always I who see when anything is seen", I could also have yielded to by saying: "whenever anything is seen, it is *this* which is seen", accompanying the word "this" by a gesture embracing my visual field (but not meaning by "this" the particular objects which I happen to see at the moment). One might say, "I am pointing at the visual field as such, not at anything in it". And this only serves to bring out the senselessness of the former expression.

Let us then discard the "always" in our expression. Then I can still express my solipsism by saying, "Only what *I* see (or: see now) is really seen". And here I am tempted to say: "Although by the word 'I' I don't mean L. W., it will do if the others understand 'I' to mean L. W., if just now I am in fact L. W." I could also express my claim by saying: "I am the vessel of life"; but mark, it is essential that everyone to whom I say this should be unable to understand me. It is essential that the other should not be able to understand 'what *I* really *mean*', though in practice he might do what I wish by conceding to me an exceptional position in his notation. But I wish it to be *logically* impossible that he should understand me, that is to say, it should be meaningless, not false, to say that he understands me. Thus my expression is one of the many which is used on various occasions by philosophers and supposed to convey something to the person who says it, though essentially incapable of conveying anything to anyone else. Now if for an expression to convey a meaning means to be accompanied by or to produce certain experiences, our expression may have all sorts of meanings, and I don't wish to say anything about them. But we are, as a matter of fact, misled into thinking that our expression has a meaning in the sense in which a non-metaphysical expression has; for we wrongly compare our case with one in which the other person can't understand what we say because he lacks a certain information. (This remark can only become clear if we understand the connection between grammar and sense and nonsense.)

The meaning of a phrase for us is characterized by the use we make of it. The meaning is not a mental accompaniment to the expression. Therefore the phrase "I think I mean something by it", or "I'm sure I mean something by it", which we so often hear in philosophical discussions to justify the use of an expression is for us no justification at all. We ask: "*What* do you mean?", i.e., "How do you use this expression?" If someone taught me the word "bench" and said that he sometimes or always put a stroke over it thus: "$\overline{\text{bench}}$", and that this meant something to him, I should say: "I don't know what sort of idea you associate with this stroke, but it doesn't interest me unless you show me that there is a use for the stroke in the kind of calculus in which you wish to use the word 'bench' ".—I want to play chess, and a man gives the white king a paper crown, leaving the use of the piece unaltered, but telling me that the crown has a meaning to him in the game, which he can't express by rules. I say: "as long as it doesn't alter the use of the piece, it hasn't what I call a meaning".

One sometimes hears that such a phrase as "This is here", when while I say it I point to a part of my visual field, has a kind of primitive meaning to me, although it can't impart information to anybody else.

When I say "Only this is seen", I forget that a sentence may come ever so natural to us without having any use in our calculus of lan-

guage. Think of the law of identity, "a = a", and of how we sometimes try hard to get hold of its sense, to visualize it, by looking at an
object and repeating to ourselves such a sentence as "This tree is the
same thing as this tree". The gestures and images by which I apparently
give this sentence sense are very similar to those which I use in the
case of "Only *this* is really seen". (To get clear about philosophical
problems, it is useful to become conscious of the apparently unimportant details of the particular situation in which we are inclined to make a
certain metaphysical assertion. Thus we may be tempted to say
"Only this is really seen" when we stare at unchanging surroundings,
whereas we may not at all be tempted to say this when we look about us
while walking.)

There is, as we have said, no objection to adopting a symbolism
in which a certain person always or temporarily holds an exceptional
place. And therefore, if I utter the sentence "Only I really see", it is
conceivable that my fellow creatures thereupon will arrange their
notation so as to fall in with me by saying "so-and-so is really seen"
instead of "L. W. sees so-and-so", etc., etc. What, however, is wrong,
is to think that I can *justify* this choice of notation. When I said, from
my heart, that only I see, I was also inclined to say that by "I" I didn't
really mean L. W., although for the benefit of my fellow men I might
say "It is now L. W. who really sees" though this is not what I really
mean. I could almost say that by "I" I mean something which just
now inhabits L. W., something which the others can't see. (I meant my
mind, but could only point to it via my body.) There is nothing wrong
in suggesting that the others should give me an exceptional place in
their notation; but the justification which I wish to give for it: that this
body is now the seat of that which really lives—is senseless. For
admittedly this is not to state anything which in the ordinary sense is
a matter of experience. (And don't think that it is an experiential
proposition which only I can know because only I am in the position
to have the particular experience.) Now the idea that the real I lives in
my body is connected with the peculiar grammar of the word "I",
and the misunderstandings this grammar is liable to give rise to.
There are two different cases in the use of the word "I" (or "my")
which I might call "the use as object" and "the use as subject".
Examples of the first kind of use are these: "My arm is broken", "I
have grown six inches", "I have a bump on my forehead", "The wind
blows my hair about". Examples of the second kind are: "*I* see so-
and-so", "*I* hear so-and-so", "*I* try to lift my arm", "*I* think it will

rain", "*I* have toothache". One can point to the difference between
these two categories by saying: The cases of the first category involve
the recognition of a particular person, and there is in these cases the
possibility of an error, or as I should rather put it: The possibility of
an error has been provided for. The possibility of failing to score has
been provided for in a pin game. On the other hand, it is not one of
the hazards of the game that the balls should fail to come up if I have
put a penny in the slot. It is possible that, say in an accident, I should
feel a pain in my arm, see a broken arm at my side, and think it is
mine, when really it is my neighbour's. And I could, looking into a
mirror, mistake a bump on his forehead for one on mine. On the
other hand, there is no question of recognizing a person when I say
I have toothache. To ask "are you sure that it's *you* who have pains?"
would be nonsensical. Now, when in this case no error is possible,
it is because the move which we might be inclined to think of as an
error, a 'bad move', is no move of the game at all. (We distinguish
in chess between good and bad moves, and we call it a mistake if we
expose the queen to a bishop. But it is no mistake to promote a pawn
to a king.) And now this way of stating our idea suggests itself: that
it is as impossible that in making the statement "I have toothache"
I should have mistaken another person for myself, as it is to moan with
pain by mistake, having mistaken someone else for me. To say, "I
have pain" is no more a statement *about* a particular person than
moaning is. "But surely the word 'I' in the mouth of a man refers to
the man who says it; it points to himself; and very often a man who
says it actually points to himself with his finger". But it was quite
superfluous to point to himself. He might just as well only have raised
his hand. It would be wrong to say that when someone points to the
sun with his hand, he is pointing both to the sun and himself because
it is *he* who points; on the other hand, he may by pointing attract
attention both to the sun and to himself.

The word "I" does not mean the same as "L. W." even if I am L. W.,
nor does it mean the same as the expression "the person who is now
speaking". But that doesn't mean: that "L. W." and "I" mean different
things. All it means is that these words are different instruments in
our language.

Think of words as instruments characterized by their use, and then
think of the use of a hammer, the use of a chisel, the use of a square,
of a glue pot, and of the glue. (Also, all that we say here can be understood only if one understands that a great variety of games is played

with the sentences of our language: Giving and obeying orders; asking questions and answering them; describing an event; telling a fictitious story; telling a joke; describing an immediate experience; making conjectures about events in the physical world; making scientific hypotheses and theories; greeting someone, etc., etc.) The mouth which says "I" or the hand which is raised to indicate that it is I who wish to speak, or I who have toothache, does not thereby point to anything. If, on the other hand, I wish to indicate the *place* of my pain, I point. And here again remember the difference between pointing to the painful spot without being led by the eye and on the other hand pointing to a scar on my body after looking for it. ("That's where I was vaccinated".)—The man who cries out with pain, or says that he has pain, *doesn't choose the mouth which says it.*

All this comes to saying that the person of whom we say "he has pain" is, by the rules of the game, the person who cries, contorts his face, etc. The place of the pain—as we have said—may be in another person's body. If, in saying "I", I point to my own body, I model the use of the word "I" on that of the demonstrative "this person" or "he". (This way of making the two expressions similar is somewhat analogous to that which one sometimes adopts in mathematics, say in the proof that the sum of the three angles of a triangle is 180°.

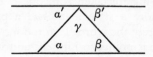

We say "$a = a'$, $\beta = \beta'$, and $\gamma = \gamma$". The first two equalities are of an entirely different kind from the third.) In "I have pain", "I" is not a demonstrative pronoun.

Compare the two cases: 1. "How do you know that *he* has pains?"—"Because I hear him moan". 2. "How do you know that you have pains?"—"Because I *feel* them". But "I feel them" means the same as "I have them". Therefore this was no explanation at all. That, however, in my answer I am inclined to stress the word "feel" and not the word "I" indicates that by "I" I don't wish to pick out one person (from amongst different persons).

The difference between the propositions "I have pain" and "he has pain" is not that of "L. W. has pain" and "Smith has pain". Rather, it corresponds to the difference between moaning and saying that some-one moans.—"But surely the word 'I' in 'I have pain' serves to dis-

tinguish me from other people, because it is by the sign 'I' that I
distinguish saying that I have pain from saying that one of the others
has". Imagine a language in which, instead of "I found nobody in
the room", one said "I found Mr. Nobody in the room". Imagine
the philosophical problems which would arise out of such a convention.
Some philosophers brought up in this language would probably feel
that they didn't like the similarity of the expressions "Mr. Nobody"
and "Mr. Smith". When we feel that we wish to abolish the "I" in
"I have pain", one may say that we tend to make the verbal expression
of pain similar to the expression by moaning.—We are inclined to
forget that it is the particular use of a word only which gives the
word its meaning. Let us think of our old example for the use of
words: Someone is sent to the grocer with a slip of paper with the
words "five apples" written on it. The use of the word *in practice*
is its meaning. Imagine it were the usual thing that the objects around
us carried labels with words on them by means of which our speech
referred to the objects. Some of these words would be proper names
of the objects, others generic names (like table, chair, etc.), others
again, names of colours, names of shapes, etc. That is to say, a label
would only have a meaning to us in so far as we made a particular
use of it. Now we could easily imagine ourselves to be impressed by
merely seeing a label on a thing, and to forget that what makes these
labels important is their use. In this way we sometimes believe that
we have named something when we make the gesture of pointing and
utter words like "This is . . ." (the formula of the ostensive definition).
We say we call something "toothache", and think that the word has
received a definite function in the dealings we carry out with language
when, under certain circumstances, we have pointed to our cheek and
said: "This is toothache". (Our idea is that when we point and the
other "only knows what we are pointing to" he knows the use of the
word. And here we have in mind the special case when 'what we point
to' is, say, a person and "to know that I point to" means to see which
of the persons present I point to.)

We feel then that in the cases in which "I" is used as subject, we
don't use it because we recognize a particular person by his bodily
characteristics; and this creates the illusion that we use this word to
refer to something bodiless, which, however, has its seat in our body.
In fact *this* seems to be the real ego, the one of which it was said,
"Cogito, ergo sum".—"Is there then no mind, but only a body?"
Answer: The word "mind" has meaning, i.e., it has a use in our

language; but saying this doesn't yet say what kind of use we make of it.

In fact one may say that what in these investigations we were concerned with was the grammar of those words which describe what are called "mental activities": seeing, hearing, feeling, etc. And this comes to the same as saying that we are concerned with the grammar of 'phrases describing sense data'.

Philosophers say it as a philosophical opinion or conviction that there are sense data. But to say that I believe that there are sense data comes to saying that I *believe* that an object may appear to be before our eyes even when it isn't. Now when one uses the word "sense datum", one should be clear about the peculiarity of its grammar. For the idea in introducing this expression was to model expressions referring to 'appearance' after expressions referring to 'reality'. It was said, e.g., that if two things *seem* to be equal, there *must* be two somethings which *are* equal. Which of course means nothing else but that we have decided to use such an expression as "the appearances of these two things are equal" synonymously with "these two things seem to be equal". Queerly enough, the introduction of this new phraseology has deluded people into thinking that they had discovered new entities, new elements of the structure of the world, as though to say "I believe that there are sense data" were similar to saying "I believe that matter consists of electrons". When we talk of the equality of appearances or sense data, we introduce a new usage of the word "equal". It is possible that the lengths A and B should appear to us to be equal, that B and C should appear to be equal, but that A and C do not appear to be equal. And in the new notation we shall have to say that though the appearance (sense datum) of A is equal to that of B and the appearance of B equal to that of C, the appearance of A is not equal to the appearance of C; which is all right if you don't mind using "equal" intransitively.

Now the danger we are in when we adopt the sense datum notation is to forget the difference between the grammar of a statement about sense data and the grammar of an outwardly similar statement about physical objects. (From this point one might go on talking about the misunderstandings which find their expression in such sentences as: "We can never see an accurate circle", "All our sense data are vague". Also, this leads to the comparison of the grammar of "position", "motion", and "size" in Euclidean and in visual space.

There is, e.g., absolute position, absolute motion and size, in visual space.)

Now we can make use of such an expression as "pointing to the *appearance* of a body" or "pointing to a visual sense datum". Roughly speaking, this sort of pointing comes to the same as sighting, say, along the barrel of a gun. Thus we may point and say: "This is the direction in which I see my image in the mirror". One can also use such an expression as "the appearance, or sense datum, of my finger points to the sense datum of the tree" and similar ones. From these cases of pointing, however, we must distinguish those of pointing in the direction a sound seems to come from, or of pointing to my forehead with closed eyes, etc.

Now when in the solipsistic way I say "*This* is what's really seen", I point before me and it is essential that I point *visually*. If I pointed sideways or behind me—as it were, to things which I don't see—the pointing would in this case be meaningless to me; it would not be pointing in the sense in which I wish to point. But this means that when I point before me saying "this is what's really seen", although I make the gesture of pointing, I don't point to one thing as opposed to another. This is as when travelling in a car and feeling in a hurry, I instinctively press against something in front of me as though I could push the car from inside.

When it makes sense to say "I see this", or "this is seen", pointing to what I see, it also makes *sense* to say "I see this", or "this is seen", pointing to something I *don't* see. When I made my solipsist statement, I pointed, but I robbed the pointing of its sense by inseparably connecting that which points and that to which it points. I constructed a clock with all its wheels, etc., and in the end fastened the dial to the pointer and made it go round with it. And in this way the solipsist's "Only this is really seen" reminds us of a tautology.

Of course one of the reasons why we are tempted to make our pseudo-statement is its similarity with the statement "I only see this", or "this is the region which I see", where I point to certain objects around me, as opposed to others, or in a certain direction in physical space (not in visual space), as opposed to other directions in physical space. And if, pointing in this sense, I say "this is what is really seen", one may answer me: "This is what *you*, L. W., see; but there is no objection to adopting a notation in which what we used to call 'things which L. W. sees' is called 'things really seen' ". If, however, I believe that by pointing to that which in my grammar has no neighbour I can convey something to myself (if not to others), I make a mistake similar to that of thinking that the sentence "I am here" makes sense to me (and, by the way, is always true) under conditions different from those very special conditions under which it does make sense. E.g., when my voice and the direction from which I speak is recognized by another person. Again an important case where you can learn that a word has meaning by the particular use we make of it.— We are like people who think that pieces of wood shaped more or less like chess or draught pieces and standing on a chess board make a game, even if nothing has been said as to how they are to be used.

To say "it approaches me" has sense, even when, physically speaking, nothing approaches my body; and in the same way it makes sense to say, "it is here" or "it has reached me" when nothing has reached my body. And, on the other hand, "I am here" makes sense if my voice is recognized and heard to come from a particular place of common space. In the sentence "it is here" the 'here' was a here in visual space. Roughly speaking, it is the geometrical eye. The sentence "I am here", to make sense, must attract attention to a place in common space. (And there are several ways in which this sentence might be used.) The philosopher who thinks it makes sense to say to himself "I am here" takes the verbal expression from the sentence in which "here" is a place in common space and thinks of "here" as the here in visual space. He therefore really says something like "Here is here".

I could, however, try to express my solipsism in a different way: I imagine that I and others draw pictures or write descriptions of what each of us sees. These descriptions are put before me. I point to the one which I have made and say: "Only this is (or was) really seen". That is, I am tempted to say: "Only this description has reality (visual reality) behind it". The others I might call—"blank descriptions". I could also express myself by saying: "*This* description only was derived from reality; only this was compared with reality". Now it has a clear meaning when we say that this picture or description is a projection, say, of this group of objects—the trees I look at—or that it has been derived from these objects. But we must look into the grammar of such a phrase as "this description is derived from my sense datum". What we are talking about is connected with that peculiar temptation to say: "I never know what the other really means by 'brown', or what he really sees when he (truthfully) says that he sees a brown object".—We could propose to one who says this to use two different words instead of the one word "brown"; one word *for his particular impression*, the other word with that meaning which other people besides himself can understand as well. If he thinks about this proposal he will see that there is something wrong in his conception of the meaning, function, of the word "brown" and others. He looks for a justification of his description where there is none. (Just as in the case when a man believes that the chain of reasons must be endless. Think of the justification by a general formula for performing mathematical operations; and of the question: Does this formula compel us to make use of it in this particular case as we do?) To say "I derive a description from visual reality" can't mean anything analogous to: "I derive a description from what I see here". I may, e.g., see a chart in which a coloured square is correlated to the word "brown", and also a patch of the same colour elsewhere; and I may say: "This chart shows me that I must use the word 'brown' for the description of this patch". This is how I may derive the word which is needed in my description. But it would be meaningless to say that I derive the word "brown" from the particular colour-impression which I receive.

Let us now ask: "Can a human *body* have pain?" One is inclined to say: "How can the body have pain? The body in itself is something dead; a body isn't conscious!" And here again it is as though we looked into the nature of pain and saw that it lies in its nature that a material object can't have it. And it is as though we saw that what has pain must be an entity of a different nature from that of a material object; that, in fact, it must be of a mental nature. But to say that the ego is mental is like saying that the number 3 is of a mental or an immaterial nature, when we recognize that the numeral "3" isn't used as a sign for a physical object.

On the other hand we can perfectly well adopt the expression "this body feels pain", and we shall then, just as usual, tell it to go to the doctor, to lie down, and even to remember that when the last time it had pains they were over in a day. "But wouldn't this form of expression at least be an indirect one?"—Is it using an indirect expression when we say "Write '3' for 'x' in this formula" instead of "Substitute 3 for *x*"? (Or on the other hand, is the first of these two expressions the only direct one, as some philosophers think?) One expression is no more direct than the other. The meaning of the expression depends entirely on how we go on using it. Let's not imagine the meaning as an occult connection the mind makes between a word and a thing, and that this connection *contains* the whole usage of a word as the seed might be said to contain the tree.

The kernel of our proposition that that which has pains or sees or thinks is of a mental nature is only, that the word "I" in "I have pains" does not denote a particular body, for we can't substitute for "I" a description of a body.

THE BROWN BOOK

THE BROWN BOOK

I

Augustine, in describing his learning of language, says that he was taught to speak by learning the names of things. It is clear that whoever says this has in mind the way in which a child learns such words as "man", "sugar", "table", etc. He does not primarily think of such words as "today", "not", "but", "perhaps".

Suppose a man described a game of chess, without mentioning the existence and operations of the pawns. His description of the game as a natural phenomenon will be incomplete. On the other hand we may say that he has completely described a simpler game. In this sense we can say that Augustine's description of learning the language was correct for a simpler language than ours. Imagine this language:—

1). Its function is the communication between a builder A and his man B. B has to reach A building stones. There are cubes, bricks, slabs, beams, columns. The language consists of the words "cube", "brick", "slab", "column". A calls out one of these words, upon which B brings a stone of a certain shape. Let us imagine a society in which this is the only system of language. The child learns this language from the grown-ups by being trained to its use. I am using the word "trained" in a way strictly analogous to that in which we talk of an animal being trained to do certain things. It is done by means of example, reward, punishment, and suchlike. Part of this training is that we point to a building stone, direct the attention of the child towards it, and pronounce a word. I will call this procedure *demonstrative* teaching of words. In the actual use of this language, one man calls out the words as orders, the other acts according to them. But learning and teaching this language will contain this procedure: The child just 'names' things, that is, he pronounces the words of the language when the teacher points to the things. In fact, there will be a still simpler exercise: The child repeats words which the teacher pronounces.

(Note. Objection: The word "brick" in language 1) has not the meaning which it has in *our* language.——This is true if it means that

77

in our language there are usages of the word "brick" different from our usages of this word in language 1). But don't we sometimes use the word "brick!" in just this way? Or should we say that when we use it, it is an elliptical sentence, a shorthand for "Bring me a brick"? Is it right to say that if *we* say "brick!" we *mean* "Bring me a brick"? Why should I translate the expression "brick!" into the expression "Bring me a brick"? And if they are synonymous, why shouldn't I say: If he says "brick!" he means "brick!" . . .? Or: Why shouldn't he be able to mean just "brick!" if he is able to mean "Bring me a brick", unless you wish to assert that while he says aloud "brick!" he as a matter of fact always says in his mind, to himself, "Bring me a brick"? But what reason could we have to assert this? Suppose someone asked: If a man gives the order, "Bring me a brick", must he mean it as four words, or can't he mean it as one composite word synonymous with the one word "brick!"? One is tempted to answer: He *means* all four words if in his language he uses that sentence in contrast with other sentences in which these words are used, such as, for instance, "Take these two bricks away". But what if I asked "But how is his sentence contrasted with these others? Must he have thought them simultaneously, or shortly before or after, or is it sufficient that he should have one time learnt them, etc.?" When we have asked ourselves this question, it appears that it is irrelevant which of these alternatives is the case. And we are inclined to say that all that is really relevant is that these contrasts should exist in the system of language which he is using, and that they need not in any sense be present in his mind when he utters his sentence. Now compare this conclusion with our original question. When we asked it, we seemed to ask a question about the state of mind of the man who says the sentence, whereas the idea of meaning which we arrived at in the end was not that of a state of mind. We think of the meaning of signs sometimes as states of mind of the man using them, sometimes as the role which these signs are playing in a system of language. The connection between these two ideas is that the mental experiences which accompany the use of a sign undoubtedly are caused by our usage of the sign in a particular system of language. William James speaks of specific feelings accompanying the use of such words as "and", "if", "or". And there is no doubt that at least certain gestures are often connected with such words, as a collecting gesture with "and", and a dismissing gesture with "not". And there obviously are visual and muscular sensations connected with these gestures. On the other hand it is clear enough that these sensations do not accompany every use of the word "not" and "and". If in some language the word "but" meant what "not" means in English, it is clear that we should not compare the meanings of these two words by comparing the sensations which they produce. Ask yourself what means we have of finding out the feelings which they produce in different people and on different occasions. Ask yourself: "When I said, 'Give me an apple *and* a pear, *and* leave the room', had I the same feeling when I pronounced the two words 'and'?" But we do not deny that the people who use the word "but" as "not" is used in English will, broadly speaking, have similar sensations accompanying the word "but" to those the English have when they use "not". And the word "but" in the two languages will on the whole be accompanied by different sets of experiences.)

2). Let us now look at an extension of language 1). The builder's man knows by heart the series of words from one to ten. On being given the order, "Five slabs!", he goes to where the slabs are kept, says the words from one to five, takes up a slab for each word, and carries them to the builder. Here both the parties use the language by speaking the words. Learning the numerals by heart will be one of the essential features of learning this language. The use of the numerals will again be taught demonstratively. But now the same word, e.g., "three", will be taught by pointing either to slabs, or to bricks, or to columns, etc. And on the other hand, different numerals will be taught by pointing to groups of stones of the same shape.

(Remark: We stressed the importance of learning the series of numerals by heart because there was no feature comparable to this in the learning of language 1). And this shows us that by introducing numerals we have introduced an entirely different *kind* of instrument into our language. The difference of kind is much more obvious when we contemplate such a simple example than when we look at our ordinary language with innumerable kinds of words all looking more or less alike when they stand in the dictionary.—

What have the demonstrative explanations of the numerals in common with those of the words "slab", "column", etc., except a gesture and pronouncing the words? The way such a gesture is used in the two cases is different. This difference is blurred if one says, "In one case we point to a shape, in the other we point to a number". The difference becomes obvious and clear only when we contemplate a *complete* example (i.e., the example of a language completely worked out in detail).)

3). Let us introduce a new instrument of communication,—a proper name. This is given to a particular object (a particular building stone) by pointing to it and pronouncing the name. If A calls the name, B brings the object. The demonstrative teaching of a proper name is different again from the demonstrative teaching in the cases 1) and 2).

(Remark: This difference does not lie, however, in the act of pointing and pronouncing the word or in any mental act (meaning?) accompanying it, but in the role which the demonstration (pointing and pronouncing) plays in the whole training and in the use which is made of it in the practice of communication by means of this language. One might think that the difference could be described by saying that in the different cases we point to different kinds of objects. But suppose I point with my hand to a blue jersey. How does pointing to its colour differ from pointing to its shape?—We are inclined to say the difference is that we *mean* something different in the two cases. And 'meaning' here is to be some sort of process taking place while we point. What particularly tempts us to this view is that a man on being asked whether he pointed to the colour or the shape is, at least in most cases, able to answer this and to be certain that his answer is correct. If on the other hand, we look for two such characteristic mental acts as meaning the colour and meaning the shape, etc., we aren't able to find any, or at least none which must always accompany pointing to colour, pointing to shape, respectively. We have only a *rough* idea of what it means to concentrate one's attention on the colour as opposed to the shape, or vice versa. The difference, one might say, does not lie in the act of demonstration, but rather in the surrounding of that act in the use of the language.)

4). On being ordered, "This slab!", B brings the slab to which A points. On being ordered, "Slab, there!", he carries a slab to the place indicated. Is the word "there" taught demonstratively? Yes and no! When a person is trained in the use of the word "there", the teacher will in training him make the pointing gesture and pronounce the word "there". But should we say that thereby he gives a place the name "there"? Remember that the pointing gesture in this case is part of the practice of communication itself.

(Remark: It has been suggested that such words as "there", "here", "now", "this" are the '*real proper names*' as opposed to what in ordinary

life we call proper names, and, in the view I am referring to, can only
be called so crudely. There is a widespread tendency to regard what in
ordinary life is called a proper name only as a rough approximation of
what ideally could be called so. Compare Russell's idea of the
'individual'. He talks of individuals as the ultimate constituents of
reality, but says that it is difficult to say which things are individuals.
The idea is that further analysis has to reveal this. We, on the other
hand, introduced the idea of a proper name in a language in which it
was applied to what in ordinary life we call "objects", "things"
("building stones").

—— "What does the word 'exactness' mean? Is it real exactness
if you are supposed to come to tea at 4.30 and come when a good
clock strikes 4.30? Or would it only be exactness if you began to
open the door at the moment the clock began to strike? But how is
this moment to be defined and how is 'beginning to open the door'
to be defined? Would it be correct to say, 'It is difficult to say what
real exactness is, for all we know is only rough approximations'?")

5).   Questions and answers: A asks, "How many slabs?" B counts
them and answers with the numeral.

Systems of communication as for instance 1), 2), 3), 4), 5) we shall
call "language games". They are more or less akin to what in ordinary
language we call games. Children are taught their native language by
means of such games, and here they even have the entertaining
character of games. We are not, however, regarding the language
games which we describe as incomplete parts of a language, but as
languages complete in themselves, as complete systems of human
communication. To keep this point of view in mind, it very often is
useful to imagine such a simple language to be the entire system of
communication of a tribe in a primitive state of society. Think of
primitive arithmetics of such tribes.

When the boy or grown-up learns what one might call special
technical languages, e.g., the use of charts and diagrams, descriptive
geometry, chemical symbolism, etc., he learns more language games.
(Remark: The picture we have of the language of the grown-up is
that of a nebulous mass of language, his mother tongue, surrounded
by discrete and more or less clear-cut language games, the technical
languages.)

6).   Asking for the name: we introduce new forms of building
stones. B points to one of them and asks, "What is this?"; A answers,

"This is a . . .". Later on A calls out this new word, say "arch", and B brings the stone. The words, "This is . . ." together with the pointing gesture we shall call ostensive explanation or ostensive definition. In case 6) a generic name was explained, in actual fact, as the name of a shape. But we can ask analogously for the proper name of a particular object, for the name of a colour, of a numeral, of a direction.

(Remark: Our use of expressions like "names of numbers", "names of colours", "names of materials", "names of nations" may spring from two different sources. One is that we might imagine the functions of proper names, numerals, words for colours, etc., to be much more alike than they actually are. If we do so we are tempted to think that the function of every word is more or less like the function of a proper name of a person, or such generic names as "table", "chair", "door", etc. The second source is this, that if we see how fundamentally different the functions of such words as "table", "chair", etc., are from those of proper names, and how different from either the functions of, say, the names of colours, we see no reason why we shouldn't speak of names of numbers or names of directions either, not by way of saying some such thing as "numbers and directions are just different forms of objects", but rather by way of stressing the analogy which lies in the lack of analogy between the functions of the words "chair" and "Jack" on the one hand, and "east" and "Jack" on the other hand.)

7).   B has a table in which written signs are placed opposite to pictures of objects (say, a table, a chair, a tea-cup, etc.). A writes one of the signs, B looks for it in the table, looks or points with his finger from the written sign to the picture opposite, and fetches the object which the picture represents.

Let us now look at the different kinds of signs which we have introduced. First let us distinguish between sentences and words. A sentence[1] I will call every complete sign in a language game, its constituent signs are words. (This is merely a rough and general remark about the way I will use the words "proposition"[1] and "word".) A proposition may consist of only one word. In 1) the signs "brick!", "column!" are the sentences. In 2) a sentence consists of two words. According to the role which propositions play in a language game, we distinguish between orders, questions, explanations, descriptions, and so on.

[1] Here Wittgenstein uses "sentence" and "proposition" interchangeably for the German "Satz".—Edd.

8).   If in a language game similar to 1) A calls out an order: "slab, column, brick!" which is obeyed by B by bringing a slab, a column and a brick, we might here talk of three propositions, or of one only. If, on the other hand,

9).   the order of words shows B the order in which to bring the building stones, we shall say that A calls out a proposition consisting of three words. If the command in this case took the form, "Slab, then column, then brick!" we should say that it consisted of four words (not of five). Amongst the words we see groups of words with similar functions. We can easily see a similarity in the use of the words "one", "two", "three", etc. and again one in the use of "slab", "column" and "brick", etc., and thus we distinguish parts of speech. In 8) all the words of the proposition belonged to the same part of speech.

10).   The order in which B had to bring the stones in 9) could have been indicated by the use of the ordinals thus: "Second, column; first, slab; third, brick!". Here we have a case in which what was the function of the order of words in one language game is the function of particular words in another.

Reflections such as the preceding will show us the infinite variety of the functions of words in propositions, and it is curious to compare what we see in our examples with the simple and rigid rules which logicians give for the construction of propositions. If we group words together according to the similarity of their functions, thus distinguishing parts of speech, it is easy to see that many different ways of classification can be adopted. We could indeed easily imagine a reason for not classing the word "one" together with "two", "three", etc., as follows:

11).   Consider this variation of our language game 2). Instead of calling out, "One slab!", "One cube!", etc., A just calls "Slab!", "Cube!", etc., the use of the other numerals being as described in 2). Suppose that a man accustomed to this form 11) of communication was introduced to the use of the word "one" as described in 2). We can easily imagine that he would refuse to classify "one" with the numerals "2", "3", etc.

(Remark: Think of the reasons for and against classifying 'o' with the other cardinals. "Are black and white colours?" In which cases would you be inclined to say so and which not?—Words can in many ways be compared to chess men. Think of the several ways of distinguishing different kinds of pieces in the game of chess (e.g., pawns and 'officers').

Remember the phrase, "two or more".)

It is natural for us to call gestures, as those employed in 4), or pictures as in 7), elements or instruments of language. (We talk sometimes of a language of gestures.) The pictures in 7) and other instruments of language which have a similar function I shall call patterns. (This explanation, as others which we have given, is vague, and meant to be vague.) We may say that words and patterns have different kinds of functions. When we make use of a pattern we compare something with it, e.g., a chair with the picture of a chair. We did not compare a slab with the word "slab". In introducing the distinction, 'word/pattern', the idea was not to set up a final logical duality. We have only singled out two characteristic kinds of instruments from the variety of instruments in our language. We shall call "one", "two", "three", etc., words. If instead of these signs we used "—", "— —", "— — —", "— — — —", we might call these patterns. Suppose in a language the numerals were "one", "one one", "one one one", etc., should we call "one" a word or a pattern? The same element may in one place be used as word and in another as pattern. A circle might be the name for an ellipse, or on the other hand a pattern with which the ellipse is to be compared by a particular method of projection. Consider also these two systems of expression:

12).   A gives B an order consisting of two written symbols, the first an irregularly shaped patch of a certain colour, say green, the second the drawn outline of a geometrical figure, say a circle. B brings an object of this outline and that colour, say a circular green object.

13).   A gives B an order consisting of one symbol, a geometrical figure painted a particular colour, say a green circle. B brings him a green circular object. In 12) patterns correspond to our names of colours and other patterns to our names of shape. The symbols in 13) cannot be regarded as combinations of two such elements. A word in inverted commas can be called a pattern. Thus in the sentence "He said 'Go to hell' ", "Go to hell" is a pattern of what he said. Compare these cases: a) Someone says "I whistled . . ." (whistling a tune);

b) Someone writes, "I whistled ". An onomatopoeic

word like "rustling" may be called a pattern. We call a very great variety
of processes "comparing an object with a pattern". We comprise many
kinds of symbols under the name "pattern". In 7) B compares a picture
in the table with the objects he has before him. But what does comparing a picture with the object consist in? Suppose the table showed:
a) a picture of a hammer, of pincers, of a saw, of a chisel; b) on the
other hand, pictures of twenty different kinds of butterflies. Imagine
what the comparison in these two cases would consist in, and note the
difference. Compare with these cases a third case c) where the pictures
in the table represent building stones drawn to scale, and the comparing
has to be done with ruler and compasses. Suppose that B's task is to
bring a piece of cloth of the colour of the sample. How are the
colours of sample and cloth to be compared? Imagine a series of
different cases:

14). A shows the sample to B, upon which B goes and fetches the
material 'from memory'.

15). A gives B the sample, B looks from the sample to the materials
on the shelves from which he has to choose.

16).   B lays the sample on each bolt of material and chooses that
one which he can't distinguish from the sample, for which the difference
between the sample and the material seems to vanish.

17).   Imagine on the other hand that the order has been, "Bring
a material slightly darker than this sample". In 14) I said that B fetches
the material 'from memory', which is using a common form of
expression. But what might happen in such a case of comparing
'from memory' is of the greatest variety. Imagine a few instances:
14a). B has a memory image before his mind's eye when he goes
for the material. He alternately looks at materials and recalls his
image. He goes through this process with, say, five of the bolts, in
some instances saying to himself, "Too dark", in some instances saying
to himself, "Too light". At the fifth bolt he stops, says, "That's it"
and takes it from the shelf.
14b). No memory image is before B's eye. He looks at four bolts,
shaking his head each time, feeling some sort of mental tension.
On reaching the fifth bolt, this tension relaxes, he nods his head,
and takes the bolt down.
14c). B goes to the shelf without a memory image, looks at five
bolts one after the other, takes the fifth bolt from the shelf.

'But this can't be all comparing consists in.'

When we call these three preceding cases, cases of comparing from memory, we feel that their description is in a sense unsatisfactory, or incomplete. We are inclined to say that the description has left out the essential feature of such a process and given us accessory features only. The essential feature it seems would be what one might call a specific experience of comparing and of recognizing. Now it is queer that on closely looking at cases of comparing, it is very easy to see a great number of activities and states of mind, all *more or less* characteristic of the act of comparing. This in fact is so, whether we speak of comparing from memory or of comparing by means of a sample before our eyes. We know a *vast* number of such processes, processes similar to each other in a vast number of different ways. We hold pieces whose colours we want to compare together or near each other for a longer or shorter period, look at them alternately or simultaneously, place them under different lights, say different things while we do so, have memory images, feelings of tension and relaxation, satisfaction and dissatisfaction, the various feelings of strain in and around our eyes accompanying prolonged gazing at the same object, and all possible combinations of these and many other experiences. The more such cases we observe and the closer we look at them, the more doubtful we feel about finding one particular mental experience characteristic of comparing. In fact, if after you had scrutinized a number of such *closely*, I admitted that there existed a peculiar mental experience which you might call the experience of comparing, and that if you insisted, I should be willing to adopt the word "comparing" only for cases in which this peculiar feeling had occurred, you would now feel that the assumption of such a peculiar experience had lost its point, because this experience was placed side by side with a vast number of other experiences which after we have scrutinized the cases seems to be that which really constitutes what connects all the cases of comparing. For the 'specific experience' we had been looking for was meant to have played the role which has been assumed by the mass of experiences revealed to us by our scrutiny: We never wanted the specific experience to be just one among a number of *more or less* characteristic experiences. (One might say that there are two ways of looking at this matter, one as it were, at close quarters, the other as though from a distance and through the medium of a peculiar atmosphere.) In fact we have found that the use which we really make of the word "comparing" is different from that which looking at it from far away we were led to expect. We find that what connects all the cases of comparing is a vast number of overlapping similarities, and as soon as we see this, we feel no longer compelled to say that there must be some one feature common to them all. What ties the ship to the wharf is a rope, and the rope consists of fibres, but it does not get its strength from any fibre which runs through it from one end to the other, but from the fact that there is a vast number of fibres over-lapping.

'But surely in case 14c) B acted entirely automatically. If all that happened was really what was described there, he did not know why he chose the bolt he did choose. He had no reason for choosing it. If he chose the right one, he did it as a machine might have done it'. Our first answer is that we did not deny that B in case 14c) had what we should call a personal experience, for we did not say that he didn't see the materials from which he chose or that which he chose, nor that he didn't have muscular and tactile sensations and suchlike while he did it. Now what would such a reason which justified his choice and made it non-automatic be like? (i.e.: What do we *imagine* it to be like?) I suppose we should say that the opposite of automatic compar-ing, as it were, the ideal case of conscious comparing, was that of having a clear memory image before our mind's eye or of seeing a real sample and of having a specific feeling of not being able to dis-tinguish in a particular way between these samples and the material chosen. I suppose that this peculiar sensation is the reason, the justification, for the choice. This specific feeling, one might say, connects the two experiences of seeing the sample, on the one hand, and the material on the other. But if so, what connects this specific experience with either? We don't deny that such an experience might intervene. But looking at it as we did just now, the distinction between automatic and non-automatic appears no longer clear-cut and final as it did at first. We don't mean that this distinction loses its practical value in particular cases, e.g., if asked under particular circumstances "Did you take this bolt from the shelf automatically, or did you think about it?", we may be justified in saying that we did not act auto-matically and give as an explanation that we had looked at the material carefully, had tried to recall the memory image of the pattern, and had uttered to ourselves doubts and decisions. This may *in the particular case* be taken to distinguish automatic from non-automatic. In another case, however, we may distinguish between an automatic and a non-automatic way of the appearance of a memory image, and so on.

If our case 14c) troubles you, you may be inclined to say: "But *why* did he bring just this bolt of material? How has he recognized it as the right one? What by?"—If you ask 'why', do you ask for the cause or for the reason? If for the cause, it is easy enough to think up a physiological or psychological hypothesis which explains this choice under the given conditions. It is the task of the experimental sciences to test such hypotheses. If on the other hand you ask for a reason the answer is, "There need not have been a reason for the choice. A reason is a step preceding the step of the choice. But why should every step be preceded by another one?"

'But then B didn't really *recognize* the material as the right one.'— You needn't reckon 14c) among the cases of recognizing, but if you have become aware of the fact that the processes which we call processes of recognition form a vast family with overlapping similarities, you will probably feel not disinclined to include 14c) in this family, too. —'But doesn't B in this case lack the criterion by which he can recognize the material? In 14a), e.g., he had the memory image and he recognized the material he looked for by its agreement with the image.'—But had he also a picture of this agreement before him, a picture with which he could compare the agreement between the pattern and the bolt to see whether it was the right one? And, on the other hand, couldn't he have been given such a picture? Suppose, e.g., that A wished B to remember that what was wanted was a bolt exactly like the sample, not, as perhaps in other cases, a material slightly darker than the pattern. Couldn't A in this case have given to B an example of the agreement required by giving him two pieces of the same colour (e.g., as a kind of reminder)? Is any such link between the order and its execution necessarily the last one?—And if you say that in 14b) at least he had the relaxing of the tension by which to recognize the right material, had he to have an image of this relaxation about him to recognize it as that by which the right material was to be recognized?—

'But supposing B brings the bolt, as in 14c), and on comparing it with the pattern it turns out to be the wrong one?'—But couldn't that have happened in all the other cases as well? Suppose in 14a) the bolt which B brought back was found not to match with the pattern. Wouldn't we in some such cases say that his memory image had changed, in others that the pattern or the material had changed, in others again that the light had changed? It is not difficult to invent cases, imagine circumstances, in which each of these judgments would be made.—'But isn't there after all an essential difference between the cases 14a) and 14c)?'—Certainly! Just that pointed out in the description of these cases.—

In 1) B learnt to bring a building stone on hearing the word "column!" called out. We could imagine what happened in such a case to be this: In B's mind the word called out brought up an image of a column, say; the training had, as we should say, established this association. B takes up that building stone which conforms to his image.—But was this *necessarily* what happened? If the training could bring it about that the idea or image—automatically—arose in B's mind, why shouldn't it bring about B's *actions* without the intervention of an image? This would only come to a slight variation of the associative mechanism. Bear in mind that the image which is brought up by the word is not arrived at by a rational process (but if it is, this only pushes our argument further back), but that this case is strictly comparable with that of a mechanism in which a button is pressed and an indicator plate appears. In fact this sort of mechanism can be used instead of that of association.

Mental images of colours, shapes, sounds, etc., etc., which play a role in communication by means of language we put in the same category with patches of colour actually seen, sounds heard.

18).   The object of the training in the use of tables (as in 7)) may be not only to teach the use of one particular table, but it may be to enable the pupil to use or construct himself tables with new co-ordinations of written signs and pictures. Suppose the first table a person was trained to use contained the four words "hammer", "pincers", "saw", "chisel" and the corresponding pictures. We might now add the picture of another object which the pupil had before him, say of a plane, and correlate with it the word "plane". We shall make the correlation between this new picture and word as similar as possible to the correlations in the previous table. Thus we might add the new word and picture on the same sheet, and place the new word under the previous words and the new picture under the previous pictures. The pupil will now be encouraged to make use of the new picture and word without the special training which we gave him when we taught him to use the first table. These acts of encouragement will be of various kinds, and many such acts will only be possible if the pupil responds, and responds in a particular way. Imagine the gestures, sounds, etc., of encouragement you use when you teach a dog to retrieve. Imagine on the other hand, that you tried to teach a cat to retrieve. As the cat will not respond to your encouragement, most of the acts of encouragement which you performed when you trained the dog are here out of the question.

19). The pupil could also be trained to give things names of his own invention and to bring the objects when the names are called. He is, e.g., presented with a table on which he finds pictures of objects around him on one side and blank spaces on the other, and he plays the game by writing signs of his own invention opposite the pictures and reacting in the previous way when these signs are used as orders. Or else

20). the game may consist in B's constructing a table and obeying orders given in terms of this table. When the use of a table is taught, and the table consists, say, of two vertical columns, the left hand one containing the names, the right hand one the pictures, a name and a picture being correlated by standing on a horizontal line, an important feature of the training may be that which makes the pupil slide his finger from left to right, as it were the training to draw a series of horizontal lines, one below the other. Such training may help to make the transition from the first table to the new item.

Tables, ostensive definitions, and similar instruments I shall call rules, in accordance with ordinary usage. The use of a rule can be explained by a further rule.

21). Consider this example: We introduce different ways of reading tables. Each table consists of two columns of words and pictures, as above. In some cases they are to be read horizontally from left to right, i.e., according to the scheme:

In others according to such schemes as:

or:

etc.

Schemes of this kind can be adjoined to our tables, as rules for reading them. Could not these rules again be explained by further rules? Certainly. On the other hand, is a rule incompletely explained if no rule for its usage has been given?

We introduce into our language games the endless series of numerals. But how is this done? Obviously the analogy between this process and that of introducing a series of twenty numerals is not the same as that between introducing a series of twenty numerals and introducing a series of ten numerals. Suppose that our game was like 2) but played with the endless series of numerals. The difference between it and 2) would not be just that more numerals were used. That is to say, suppose that as a matter of fact in playing the game we had actually made use of, say, 155 numerals, the game we play would not be that which could be described by saying that we played the game 2), only with 155 instead of 10 numerals. But what does the difference consist in? (The difference would seem to be almost one of the spirit in which the games are played.) The difference between games can lie, say, in the number of the counters used, in the number of squares of the playing board, or in the fact that we use squares in one case and hexagons in the other, and suchlike. Now the difference between the finite and infinite game does not seem to lie in the material tools of the game; for we should be inclined to say that infinity can't be expressed in them, that is, that we can only conceive of it in our thoughts, and hence that it is in these thoughts that the finite and infinite game must be distinguished. (It is queer though that these thoughts should be capable of being expressed in signs.)

Let us consider two games. They are both played with cards carrying numbers, and the highest number takes the trick.

22).   One game is played with a fixed number of such cards, say 32. In the other game we are under certain circumstances allowed to increase the number of cards to as many as we like, by cutting pieces of paper and writing numbers on them. We will call the first of these games bounded, the second unbounded. Suppose a hand of the second game was played and the number of cards actually used was 32. What is the difference in this case between playing a hand *a*) of the unbounded game and playing a hand *b*) of the bounded game?

The difference will not be that between a hand of a bounded game with 32 cards and a hand of a bounded game with a greater number of cards. The number of cards used was, we said, the same. But there will be differences of another kind, e.g., the bounded game is played with a normal pack of cards, the unbounded game with a large supply of blank cards and pencils. The unbounded game is opened with the question, "How high shall we go?" If the players look up the rules of this game in a book of rules, they will find the phrase "and so on" or "and so on *ad inf.*" at the end of certain series of rules. So the difference between the two hands *a*) and *b*) lies in the tools we use, though admittedly not in the cards they are played with. But this difference seems trivial and not the essential difference between the games. We feel that there must be a big and essential difference somewhere. But if you look closely at what happens when the hands are played, you find that you can only detect a number of differences in details, each of which would seem inessential. The acts, e.g., of dealing and playing the cards *may* in both cases be identical. In the course of playing the hand *a*), the players may have considered making up more cards, and again discarded the idea. But what was it like to consider this? It could be some such process as saying to themselves or aloud "I wonder whether I should make up another card". Again, no such consideration may have entered the minds of the players. It is possible that the whole difference in the events of a hand of the bounded, and a hand of the unbounded, game lay in what was said before the game started, e.g., "Let's play the bounded game".

'But isn't it correct to say that hands of the two different games belong to two different systems?' Certainly. Only the facts which we are referring to by saying that they belong to different systems are much more complex than we might expect them to be.

Let us now compare language games of which we should say that they are played with a limited set of numerals, with language games of which we should say that they are played with the endless series of numerals.

23). Like 2) A orders B to bring him a number of building stones. The numerals are the signs "1", "2", ... "9", each written on a card. A has a set of these cards and gives B the order by showing him one of the set and calling out one of the words, "slab", "column", etc.

24). Like 23), only there is no set of indexed cards. The series of numerals 1 ... 9 is learned by heart. The numerals are called out in the orders, and the child learns them by word of mouth.

25). An abacus is used. A sets the abacus, gives it to B, B goes with it to where the slabs lie, etc.

26). B is to count the slabs in a heap. He does it with an abacus, the abacus has twenty beads. There are never more than 20 slabs in a heap. B sets the abacus for the heap in question and shows A the abacus thus set.

27). Like 26). The abacus has 20 small beads and one large one. if the heap contains more than 20 slabs, the large bead is moved. (So the large bead in some way corresponds to the word "many".)

28). Like 26). If the heap contains n slabs, n being more than 20 but less than 40, B moves n-20 beads, shows A the abacus thus set and claps his hands once.

29). A and B use the numerals of the decimal system (written or spoken) up to 20. The child learning this language learns these numerals by heart, as in 2).

30). A certain tribe has a language of the kind 2). The numerals used are those of our decimal system. No one numeral used can be observed to play the predominant role of the last numeral in some of the above games (27), 28)). (One is tempted to continue this sentence by saying, "although there is of course a highest numeral actually used".) The children of the tribe learn the numerals in this way: They are taught the signs from 1 to 20 as in 2) and to count rows of beads of no more than 20 on being ordered, "Count these". When in counting the pupil arrives at the numeral 20, one makes a gesture suggestive of "Go on", upon which the child says (in most cases at any rate) "21". Analogously, the children are made to count to 22 and to higher numbers, no particular number playing in these exercises the predominant role of a last one. The last stage of the training is that the child is ordered to count a group of objects, well above 20, without the suggestive gesture being used to help the child over the numeral 20. If a child does not respond to the suggestive gesture, it is separated from the others and treated as a lunatic.

31). Another tribe. Its language is like that in 30). The highest numeral observed in use is 159. In the life of this tribe the numeral 159 plays a peculiar role. Supposing I said, "They treat this number as their highest",—— but what does this mean? Could we answer: "They just say that it is the highest"?—They say certain words, but how do we know what they mean by them? A criterion for what they mean would be the occasions on which the word we are inclined to translate into our word "highest" is used, the role, we might say, which we observe this word to play in the life of the tribe. In fact we could easily imagine the numeral 159 to be used on such occasions, in connection with such gestures and forms of behaviour as would make us say that this numeral plays the role of an unsurmountable limit, even if the tribe had no word corresponding to our "highest", and the criteria for numeral 159 being the highest numeral did not consist of anything that was *said* about the numeral.

32).   A tribe has two systems of counting. People learned to count with the alphabet from A to Z and also with the decimal system as in 30.) If a man is to count objects with the first system, he is ordered to count "*in the closed way*", in the second case, "*in the open way*"; and the tribe uses the words "closed" and "open" also for a closed and open door.

(Remarks: 23) is limited in an obvious way by the set of cards. 24): Note analogy and lack of analogy between the *limited supply* of cards in 23) and of words in our memory in 24). Observe that the limitation in 26) on the one hand lies in the *tool* (the abacus of 20 beads) and its usage in our game, on the other hand (in a totally different way) in the fact that in the actual practice of playing the game no more than 20 objects are ever to be counted. In 27) that latter kind of limitation was absent, but the large bead rather stressed the limitation of our means. Is 28) a limited or an unlimited game? The practice we have described gives the limit 40. We are inclined to say this game 'has it in it' to be continued indefinitely, but remember that we could also have construed the preceding games as beginnings of a system. In 29) the systematic aspect of the numerals used is even more conspicuous than in 28). One might say that there was no limitation imposed by the tools of this game, if it were not for the remark that the numerals up to 20 are learnt by heart. This suggests the idea that the child is not taught to '*understand*' the system which we see in the decimal notation. Of the tribe in 30) we should certainly say that they are trained to construct numerals indefinitely, that the arithmetic of their language is not a finite one, that their series of numbers has no end. (It is just in such a case when numerals are constructed 'indefinitely' that we say that people have the infinite series of numbers.) 31) might show you what a vast variety of cases can be imagined in which we should be inclined to say that the arithmetic of the tribe deals with a finite series of numbers, even in spite of the fact that the way in which the children are trained in the use of numerals suggests no upper limit. In 32) the terms "closed" and "open" (which could by a slight variation of the example be replaced by "limited" and "unlimited") are introduced into the language of the tribe itself. Introduced in that simple and clearly circumscribed game, there is of course nothing mysterious about the use of the word "open". But this word corresponds to our "infinite", and the games we play with the latter differ from 31) only by being vastly more complicated. In other words, our use of the word "infinite" is just as *straightforward* as that of "open" in 31), and our idea that its meaning is 'transcendent' rests on a misunderstanding.)

We might say roughly that the unlimited cases are characterized by this: that they are not played with a *definite supply* of numerals, but instead with a *system* for constructing numerals (indefinitely). When we say that someone has been supplied with a system for constructing numerals, we generally think of one of three things: a) of giving him a *training* similar to that described in 30), which, experience teaches us, will make him pass tests of the kind mentioned there; b) of creating a *disposition* in the same man's mind, or brain, to react in that way; c) of supplying him with a *general* rule for the construction of numerals.

What do we call a rule? Consider this example:

33). B moves about according to rules which A gives him.

B is supplied with the following table:

a	→
b	←
c	↑
d	↓

A gives an order made up of the letters in the table, say: "aacaddd". B looks up the arrow corresponding to each letter of the order and

moves accordingly; in our example thus: →→↑→↓↓↓

The table 33) we should call a rule (or else "the expression of a rule". Why I give these synonymous expressions will appear later.) We shan't be inclined to call the sentence "aacaddd" itself a rule. It is of course the description of the way B has to take. On the other hand, such a description would under certain circumstances be called a rule, e.g., in the following case:

34).   B is to draw various ornamental linear designs. Each design is a repetition of one element which A gives him. Thus if A gives the order "cada", B draws a line thus: ⌐⌐⌐⌐⌐⌐
In this case I think we should say that "cada" is the rule for drawing the design. Roughly speaking, it characterizes what we call a rule to be applied repeatedly, in an indefinite number of instances. Cf., e.g., the following case with 34):

35).   A game played with pieces of various shapes on a chess board. The way each piece is allowed to move is laid down by a rule. Thus the rule for a particular piece is "ac", for another piece "acaa", and so on. The first piece then can make a move like this: $\xrightarrow{\uparrow}$, the second, like this: $\rightarrow\uparrow^{\longrightarrow}$. Both a formula like "ac" or a diagram like that corresponding to such a formula might here be called a rule.

36).   Suppose that after playing the game 33) several times as described above, it was played with this variation: that B no longer looked at the table, but reading A's order the letters call up the images of the arrows (by association), and B acts according to these imagined arrows.

37).   After playing it like this for several times, B moves about according to the written order as he would have done had he looked up or imagined the arrows, but actually without any such picture intervening. Imagine even this variation:

38).   B in being trained to follow a written order, is shown the table of 33) once, upon which he obeys A's orders without further intervention of the table in the same way in which B in 33) does with the help of the table on each occasion.
In each of these cases, we might say that the table 33) is a rule of the game. But in each one this rule plays a different role. In 33) the table is an instrument used in what we should call *the practice* of the game. It is replaced in 36) by the working of association. In 37) even this shadow of the table has dropped out of the practice of the game, and in 38) the table is admittedly an instrument for the *training* of B only.
But imagine this further case:

39).   A certain system of communication is used by a tribe. I will describe it by saying that it is similar to our game 38) except that no table is used in the training. The training *might* have consisted in several times leading the pupil by the hand along the path one wanted him to go. But we could also imagine a case:

40).   where even this training is not necessary, where, as we should say, the look of the letters abcd naturally produced an urge to move in the way described. This case at first sight looks puzzling. We seem to be assuming a most unusual working of the mind. Or we may ask, "How on earth is he to know which way to move if the letter a is shown him?". But isn't B's reaction in this case the very reaction described in 37) and 38), and in fact our usual reaction when for instance we hear and obey an order? For, the fact that the training in 38) and 39) *preceded* the carrying out of the order does not change the process of carrying out. In other words the 'curious mental mechanism' assumed in 40) is no other than that which we assumed to be created by the training in 37) and 38). 'But *could* such a mechanism be born with you?' But did you find any difficulty in assuming that *that* mechanism was born with B, which enabled him to respond to the training in the way he did? And remember that the rule or explanation given in table 33) of the signs abcd was not essentially the last one, and that we might have given a table for the use of such tables, and so on. (Cf. 21).)

How does one explain to a man how he should carry out the order, "Go *this* way!" (pointing with an arrow the way he should go)? Couldn't this mean going the direction which we should call the opposite of that of the arrow? Isn't every explanation of how he should follow the arrow in the position of another arrow? What would you say to this explanation: A man says, "If I point this way (pointing with his right hand) I mean you to go like this" (pointing with his left hand the same way)? This just shows you the extremes between which the uses of signs vary.

Let us return to 39). Someone visits the tribe and observes the use of the signs in their language. He describes the language by saying that its sentences consist of the letters abcd used according to the table (of 33)). We see that the expression, "A game is played according to the rule so and so" is used not only in the variety of cases exemplified by 36), 37), and 38), but even in cases where the rule is neither an instrument of the training nor of the practice of the game, but stands in the relation to it in which our table stands to the practice of our game 39). One might in this case call the table a natural law describing the behaviour of the people of this tribe. Or we might say that the table is a record belonging to the natural history of the tribe.

Note that in the game 33) I distinguished sharply between the order to be carried out and the rule employed. In 34), on the other hand, we called the sentence "cada" a rule, and it was the order. Imagine also this variation:

41).   The game is similar to 33), but the pupil is not just trained to use a single table; but the training aims at making the pupil use any table correlating letters with arrows. Now by this I mean no more than that the training is of a peculiar kind, roughly speaking one analogous to that described in 30). I will refer to a training more or less similar to that in 30) as a "*general training*". General trainings form a family whose members differ greatly from one another. The kind of thing I'm thinking of now mainly consists: *a*) of a training in a limited range of actions, *b*) of giving the pupil a lead to extend this range, and *c*) of random exercises and tests. After the general training the order is now to consist in giving him a sign of this kind:

He carries out the order by moving thus:

Here I suppose we should say the table, the rule, is *part* of the order.

Note, we are not saying '*what a rule is*' but just giving different applications of the word "rule": and we certainly do this by giving applications of the words "expression of a rule".

Note also that in 41) there is no clear case against calling the whole symbol given the sentence, though we *might* distinguish in it between the sentence and the table. What in this case more particularly tempts us to this distinction is the linear writing of the part outside the table. Though from certain points of view we should call the linear character of the sentence merely external and inessential, this character and similar ones play a great role in what as logicians we are inclined to say about sentences and propositions. And therefore if we conceive of the symbol in 41) as a unit, this may make us realize what a sentence *can* look like.

Let us now consider these two games:

42).   A gives orders to B: They are written signs consisting of dots and dashes, and B executes them by doing a figure in dancing with a particular step. Thus the order "—·" is to be carried out by taking a step and a hop alternately; the order "··———" by alternately taking two hops and three steps, etc. The training in this game is 'general' in the sense explained in 41); and I should like to say, "The orders given don't move in a limited range. They comprise combinations of any number of dots and dashes".—But what does it mean to say that the orders don't move in a limited range? Isn't this nonsense? Whatever orders are given in the practice of the game constitute the limited range.—Well, what I meant to say by "The orders don't move in a limited range" was that neither in the teaching of the game nor in the practice of it a limitation of the range plays a 'predominant' role (see 30)), or, as we might say, the range of the game (it is superfluous to say limited) is just the extent of its actual ('accidental') practice. (Our game is in this way like 30).) Cf. with this game the following:

43).   The orders and their execution as in 42); but only these three signs are used: "—", "—··", "·——". We say that in 42) B, in executing the order, is *guided* by the sign given to him. But if we ask ourselves whether the three signs in 43) guide B in executing the orders, it seems that we can say both yes and no according to the way we look at the execution of the orders.

If we try to decide whether B in 43) is guided by the signs or not, we are inclined to give such answers as the following: *a*) B is guided if he doesn't just look at an order, say "·——" as a whole and then act, but if he reads it 'word by word' (the words used in our language being "·" and "—") and acts according to the words he has read.

We could make these cases clearer if we imagine that the 'reading word by word' consisted in pointing to each word of the sentence in turn with one's finger as opposed to pointing at the whole sentence at once, say by pointing to the beginning of the sentence. And the 'acting according to the words' we shall for the sake of simplicity imagine to consist in acting (stepping or hopping) after each word of the sentence in turn.— *b*) B is guided if he goes through a conscious process which makes a connection between the pointing to a word and the act of hopping and stepping. Such a connection could be imagined in many different ways. E.g., B has a table in which a dash is correlated to the picture of a man making a step and a dot to a picture of a man hopping. Then the conscious acts connecting reading the order and carrying it out might consist in consulting the table, or in consulting a memory image of it 'with one's mind's eye'. *c*) B is guided if he does not just react to looking at each word of the order, but experiences the peculiar strain of 'trying to remember what the sign means', and further, the relaxing of this strain when the meaning, the right action, comes before his mind.

All these explanations seem in a peculiar way unsatisfactory, and it is the limitation of our game which makes them unsatisfactory. This is expressed by the explanation that B is guided by the particular combination of words in one of our three sentences if he *could* also have carried out orders consisting in other combinations of dots and dashes. And if we say this, it seems to us that the '*ability*' to carry out other orders is a particular state of the person carrying out the orders of 42). And at the same time we can't in this case find anything which we should call such a state.

Let us see what role the words "can" or "to be able to" play in our language. Consider these examples:

44). Imagine that for some purpose or other people use a kind of instrument or tool; this consists of a board with a slot in it guiding the movement of a peg. The man using the tool slides the peg along the slot. There are such boards with straight slots, circular slots, elliptic slots, etc. The language of the people using this instrument has expressions for describing the activity of moving the peg in the slot. They talk of moving it in a circle, in a straight line, etc. They also have a means of describing the board used. They do it in this form: "This is a board in which the peg *can* be moved in a circle". One could in this case call the word "can" an operator by means of which the form of expression describing an action is transformed into a description of the instrument.

45). Imagine a people in whose language there is no such form of sentence as "the book is in the drawer" or "water is in the glass", but wherever we should use these forms they say, "The book can be taken out of the drawer", "The water can be taken out of the glass".

46). An activity of the men of a certain tribe is to test sticks as to their hardness. They do it by trying to bend the sticks with their hands. In their language they have expressions of the form, "This stick can be bent easily", or "This stick can be bent with difficulty". They use these expressions as we use "This stick is soft", or "This stick is hard". I mean to say that they don't use the expression, "This stick can be bent easily" as we should use the sentence, "I am bending the stick with ease". Rather they use their expression in a way which would make us say that they are describing a state of the stick. I.e., they use such sentences as, "This hut is built of sticks that can be bent easily". (Think of the way in which we form adjectives out of verbs by means of the ending "able", e.g., "deformable".)

Now we might say that in the last three cases the sentences of the form "so and so can happen" described the state of objects, but there are great differences between these examples. In 44) we saw the state described before our eyes. We saw that the board had a circular or a straight slot, etc. In 45), in some instances at least this was the case, we could see the objects in the box, the water in the glass, etc. In such cases we use the expression "state of an object" in such a way that there corresponds to it what one might call a stationary sense experience.

When, on the other hand, we talk of the state of a stick in 46), observe that to this 'state' there does not correspond a particular sense experience which lasts while the state lasts. Instead of that, the defining criterion for something being in this state consists in certain *tests*.

We may say that a car travels 20 miles an hour even if it only travels for half an hour. We can explain our form of expression by saying that the car travels with a speed which enables it to make 20 miles an hour. And here also we are inclined to talk of the velocity of the car as of a state of its motion. I think we should not use this expression if we had no other 'experiences of motion' than those of a body being in a particular place at a certain time and in another place at another time; if, e.g., our experiences of motion were of the kind which we have when we see that the hour hand of the clock has moved from one point of the dial to the other.

47).   A tribe has in its language commands for the execution of certain actions of men in warfare, something like "Shoot!", "Run!", "Crawl!", etc. They also have a way of describing a man's build. Such a description has the form "He can run fast", "He can throw the spear far". What justifies me in saying that these sentences are descriptions of the man's build is the use which they make of sentences of this

form. Thus if they see a man with bulging leg muscles but who as
we should say has not the use of his legs for some reason or other,
they say he is a man who can run fast. The drawn image of a man
which shows large biceps they describe as representing a man "who
can throw a spear far".

48).   The men of a tribe are subjected to a kind of medical
examination before going into war. The examiner puts the men
through a set of standardized tests. He lets them lift certain weights,
swing their arms, skip, etc. The examiner then gives his verdict
in the form "So and so can throw a spear" or "can throw a boomerang"
or "is fit to pursue the enemy", etc. There are no special expressions in
the language of this tribe for the activities performed in the tests;
but these are referred to only as the tests for certain activities in warfare.

It is an important remark concerning this example and others which
we give that one may object to the description which we give of the
language of a tribe, that in the specimens we give of their language
we let[1] them speak English, thereby already presupposing the whole
background of the English language, that is, our usual meanings
of the words. Thus if I say that in a certain language there is no
special verb for "skipping", but that this language uses instead the
form "making the test for throwing the boomerang", one may ask how
I have characterized the use of the expressions, "make a test for" and
"throwing the boomerang", to be justified in substituting these English
expressions for whatever their actual words may be. To this we must
answer that we have only given a very sketchy description of the
practices of our fictitious languages, in some cases only hints, but that
one can easily make these descriptions more complete. Thus in 48)
I could have said that the examiner uses orders for making the men
go through the tests. These orders all begin with one particular
expression which I could translate into the English words, "Go
through the test". And this expression is followed by one which in
actual warfare is used for certain actions. Thus there is a command
upon which men throw their boomerangs and which therefore I
should translate into, "Throw the boomerangs". Further, if a man
gives an account of the battle to his chief, he again uses the expression
I have translated into "throw a boomerang", this time in a description.
Now what characterizes an order as such, or a description as such,

---

[1] German *lassen*, i.e. 'make'.—*Edd.*

or a question as such, etc., is—as we have said—the role which the utterance of these signs plays in the whole practice of the language. That is to say, whether a word of the language of our tribe is rightly translated into a word of the English language depends upon the role this word plays in the whole life of the tribe; the occasions on which it is used, the expressions of emotion by which it is generally accompanied, the ideas which it generally awakens or which prompt its saying, etc., etc. As an exercise ask yourself: in which cases would you say that a certain word uttered by the people of the tribe was a greeting? In which cases should we say it corresponded to our "Good-bye", in which to our "Hello"? In which cases would you say that a word of a foreign language corresponded to our "perhaps"?—to our expressions of doubt, trust, certainty? You will find that the justifications for calling something an expression of doubt, conviction, etc., largely, though of course not wholly, consist in descriptions of gestures, the play of facial expressions, and even the tone of voice. Remember at this point that the personal experiences of an emotion must in part be strictly localized experiences; for if I frown in anger I feel the muscular tension of the frown in my forehead, and if I weep, the sensations around my eyes are obviously part, and an important part, of what I feel. This is, I think, what William James meant when he said that a man doesn't cry because he is sad but that he is sad because he cries. The reason why this point is often not understood, is that we think of the utterance of an emotion as though it were some artificial device to let others know that we have it. Now there is no sharp line between such 'artificial devices' and what one might call the natural expressions of emotion. Cf. in this respect: *a*) weeping, *b*) raising one's voice when one is angry, *c*) writing an angry letter, *d*) ringing the bell for a servant you wish to scold.

49)   Imagine a tribe in whose language there is an expression corresponding to our "He has done so and so", and another expression corresponding to our "He can do so and so", this latter expression, however, being only used where its use is justified by the same fact which would also justify the former expression. Now what can make me say this? They have a form of communication which we should call narration of past events because of the circumstances under which it is employed. There are also circumstances under which we should ask and answer such questions as "Can so and so do this?" Such circumstances can be described, e.g., by saying that a chief picks men

suitable for a certain action, say crossing a river, climbing a mountain,
etc. As the defining criteria of "the chief picking men suitable for
this action", I will not take what he says but only the other features of
the situation. The chief under these circumstances asks a question
which, as far as its practical consequences go, would have to be
translated by our "Can so and so swim across this river?" This question
however, is only answered affirmatively by those who actually have
swum across this river. This answer is not given in the same words in
which under the circumstances characterizing narration he would say
that he has swum across this river, but it is given in the terms of the
question asked by the chief. On the other hand, this answer is not
given in cases in which we should certainly give the answer, "I can
swim across this river", if, e.g., I had performed more difficult feats of
swimming though not just that of swimming across this particular
river.

By the way, have the two phrases "He has done so and so" and
"He can do so and so" the same meaning in this language or have they
different meanings? If you think about it, something will tempt you
to say the one, something to say the other. This only shows that the
question has here no clearly defined meaning. All I can say is: If the
fact that they only say "He can . . ." if he has done . . . is your criterion
for the same meaning, then the two expressions have the same meaning.
If the circumstances under which an expression is used make its
meaning, the meanings are different. The use which is made of the
word "can"—the expression of possibility in 49)—can throw a light
upon the idea that what can happen must have happened before
(Nietzsche). It will also be interesting to look, in the light of our
examples, on the statement that what happens can happen.

Before we go on with our consideration of the use of 'the expression
of possibility', let us get clearer about that department of our language
in which things are said about past and future, that is, about the use of
sentences containing such expressions as "yesterday", "a year ago",
"in five minutes", "before I did this", etc. Consider this example:

50).   Imagine how a child might be trained in the practice of
'narration of past events'. He was first trained in asking for certain
things (as it were, in giving orders. See 1)). Part of this training was
the exercise of 'naming the things'. He has thus learnt to name (and
ask for) a dozen of his toys. Say now that he has played with three of
them (e.g., a ball, a stick, and a rattle), then they are taken away from

him, and now the grown up says such a phrase as, "He's had a ball, a stick, and a rattle". On a similar occasion he stops short in the enumeration and induces the child to complete it. On another occasion, perhaps, he only says, "He's had . . . " and leaves the child to give the whole enumeration. Now the way of 'inducing the child to go on' can be this: He stops short in his enumeration with a facial expression and a raised tone of voice which we should call one of expectancy. All then depends on whether the child will react to this 'inducement' or not. Now there is a queer misunderstanding we are most liable to fall into, which consists in regarding the 'outward means' the teacher uses to induce the child to go on as what we might call an indirect means of making himself understood to the child. We regard the case as though the child already possessed a language in which it thought and that the teacher's job is to induce it to guess his meaning in the realm of meanings before the child's mind, as though the child could in his own private language ask himself such a question as, "Does he want me to continue, or repeat what he said, or something else?" (Cf. with 30).)

51).   Another example of a primitive kind of narration of past events: we live in a landscape with characteristic natural landmarks against the horizon. It is therefore easy to remember the place at which the sun rises at a particular season, or the place above which it stands when at its highest point, or the place at which it sets. We have some characteristic pictures of the sun in different positions in our landscape. Let us call this series of pictures the sun series. We have also some characteristic pictures of the activities of a child, lying in bed, getting up, dressing, lunching, etc. This set I'll call the life pictures. I imagine that the child can frequently see the position of the sun while about the day's activities. We draw the child's attention to the sun's standing in a certain place while the child is occupied in a particular way. We then let it look both at a picture representing its occupation and at a picture showing the sun in its position at that time. We can thus roughly tell the story of the child's day by laying out a row of the life pictures, and above it what I called the sun series, the two rows in the proper correlation. We shall then proceed to let the child supplement such a picture story, which we leave incomplete. And I wish to say at this point that this form of training (see 50) and 30)) is one of the big characteristic features in the use of language, or in thinking.

52).   A variation of 51). There is a big clock in the nursery, for simplicity's sake imagine it with an hour hand only. The story of the child's day is narrated as above, but there is no sun series; instead we write one of the numbers of the dial against each life picture.

53).   Note that there would have been a similar game in which also, as we might say, time was involved, that of just laying out a series of life pictures. We might play this game with the help of words which would correspond to our "before" and "after". In this sense we may say that 53) involves the ideas of before and after, but not the idea of a measurement of time. I needn't say that an easy step would lead us from the narrations in 51), 52), and 53) to narrations in words. Possibly someone considering such forms of narration might think that in them the real idea of time isn't yet involved at all, but only some crude substitute for it, the positions of a clock hand and suchlike. Now if a man claimed that there is an idea of five o'clock which does not bring in a clock, that the clock is only the coarse instrument indicating when it is five o'clock or that there is an idea of an hour which does not bring in an instrument for measuring the time, I will not contradict him, but I will ask him to explain to me what his use of the term "an hour" or "five o'clock" is. And if it is not that involving a clock, it is a different one; and then I will ask him why he uses the terms "five o'clock", "an hour", "a long time", "a short time", etc., in one case in connection with a clock, in the other independent of one; it will be because of certain analogies holding between the two uses, but we have now two uses of these terms, and no reason to say that one of them is less real and pure than the other. This might get clearer by considering the following example:

54).   If we give a person the order "Say a number, any one which comes into your mind", he can generally comply with it at once. Suppose it were found that the numbers thus said on request increased—with every normal person—as the day went on; a man starts out with some small number every morning and reaches the highest number before falling asleep at night. Consider what could tempt one to call the reactions described "a means of measuring time" or even to say that they are the *real* milestones in the passage of time, the sun clocks, etc., being only indirect markers. (Examine the statement that the human heart is the real clock behind all the other clocks.)

Let us now consider further language games into which temporal expressions enter.

55). This arises out of 1). If an order like "slab!", "column!", etc. is called out, B is trained to carry it out immediately. We now introduce a clock into this game, an order is given, and we train the child not to carry it out until the hand of our clock reaches a point indicated before with the finger. (This might, e.g., be done in this way: You first trained the child to carry out the order immediately. You then give the order, but hold the child back, releasing it only when the hand of the clock has reached the point of the dial to which we point with our fingers.)

We could at this stage introduce such a word as "now". We have two kinds of orders in this game, the orders used in 1), and orders consisting of these, together with a gesture indicating a point of the clock dial. In order to make the distinction between these two kinds more explicit, we may affix a particular sign to the orders of the first kind and, e.g., say: "slab, now!".

It would be easy now to describe language games with such expressions as "in five minutes", "half an hour ago".

56). Let us now have the case of a *description* of the future, a forecast. One might, e.g., awaken the tension of expectation in a child by keeping his attention for a considerable time on some traffic lights changing their colour periodically. We also have a red, a green, and a yellow disc before us and alternately point to one of these discs by way of forecasting the colour which will appear next. It is easy to imagine further developments of this game.

Looking at these language games, we don't come across the ideas of the past, the future and the present in their problematic and almost mysterious aspect. What this aspect is and how it comes about that it appears can be almost characteristically exemplified if we look at the question "Where does the present go when it becomes past, and where is the past?"—Under what circumstances has this question an allurement for us? For under certain circumstances it hasn't, and we should wave it away as nonsense.

It is clear that this question most easily arises if we are preoccupied with cases in which there are things flowing by us,—as logs of wood float down a river. In such a case we can say the logs which *have passed* us are all down towards the left and the logs which *will pass* us are all up towards the right. We then use this situation as a simile for all happening in time and even embody the simile in our language, as when we say that 'the present event passes by' (a log passes by), 'the future event is to come' (a log is to come). We talk about the flow of events; but also about the flow of time—the river on which the logs travel.

Here is one of the most fertile sources of philosophic puzzlement: we talk of the future event of something coming into my room, and also of the future coming of this event.

We say, "*Something* will happen", and also, "Something comes towards me"; we refer to the log as "something", but also the log's coming towards me.

Thus it can come about that we aren't able to rid ourselves of the implications of our symbolism, which seems to admit of a question like "Where does the flame of a candle go to when it's blown out?" "Where does the light go to?", "Where does the past go to"? We have become obsessed with our symbolism.—We may say that we are led into puzzlement by an analogy which irresistibly drags us on.—And this also happens when the meaning of the word "now" appears to us in a mysterious light. In our example 55) it appears that the function of "now" is in no way comparable to the function of an expression like "five o'clock", "midday", "the time when the sun sets", etc. This latter group of expressions I might call "specifications of times". But our ordinary language uses the word "now" and specifications of time in similar contexts. Thus we say

"The sun sets at six o'clock".
"The sun is setting now".

We are inclined to say that both "now" and "six o'clock" 'refer to points of time'. This use of words produces a puzzlement which one might express in the question "What is the 'now'?—for it is a moment of time and yet it can't be said to be either the 'moment at which I speak' or 'the moment at which the clock strikes', etc., etc."—Our answer is: The function of the word "now" is entirely different from that of a specification of time.—This can easily be seen if we look at the role this word really plays in our usage of language, but it is obscured when instead of looking at the *whole language game*, we only look at the contexts, the phrases of language in which the word is used. (The word "today" is not a date, but it isn't anything like it either. It doesn't differ from a date as a hammer differs from a mallet, but as a hammer differs from a nail; and surely we may say there is both a connection between a hammer and a mallet and between a hammer and a nail.)

One has been tempted to say that "now" is the name of an instant of time, and this, of course, would be like saying that "here" is the name of a place, "this" the name of a thing, and "I" the name of a man. (One could, of course, also have said "a year ago" was the name of a time, "over there" the name of a place, and "you" the name of a person.) But nothing is more unlike than the use of the word "this" and the use of a proper name—I mean *the games* played with these words, not the phrases in which they are used. For we do say "This is short" and "Jack is short"; but remember that "This is short" without the pointing gesture and without the thing we are pointing to would be meaningless.—What can be compared with a name is not the word "this" but, if you like, the symbol consisting of this word, the gesture, and the sample. We might say: Nothing is more characteristic of a proper name A than that we can use it in such a phrase as "This is A"; and it makes no sense to say "This is this" or "Now is now" or "Here is here".

The idea of a proposition saying something about what will happen in the future is even more liable to puzzle us than the idea of a proposition about the past. For comparing future events with past events, one may almost be inclined to say that though the past events do not really exist in the full light of day, they exist in an underworld into which they have passed out of the real life; whereas the future events do not even have this shadowy existence. We could, of course, imagine a realm of the unborn, future events, whence they come into reality and pass into the realm of the past; and, if we think in terms of this metaphor, we may be surprised that the future should appear less existent than the past. Remember, however, that the grammar of our temporal expressions is not symmetrical with respect to an origin corresponding with the present moment. Thus the grammar of the expressions relating to memory does not reappear 'with opposite sign' in the grammar of the future tense. This is the reason why it has been said that propositions concerning future events are not really propositions. And to say this is all right as long as it isn't meant to be more than a decision about the use of the term "proposition"; a decision which, though not agreeing with the common usage of the word "proposition", may come natural to human beings under certain circumstances. If a philosopher says that propositions about the future are not real propositions, it is because he has been struck by the asymmetry in the grammar of temporal expressions. The danger is, however, that he imagines he has made a kind of scientific statement about 'the nature of the future'.

57). A game is played in this way: A man throws a die, and before throwing he draws on a piece of paper some one of the six faces of the die. If, after having thrown, the face of the die turning up is the one he has drawn, he feels (expresses) satisfaction. If a different face turns up, he is dissatisfied. Or, let there be two partners and every time one guesses correctly what he will throw his partner pays him a penny, and if incorrectly, he pays his partner. Drawing the face of the die will under the circumstances of this game be called "making a guess" or "a conjecture".

58). In a certain tribe contests are held in running, putting the weight, etc., and the spectators stake possessions on the competitors. The pictures of all the competitors are placed in a row, and what I called the spectator's staking property on one of the competitors consists in laying this property (pieces of gold) under one of the pictures. If a man has placed his gold under the picture of the winner in the competition he gets back his stake doubled. Otherwise he loses his stake. Such a custom we should undoubtedly call betting, even if we observed it in a society whose language held no scheme for stating 'degrees of probability', 'chances' and the like. I assume that the behaviour of the spectators expresses great keenness and excitement before and after the outcome of the bet is known. I further imagine that on examining the placing of the bets I can under-stand '*why*' they were thus placed. I mean: In a competition between two wrestlers, mostly the bigger man is the favourite; or if the smaller, I find that he has shown greater strength on previous occasions, or that the bigger had recently been ill, or had neglected his training, etc. Now this may be so although the language of the tribe does not express reasons for the placing of the bets. That is to say, nothing in their language corresponds to our saying, e.g., "I bet on this man because he has kept fit, whereas the other has neglected his training", and such like. I might describe this state of affairs by saying that my observation has taught me certain *causes* for their placing their bets as they do, but that the bettors used no *reasons* for acting as they did.

The tribe may, on the other hand, have a language which comprises 'giving reasons'. Now this game of giving the reason why one acts in a particular way does not involve finding the causes of one's actions (by frequent observations of the conditions under which they arise). Let us imagine this:

59).   If a man of our tribe has lost his bet and upon this is chaffed or scolded, he points out, possibly exaggerating, certain features of the man on whom he has laid his bet.   One can imagine a discussion of pros and cons going on in this way: two people pointing out alternately certain features of the two competitors whose chances, as we should say, they are discussing; A pointing with a gesture to the great height of the one, B in answer to this shrugging his shoulders and pointing to the size of the other's biceps, and so on. I could easily add more details which would make us say that A and B are giving reasons for laying a bet on one person rather than on the other.

Now one might say that giving reasons in this way for laying their bets certainly presupposes that they have observed causal connections between the result of a fight, say, and certain features of the bodies of the fighters, or of their training. But this is an assumption which, whether reasonable or not, I certainly have not made in the description of our case. (Nor have I made the assumption that the bettors give reasons for their reasons.) We should in a case like that just described not be surprised if the language of the tribe contained what we should call expressions of degrees of belief, conviction, certainty. These expressions we could imagine to consist in the use of a particular word spoken with different intonations, or a series of words. (I am not thinking, however, of the use of a scale of probabilities.)—It is also easy to imagine that the people of our tribe accompany their betting by verbal expressions which we translate into "I believe that so and so *can* beat so and so in wrestling," etc.

60).   Imagine in a similar way conjectures being made as to whether a certain load of gunpowder will be sufficient to blast a certain rock, and the conjecture to be expressed in a phrase of the form "This quantity of gunpowder can blast this rock".

61).   Compare with 60) the case in which the expression "I shall be able to lift this weight", is used as an abbreviation for the conjecture "My hand holding this weight will rise if I go through the process (experience) of 'making an effort to lift it' ".   In the last two cases the word "can" characterized what we should call the expression of a conjecture. (Of course I don't mean that we call the sentence a conjecture because it contains the word "can"; but in calling a sentence a conjecture we referred to the role which the sentence played in the language game; and we translate a word our tribe uses by "can" if

"can" is the word we should use under the circumstances described.)
Now it is clear that the use of "can" in 59), 60), 61) is closely related
to the use of "can" in 46) to 49); differing, however in this, that in 46)
to 49) the sentences saying that something *could* happen were not
expressions of conjecture. Now one might object to this by saying:
Surely we are only willing to use the word "can" in such cases as 46)
to 49) because it is reasonable to conjecture in these cases what a man
will do in the future from the tests he has passed or from the state
he is in.

Now it is true that I have deliberately made up the cases 46) to 49)
so as to make a conjecture of this kind seem reasonable. But I have
also deliberately made them up so as *not* to contain a conjecture.
We can, if we like, make the hypothesis that the tribe would never use
such a form of expression as that used in 49), etc. if experience had
not shown them that . . . etc. But this is an assumption which,
though possibly correct, is in no way presupposed in the games 46)
to 49) as I have actually described them.

62).   Let the game be this: A writes down a row of numbers.
B watches him and tries to find a system in the sequence of these
numbers. When he has done so he says: "Now I can go on". This
example is particularly instructive because 'being able to go on' here
seems to be something setting in suddenly in the form of a clearly
outlined event.—Suppose then that A had written down the row
1, 5, 11, 19, 29. At that point B shouts "Now I can go on". What was it
that happened when suddenly he saw how to go on? A great many
different things might have happened. Let us assume then that in the
present case, while A wrote one number after the other, B busied himself with trying out several algebraic formulae to see whether they
fitted. When A had written "19" B had been led to try the formula
$a_n = n^2 + n - 1$. A's writing 29 confirms his guess.

63).   Or, no formula came into B's mind. After looking at the
growing row of numbers A was writing, possibly with a feeling of
tension and with hazy ideas floating in his mind, he said to himself
the words "He's squaring and always adding one more"; then he made
up the next number of the sequence and found it to agree with the
numbers A then wrote down.—

64).   Or, the row A wrote down was 2, 4, 6, 8. B looks at it,
and says "Of course I can go on", and continues the series of even

numbers. Or he says nothing, and just goes on. Perhaps when looking at the row 2, 4, 6, 8 which A had written down, he had some sensation, or sensations, often accompanying such words as "That's easy!" A sensation of this kind is, for instance, the experience of a slight, quick intake of breath, what one might call a slight start.

Now, should we say that the proposition "B can continue the series", means that one of the occurrences just described takes place? Isn't it clear that the statement "B can continue . . ." is not the same as the statement that the formula $a_n = n^2 + n - 1$ comes into B's mind? This occurrence might have been all that actually took place. (It is clear, by the way, that it can make no difference to us here whether B has the experience of this formula appearing before his mind's eye, or the experience of writing or speaking the formula, or of picking it out with his eyes from amongst several formulae written down beforehand.) If a parrot had uttered the formula, we should not have said that he could continue the series.—Therefore, we are inclined to say "to be able to . . ." must mean more than just uttering the formula— and in fact more than any one of the occurrences we have described. And this, we go on, shows that saying the formula was only a symptom of B's being able to go on, and that it was not the ability of going on itself. Now what is misleading in this is that we seem to intimate that there is one peculiar activity, process, or state called "being able to go on" which somehow is hidden from our eyes but manifests itself in those occurrents which we call symptoms (as an inflammation of the mucous membranes of the nose produces the symptom of sneezing). This is the way talking of symptoms, in this case, misleads us. When we say "Surely there must be something else behind the mere uttering of the formula, as this alone we should not call 'being able to . . .' ", the word "behind" here is certainly used metaphorically, and 'behind' the utterance of the formula may be the circumstances under which it is uttered. It is true, "B can continue . . ." is not the same as to say "B says the formula . . .", but it doesn't follow from this that the expression "B can continue . . ." refers to an activity other than that of saying the formula, in the way in which "B says the formula" refers to the well-known activity. The error we are in is analogous to this: Someone is told the word "chair" does not mean this particular chair I am pointing to, upon which he looks round the room for the object which the word "chair" does denote. (The case would be even more a striking illustration if he tried to look inside the chair in order to find the real meaning of the word "chair".) It is clear that when with

reference to the act of writing or speaking the formula etc., we use
the sentence "He can continue the series", this must be because of some
connection between writing down a formula and actually continuing
the series. And the connection in experience of these two processes
or activities is clear enough. But this connection tempts us to suggest
that the sentence "B can continue . . ." means something like "B does
something which, experience has shown us, generally leads to his continuing the series". But does B, when he says "Now I can go on"
really mean "Now I am doing something which, as experience has
shown us, etc., etc."? Do you mean that he had this phrase in his mind
or that he would have been prepared to give it as an explanation of
what he had said? To say the phrase "B can continue . . ." is correctly
used when prompted by such occurrences as described in 62), 63), 64)
but that these occurrences justify its use only under certain circumstances (e.g. when experience has shown certain connections) is not to
say that the sentence "B can continue . . ." is short for the sentence
which describes all these circumstances, i.e. the whole situation which
is the background of our game.

On the other hand we should *under certain circumstances* be ready to
substitute "B knows the formula", "B has said the formula" for "B can
continue the series". As when we ask a doctor "Can the patient walk?",
we shall sometimes be ready to substitute for this "Is his leg healed?"—
"Can he speak?" under circumstances means "Is his throat all right?",
under others (e.g., if he is a small child) it means "Has he learned to
speak?"—To the question "Can the patient walk?", the doctor's answer
may be "His leg is all right".—We use the phrase "He can walk, as
far as the state of his leg is concerned", especially when we wish to
oppose this condition for his walking to some other condition, say
the state of his spine. Here we must beware of thinking that there is
in the nature of the case something which we might call the complete
set of conditions, e.g., for his walking; so that the patient, as it were,
can't help walking, *must* walk, if all these conditions are fulfilled.

We can say: The expression "B can continue the series" is used
under different circumstances to make different distinctions. Thus
it may distinguish *a*) between the case when a man knows the formula
and the case when he doesn't; or *b*) between the case when a man
knows the formula and hasn't forgotten how to write the numerals
of the decimal system, and the case when he knows the formula and has
forgotten how to write the numerals; or *c*) (as perhaps in 64)) between
the case when a man is feeling his normal self and the case when he is

still in a condition of shell-shock; or *d*) between the case of a man who has done this kind of exercise before and the case of a man who is new at it. These are only a few of a large family of cases.

The question whether "He can continue . . ." means the same as "He knows the formula" can be answered in several different ways: We can say "They don't mean the same, i.e., they are not in general used as synonyms as, e.g., the phrases 'I am well' and 'I am in good health' "; or we may say *"Under certain circumstances* 'He can continue . . .' means he knows the formula". Imagine the case of a language (somewhat analogous to 49)) in which two forms of expression, two different sentences, are used to say that a person's legs are in working order. The one form of expression is exclusively used under circumstances when preparations are going on for an expedition, a walking tour, or the like; the other is used in cases when there is no question of such preparations. We shall here be doubtful whether to say the two sentences have the same meaning or different meanings. In any case the true state of affairs can only be seen when we look into the detail of the usage of our expressions.—And it is clear that if in our present case we should decide to say that the two expressions have different meanings, we shall certainly not be able to say that the difference is that the fact which makes the second sentence true is a different one from the fact which makes the first sentence true.

We are justified in saying that the sentence "He can continue . . ." has a different meaning from this: "He knows the formula". But we mustn't imagine that we can find a particular state of affairs 'which the first sentence refers to', as it were on a plane above that on which the special occurrences (like knowing the formula, imagining certain further terms, etc.) take place.

Let us ask the following question: Suppose that, on one ground or another, B has said "I can continue the series", but on being asked to continue it he had shown himself unable to do so——should we say that this proved that his statement, that he could continue, was wrong, or should we say that he was able to continue when he said he was? Would B himself say "I see I was wrong", or "What I said was true, I could do it then but I can't now"?—There are cases in which he would correctly say the one and cases in which he would correctly say the other. Suppose *a*) when he said he could continue he saw the formula before his mind, but when he was asked to continue he found he had forgotten it;—or, *b*) when he said he could continue he had said to himself the next five terms of the series, but now finds that they don't come into his mind;—or, *c*) before, he had continued the series calculating five more places, now he still remembers these five numbers but has forgotten how he had calculated them;—or, *d*) he says "Then I felt I could continue, now I can't";—or, *e*) "When I said I could lift the weight my arm didn't hurt, now it does"; etc.

On the other hand we say "I thought I could lift this weight, but I see I can't", "I thought I could say this piece by heart, but I see I was mistaken".

These illustrations of the use of the word "can" should be supplemented by illustrations showing the variety of uses we make of the terms "forgetting" and "trying", for these uses are closely connected with those of the word "can". Consider these cases: *a*) Before, B had said to himself the formula, now, "he finds a complete blank there". *b*) Before, he had said to himself the formula, now, for a moment he isn't sure 'whether it was 2^n or 3^n'. *c*) He has forgotten a name and it is 'on the tip of his tongue'. Or, *d*) he is not certain whether he has ever known the name or has forgotten it.

Now look at the way in which we use the word "trying": *a*) A man is trying to open a door by pulling as hard as he can. *b*) He is trying to open the door of a safe by trying to find the combination. *c*) He is trying to find the combination by trying to remember it, or *d*) by turning the knobs and listening with a stethoscope. Consider the various processes we call "trying to remember". Compare *e*) trying to move your finger against a resistance (e.g., when someone is holding it), and *f*) when you have intertwined the fingers of both hands in a particular way and feel 'you don't know what to do in order to make a particular finger move'.

(Consider also the class of cases in which we say "I can do so and so but I won't": "I could if I tried"—e.g., lift 100 pounds; "I could if I wished"—e.g., say the alphabet.)

One might perhaps suggest that the only case in which it is correct to say, without restriction, that I can do a certain thing, is that in which while saying that I can do it, I actually do it, and that otherwise I ought to say "I can do it as far as . . . is concerned". One may be inclined to think that only in the above case has a person given a real proof of being able to do a thing.

65).   But if we look at a language game in which the phrase "I can . . . " is used in this way (i.e., a game in which doing a thing is taken as the only justification for saying that one is able to do it), we see that there is not the *metaphysical* difference between this game and one in which other justifications are accepted for saying "I can do so and so". A game of the kind 65), by the way, shows us the real use of the phrase "If something happens it certainly can happen"; an almost useless phrase in our language. It sounds as though it had some very clear and deep meaning, but like most of the general philosophical propositions it is meaningless except in very special cases.

66).   Make this clear to yourself by imagining a language (similar to 49)) which has two expressions for such sentences as "I am lifting a fifty pound weight"; one expression is used whenever the action is performed as a test (say, before an athletic competition), the other expression is used when the action is not performed as a test.

We see that a vast net of family likenesses connects the cases in which the expressions of possibility, "can", "to be able to", etc. are used. Certain characteristic features, we may say, appear in these cases in different combinations: there is, e.g., the element of conjecture (that something will behave in a certain way in the future); the description of the state of something (as a condition for its behaving in a certain way in the future); the account of certain tests someone or something has passed.—

There are, on the other hand, various reasons which incline us to look at the fact of something being possible, someone being able to do something, etc., as the fact that he or it is in a particular state. Roughly speaking, this comes to saying that "A is in the state of being able to do something" is the form of representation we are most strongly tempted to adopt; or, as one could also put it, we are strongly inclined to use the metaphor of something being in a peculiar state for saying that something can behave in a particular way. And this way of representation, or this metaphor, is embodied in the expressions "He is capable of . . .", "He is able to multiply large numbers in his head", "He can play chess": in these sentences the verb is used in the *present tense*, suggesting that the phrases are descriptions of states which exist at the moment when we speak.

The same tendency shows itself in our calling the ability to solve a mathematical problem, the ability to enjoy a piece of music, etc., certain states of the mind; we don't mean by this expression 'conscious mental phenomena'. Rather, a state of the mind in this sense is the state of a hypothetical mechanism, a mind model meant to explain the conscious mental phenomena. (Such things as unconscious or subconscious mental states are features of the mind *model*.) In this way also we can hardly help conceiving of memory as of a kind of storehouse. Note also how sure people are that to the ability to add or to multiply or to say a poem by heart, etc., there *must* correspond a peculiar state of the person's brain, although on the other hand they know next to nothing about such psycho-physiological correspondences. We regard these phenomena as manifestations of this mechanism, and their possibility is the particular construction of the mechanism itself.

Now looking back to our discussion of 43), we see that it was no real explanation of B's being guided by the signs when we said that B was guided if he *could* also have carried out orders consisting in other combinations of dots and dashes than those of 43). In fact, when we considered the question whether B in 43) was guided by the signs, we were all the time inclined to say some such thing as that we could only decide this question with certainty if we could look into the actual mechanism connecting seeing the signs with acting according to them. For we have a definite picture of what in a mechanism we should call certain parts being guided by others. In fact, the mechanism which immediately suggests itself when we wish to show what in such a case as 43) we should call "being guided by the signs" is a mechanism of the type of a pianola. Here, in the working of the pianola we have a clear case of certain actions, those of the hammers of the piano, being guided by the pattern of the holes in the pianola roll. We could use the expression "The pianola is *reading off* the record made by the perforations in the roll", and we might call patterns of such perforations *complex signs* or *sentences*, opposing their function in a pianola to the function which similar devices have in mechanisms of a different type, e.g., the combination of notches and teeth which form a key bit. The bolt of a lock is caused to slide by this particular combination, but we should not say that the movement of the bolt was guided by the way in which we combined teeth and notches, i.e., we should not say that the bolt moved *according* to the pattern of the key bit. You see here the connection between the idea of being guided and the idea of being able to read new combinations of signs; for we should say that the pianola *can* read *any* pattern of perforations, of a particular kind, it is not built for one particular tune or set of tunes (like a musical box),—whereas the bolt of the lock reacts to that pattern of the key bit only which is predetermined in the construction of the lock.

We could say that the notches and teeth forming a key bit are not comparable to the words making up a sentence but to the letters making up a word, and that the pattern of the key bit in this sense did not correspond to a complex sign, to a sentence, but to a word.

It is clear that although we might use the ideas of such mechanisms as similes for describing the way in which B acts in the games 42) and 43), no such mechanisms are actually involved in these games. We shall have to say that the use which we made of the expression "to be guided" in our examples of the pianola and of the lock is only one use within a family of usages, though these examples may serve as metaphors, ways of representation, for other usages.

Let us study the use of the expression "to be guided" by studying the use of the word "reading". By "reading" I here mean the activity of translating script into sounds, also of writing according to dictation or of copying in writing a page of print, and suchlike; reading in this sense does not involve any such thing as understanding what you read. The use of the word "reading" is, of course, extremely familiar to us in the circumstances of our ordinary life (it would be extremely difficult to describe these circumstances even roughly). A person, say an Englishman, has as a child gone through one of the normal ways of training in school or at home, he has learned to read his language, later on he reads books, newspapers, letters, etc. What happens when he reads the newspaper?—His eyes glide along the printed words, he pronounces them aloud or to himself, but he pronounces certain words just taking their pattern in as a whole, other words he pronounces after having seen their first few letters only, others again he reads out letter by letter. We should also say that he had read a sentence if while letting his eyes glide along it he had said nothing aloud or to himself, but on being asked afterwards what he had read he was able to reproduce the sentence verbatim or in slightly different words. He may also act as what we might call a mere reading machine, I mean, paying no attention to what he spoke, perhaps concentrating his attention on something totally different. We should in this case say that he read if he acted faultlessly like a reliable machine.—Compare with this case the case of a beginner. He reads the words by spelling them out painfully. Some of the words, however, he just guesses from their contexts, or possibly he knows the piece by heart. The teacher then says that he is pretending to read the words, or just that he is not really reading them. If, looking at this example, we asked ourselves what reading was, we should be inclined to say that it was a particular conscious mental act. This is the case in which we say "Only he knows whether he is reading; nobody else can really know it". Yet we must admit that as far as the reading of a particular word goes, exactly the same thing might have happened in the beginner's mind when he 'pretended' to read as what happened in the mind of the fluent reader when he read the word. We are using the word "reading" in a different way when we talk about the accomplished reader on the one hand and the beginner on the other hand. What in the one case we call an instance of reading we don't call an instance of reading in the other.—Of course we are inclined to say that what happened in the accomplished reader and in the beginner when they pronounced the word could not have been the same. The difference lying, if not in their conscious states, then in the unconscious regions of their minds, or in their brains. We here imagine two mechanisms, the internal working of which we can see, and this internal working is the real criterion for a person's reading or not reading. But in fact no such mechanisms are known to us in these cases. Look at it in this way:

67).   Imagine that human beings or animals were used as reading machines; assume that in order to become reading machines they need a particular training. The man who trains them says of some of them that they already can read, of others that they can't. Take a case of one who has so far not responded to the training. If you put before him a printed word he will sometimes make sounds, and every now and then it happens 'accidentally' that these sounds more or less correspond to the printed word. A third person hears the creature under training uttering the right sound on looking at the word "table". The third person says "He's reading", but the teacher answers "No, he isn't, it is mere accident". But supposing now that the pupil on being shown other words and sentences goes on reading them correctly. After a time the teacher says "Now he can read".—But what about the first word "table"? Should the teacher say "I was wrong. He read that, too"?, or should he say "No, he only started reading later"? When did he really begin to read, or: Which was the first word, or the first letter, which he read? It is clear that this question here makes no sense unless I give an 'artificial' explanation such as: "The first word which he reads = the first word of the first hundred consecutive words he reads correctly."—Suppose on the other hand that we used the word "reading" to distinguish between the case when a particular conscious process of spelling out the words takes place in a person's mind from the case in which this does not happen.—Then, at least the person who is reading could say that such and such a word was the first which he actually read.—Also, in the different case of a reading machine which is a mechanism connecting signs with the reactions to these signs, e.g., a pianola, we could say "Only after such and such a thing had been done to the machine, e.g., certain parts had been connected by wires, the machine actually read; the first letter which it read was a *d*".—

In the case 67), by calling certain creatures "reading machines" we meant only that they react in a particular way to seeing printed signs. No connection between seeing and reacting, no internal mechanism enters into this case. It would be absurd if the trainer had answered to the question whether he read the word "table" or not, "Perhaps he read it", for there is no doubt in this case about what he actually did. The change which took place was one which we might call a change in the general behaviour of the pupil, and we have in this case not given a meaning to the expression "the first word in the new era". (Compare with this the following case:

. . . .

In our figure a row of dots with large intervals succeeds a row of dots with small intervals. Which is the last dot in the first sequence and which the first dot in the second? Imagine our dots were holes in the revolving disc of a siren. Then we should hear a tone of low pitch following a tone of high pitch (or vice versa). Ask yourself: At which moment does the tone of low pitch begin and the other end?)

There is a great temptation on the other hand to regard the conscious mental act as the only real criterion distinguishing reading from not reading. For we are inclined to say "Surely a man always knows whether he is reading or pretending to read", or "Surely a man always knows when he is really reading". If A tries to make B believe that he is able to read Cyrillic script, cheating him by learning a Russian sentence by heart and then saying it while looking at the printed sentence, we may certainly say that A knows that he is pretending and that his not reading in this case is characterized by a particular personal experience, namely, that of saying the sentence by heart. Also, if A makes a slip in saying it by heart, this experience will be different from that which a person has who makes a slip in *reading*.

68).   But supposing now that a man who could read fluently and who was made to read sentences which he had never read before read these sentences, but all the time with the peculiar feeling of knowing the sequence of words by heart. Should we in this case say that he was not reading, i.e., should we regard his personal experience as the criterion distinguishing between reading and not reading?

69).   Or imagine this case: A man under the influence of a certain drug is shown a group of five signs, not letters of an existing alphabet; and looking at them with all the outward signs and personal experiences of spelling out a word, pronounces the word "ABOVE". (This sort of thing happens in dreams. After waking up we then say, "It seemed to me that I was reading these signs though they weren't really signs at all".) In such a case some people might be inclined to say that he is reading, others that he isn't. We could imagine that after he had spelt out the word "above" we showed him other combinations of the five signs and that he read them consistently with his reading of the first permutation of signs shown to him. By a series of similar tests we might find that he used what we might call an imaginary alphabet. If this was so, we should be more ready to say "He is reading" than "He imagines that he reads, but he doesn't really".

Note also that there is a continuous series of intermediary cases between the case when a person knows by heart what is in print before him, and the case in which he spells out the letters of every word without any such help as guessing from the context, knowing by heart, and such like.

Do this: Say by heart the series of cardinals from one to twelve.— Now look at the dial of your watch and *read* this sequence of numbers. Ask yourself what in this case you called reading, that is, what did you do to make it reading?

Let us try this explanation: A person reads if he *derives* the copy which he is producing from the model which he is copying. (I will use the word "model" to mean that which he is reading off, e.g., the printed sentences which he is reading or copying in writing, or such signs as "– – · · –" in 42) and 43) which he is "reading" by his movements, or the scores which a pianist plays off, etc. The word "copy" I use for the sentence spoken or written from the printed one, for the movements made according to such signs as " – – · · –", for the movements of the pianist's fingers or the tune which he plays from the scores, etc.) Thus if we had taught a person the Cyrillic alphabet and had taught him how each letter was pronounced, if then we gave him a piece printed in the Cyrillic script and he spelt it out according to the pronunciation of each letter as we had taught it, we should undoubtedly say that he was deriving the sound of every word from the written and spoken alphabet taught him. And this also would be a clear case of reading. (We might use the expression, "We have taught him the *rule* of the alphabet".)

But let us see; what made us say that he *derived* the spoken words from the printed by means of the rule of the alphabet? Isn't all we know that we told him that this letter was pronounced this way, that letter that way, etc., and that he afterwards read out words in the Cyrillic script? What suggests itself to us as an answer is that he must have shown somehow that he did actually make the transition from the printed to the spoken words by means of the rule of the alphabet which we had given him. And what we mean by his showing this will certainly get clearer if we alter our example and:

70) assume that he reads off a text by transcribing it, say, from block letters into cursive script. For in this case we can assume the rule of the alphabet to have been given in the form of a table which shows the block alphabet and the cursive alphabet in parallel columns. Then the *deriving* the copy from the text we should imagine this way: The person who copies looks up the table for each letter at frequent intervals, or he says to himself such things as, "Now what's a small *a* like?", or he tries to visualize the table, refraining from actually looking at it.—

71). But what if, doing all this, he then transcribed an "A" into a "b", a "B" into a "c", and so on? Should we not call this "reading", "deriving", too? We might in this case describe his procedure by saying that he used the table as we should have used it had we not looked straight from left to right like this:

but like this:

though he actually when looking up the table passed with his eyes or finger horizontally from left to right.—But let us suppose now

72)   that going through the normal process of looking up, he transcribed an "A" into an "n", a "B" into an "x", in short, acted, as we might say, according to a scheme of arrows which showed no simple regularity. Couldn't we call this "deriving" too?—But suppose that

73)   he didn't stick to this way of transcribing. In fact he changed it, but according to a simple rule: After having transcribed "A" into "n", he transcribes the next "A" into "o", and the next "A" into "p", and so on. But where is the sharp line between this procedure and that of producing a transcription without any system at all? Now you might object to this by saying "In the case 71), you obviously assumed that he *understood the table differently*; he didn't understand it in the normal way". But what do we call "understanding the table in a particular way?" But whatever process you imagine this 'understanding' to be, it is only another link interpcsed between the outward and inward processes of deriving I have described and the actual transcription. In fact this process of understanding could obviously be described by means of a schema of the kind used in 71), and we could then say that in a particular case he looked up the table like this:

understood the table like this:

and transcribed it like this:

But does this mean that the word "deriving" (or "understanding") has really no meaning, as by following up its meaning this seems to trail off into nothing? In case 70) the meaning of "deriving" stood out quite clearly, but we told ourselves that this was only one special case of deriving. It seemed to us that the essence of the process of deriving was here presented in a particular dress and that by stripping it of this we should get at the essence. Now in 71), 72), 73) we tried to strip our case of what had seemed but its peculiar costume only to find that what had seemed mere costumes were the essential features of the case. (We acted as though we had tried to find the real artichoke by stripping it of its leaves.) The use of the word "deriving" is indeed exhibited in 70), i.e., this example showed us one of the family of cases in which this word is used. And the explanation of the use of this word, as that of the use of the word "reading" or "being guided by symbols", essentially consists in describing a selection of examples exhibiting characteristic features, some examples showing these features in exaggeration, others showing transitions, certain series of examples showing the trailing off of such features. Imagine that someone wished to give you an idea of the facial characteristics of a certain family, the So and so's, he would do it by showing you a set of family portraits and by drawing your attention to certain characteristic features, and his main task would consist in the proper *arrangement* of these pictures, which, e.g., would enable you to see how certain influences gradually changed the features, in what characteristic ways the members of the family aged, what features appeared more strongly as they did so.

It was not the function of our examples to show us the essence of 'deriving', 'reading', and so forth through a veil of inessential features; the examples were not descriptions of an outside letting us guess at an inside which for some reason or other could not be shown in its nakedness. We are tempted to think that our examples are *indirect* means for producing a certain image or idea in a person's mind,— that they *hint* at something which they cannot show. This would be so in some such case as this: Suppose I wish to produce in someone a mental image of the inside of a particular eighteenth-century room which he is prevented from entering. I therefore adopt this method: I show him the house from the outside, pointing out the windows of the room in question, I further lead him into other rooms of the same period.—

Our method is *purely descriptive*; the descriptions we give are not hints of explanations.

II

1.   Do we have a feeling of familiarity whenever we look at familiar objects? Or do we have it usually?

When do we actually have it?

It helps us to ask: What do we contrast the feeling of familiarity with?

One thing we contrast it with is surprise.

One could say: "Unfamiliarity is much more of an experience than familiarity".

We say: A shows B a series of objects. B is to tell A whether the object is familiar to him or not. *a*) The question may be "Does B know what the objects are?" or *b*) "Does he recognize the particular object?"

1).   Take the case that B is shown a series of apparatus—a balance, a thermometer, a spectroscope, etc.

2).   B is shown a pencil, a pen, an inkpot, and a pebble. Or:

3).   Besides familiar objects he is shown an object of which he says "That looks as though it served some purpose, but I don't know what purpose".

What happens when B recognizes something as a pencil?

Suppose A had shown him an object looking like a stick. B handles this object, suddenly it comes apart, one of the parts being a cap, the other a pencil. B says "Oh, this is a pencil". He has recognized the object as a pencil.

4).   We could say "B always knew what a pencil looked like; he could, e.g., have drawn one on being asked to. He didn't know that the object he was given contained a pencil which he could have drawn any time". Compare with this case 5):

5).   B is shown a word written on a piece of paper held upside down. He does not recognize the word. The paper is gradually turned round until B says "Now I see what it is. It is 'pencil' ".

We might say "He always knew what the word 'pencil' looked like. He did not know that the word he was shown would, when turned round, look like 'pencil' ".

In both cases 4) and 5) you might say something was hidden. But note the different application of "hidden".

6). Compare with this: You read a letter and can't read one of its words. You guess what it must be from the context, and now can read it. You recognize this scratch as an *e*, the second as an *a*, the third as a *t*. This is different from the case where the word "eat" was covered by a blotch of ink, and you only guessed that the word "eat" must have been in this place.

7). Compare: You see a word and can't read it. Someone alters it slightly by adding a dash, lengthening a stroke, or such like. Now you can read it. Compare this alteration with the turning in 5), and note that there is a sense in which while the word was turned round you saw that it was *not* altered. I.e., there is a case in which you say "I looked at the word while it was turned, and I know that it is the same now as it was when I didn't recognize it".

8). Suppose the game between A and B just consisted in this, that B should say whether he knows the object or not but does not say what it is. Suppose he was shown an ordinary pencil, after having been shown a hygrometer which he had never seen before. On being shown the hygrometer he said that he was not familiar with it, on being shown the pencil, that he knew it. What happened when he recognized it? Must he have told himself, though he didn't tell A, that what he saw was a pencil? Why should we assume this?

Then, when he recognized the pencil, what did he recognize it as?

9). Suppose even that he had said to himself "Oh, this is a pencil", could you compare this case with 4) or 5)? In these cases one might have said "He recognized this as that" (pointing, e.g., for "this" to the covered up pencil and for "that" to an ordinary pencil, and similarly in 5)).

In 8) the pencil underwent no change and the words "Oh, this is a pencil" did not refer to a paradigm, the similarity of which with the pencil shown B had recognized.

Asked "What is a pencil?", B would not have pointed to another object as the paradigm or sample, but could straight away have pointed to the pencil shown to him.

"But when he said 'Oh, this is a pencil', how did he know that it was if he didn't recognize it as something?"—This really comes to saying "How did he recognize 'pencil' as the name of this sort of thing?" Well, how did he recognize it? He just reacted in this particular way by saying this word.

10). Suppose someone shows you colours and asks you to name them.

Pointing to a certain object you say "This is red". What would you answer if you were asked "How do you know that this is red?"?

Of course there is the case in which a general explanation was given to B, say, "We shall call 'pencil' anything that one can easily write with on a wax tablet." Then A shows B amongst other objects a small pointed object, and B says "Oh, this is a pencil", after having thought "One could write with this quite easily". In this case, we may say, a *derivation* takes place. In 8), 9), 10) there is no derivation. In 4) we might say that B derived that the object shown to him was a pencil by means of a paradigm, or else no such derivation might have taken place.

Now should we say that B on seeing the pencil after seeing instruments which he didn't know had a feeling of familiarity? Let us imagine what really might have happened. He saw a pencil, smiled, felt relieved, and the name of the object he saw came into his mind or mouth.

Now isn't the feeling of relief just that which characterizes the experience of passing from unfamiliar to familiar things?

2. We say we experience tension and relaxation, relief, strain and rest in cases as different as these: A man holds a weight with outstretched arm; his arm, his whole body is in a state of tension. We let him put down the weight, the tension relaxes. A man runs, then rests. He thinks hard about the solution of a problem in Euclid, then finds it, and relaxes. He tries to remember a name, and relaxes on finding it.

What if we asked "What do all these cases have in common that makes us say that they are cases of strain and relaxation?"?

What makes us use the expression "seeking in our memory", when we try to remember a word?

Let us ask the question "What is the similarity between looking for a word in your memory and looking for my friend in the park?" What would be the answer to such a question?

One kind of answer certainly would consist in describing a series of intermediate cases. One might say that the case which looking in your memory for something is most similar to is not that of looking for my friend in the park, but, say, that of looking up the spelling of a word in a dictionary. And one might go on interpolating cases. Another way of *pointing out* the similarity would be to say, e.g., "In both these cases at first we can't write down the word and then we can". This is what we call pointing out a common feature.

Now it is important to note that we needn't be aware of such similarities thus pointed out when we are prompted to use the words "seeking", "looking for", etc., in the case of trying to remember.

One might be inclined to say "Surely a similarity must strike us, or we shouldn't be moved to use the same word".—Compare that statement with this: "A similarity between these cases must strike us in order that we should be inclined to use the same picture to represent both". This says that some act must precede the act of using this picture. But why shouldn't what we call "the similarity striking us" consist partially or wholly in our using the same picture? And why shouldn't it consist partially or wholly in our being prompted to use the same phrase?

We say: "This picture (or this phrase) suggests itself to us irresistibly". Well, isn't this an experience?

We are treating here of cases in which, as one might roughly put it, the grammar of a word seems to suggest the 'necessity' of a certain intermediary step, although in fact the word is used in cases in which there is no such intermediary step. Thus we are inclined to say: "A man *must* understand an order before he obeys it", "He must know where his pain is before he can point to it", "He must know the tune before he can sing it", and suchlike.

Let us ask the question: Suppose I had explained to someone the word "red" (or the meaning of the word "red") by having pointed to various red objects and given the ostensive explanation.—What does it mean to say "Now if he has understood the meaning, he will bring me a red object if I ask him to"? This seems to say: If he has really got hold of what is in common between all the objects I have shown him, he will be in the position to follow my order. But what is it that is in common to these objects?

Could you tell me what is in common between a light red and a dark red? Compare with this the following case: I show you two pictures of two different landscapes. In both pictures, amongst many other objects, there is the picture of a bush, and it is exactly alike in both. I ask you "Point to what these two pictures have in common", and as an answer you point to this bush.

Now consider this explanation: I give someone two boxes containing various things, and say "The object which both boxes have in common is called a toasting fork". The person I give this explanation has to

sort out the objects in the two boxes until he finds the one they
have in common, and thereby, we may say, he arrives at the ostensive
explanation.   Or, this explanation: "In these two pictures you see
patches of many colours; the one colour which you find in both is
called 'mauve' ".—In this case it makes a clear sense to say "If he has
seen (or found) what is in common between these two pictures, he
can now bring me a mauve object".

There is also this case: I say to someone "I shall explain to you
the word 'w' by showing you various objects. What's in common to
them all is what 'w' means." I first show him two books, and he
asks himself "Does 'w' mean 'book'?" I then point to a brick, and
he says to himself "Perhaps 'w' means 'parallelepiped' ". Finally I
point to glowing coal, and he says to himself "Oh, it's 'red' he means,
for all these objects had something red about them". It would be
interesting to consider another form of this game where the person
has at each stage to *draw* or *paint* what he thinks I mean. The interest
of this version lies in this, that in some cases it would be quite obvious
what he has got to draw, say, when he sees that all the objects I have
shown him so far bear a certain trademark (he'd draw the trade mark).
—What, on the other hand, should be paint if he recognizes that there
is something red about each object? A red patch? And of what shape
and shade? Here a convention would have to be laid down, say,
that painting a red patch with ragged edges does not mean that the
objects have that red patch with ragged edges in common, but *something* red.

If, pointing to patches of various shades of red, you asked a man
"What have these in common that makes you call them red?", he'd
be inclined to answer "Don't you see?" And this of course would not
be pointing out a common element.

There are cases where experience teaches us that a person is not
able to carry out an order, say, of the form "Bring me x" if he did not
see what was in common between the various objects to which I
pointed as an explanation of "x". And 'seeing what they have in
common' in some cases consisted in pointing to it, in letting one's
glance rest on a coloured patch after a process of scrutiny and comparing, in saying to oneself "Oh, it's red he means", and perhaps at the
same time glancing at all the red patches on the various objects, and
so on.—There are cases, on the other hand, in which no process takes
place comparable with this intermediary 'seeing what's in common',
and where we still use this phrase, though this time we ought to say

"If after showing him these things he brings me another red object, then *I shall say* that he has seen the common feature of the objects I showed him". Carrying out the order is now the criterion for his having understood.

3. 'Why do you call "strain" all these different experiences?'—'Because they have some element in common.'—'What is it that bodily and mental strain have in common?'—'I don't know, but obviously there is some similarity.'

Then why did you say the experiences had something in common? Didn't this expression just compare the present case with those cases in which we primarily say that two experiences have something in common? (Thus we might say that some experiences of joy and of fear have the feeling of heart-beat in common.) But when you said that the two experiences of strain had something in common, these were only different words for saying that they were similar. It was then no explanation to say that the similarity consisted in the occurrence of a common element.

Also, shall we say that you had a feeling of similarity when you compared the two experiences, and that this made you use the same word for both? If you say you have a feeling of similarity, let us ask a few questions about it:

Could you say the feeling was located here or there?

When did you actually have this feeling? For, what we call comparing the two experiences is quite a complicated activity: perhaps you called the two experiences before your mind, and imagining a bodily strain, and imagining a mental strain, was each in itself imagining a process and not a state uniform through time. Then ask yourself at what time during all this you had the feeling of similarity.

'But surely I wouldn't say they are similar if I had no experience of their similarity.'—But must this experience be anything you should call a feeling? Suppose for a moment it were the experience that the word "similar" suggested itself to you. Would you call this a feeling?

'But is there no feeling of similarity?'—I think there are feelings which one might call feelings of similarity. But you don't always have any such feeling if you 'notice similarity'. Consider some of the different experiences which you have if you do so.

a) There is a kind of experience which one might call being hardly able to distinguish. You see, e.g., two lengths, two colours, almost exactly alike. But if I ask myself "Does this experience consist in having a peculiar feeling?", I should have to say that it certainly isn't characterized by any such feeling alone, that a most important part of the experience is that of letting my glance oscillate between the two objects, fixing it intently now on the one, now on the other, perhaps saying words expressive of doubt, shaking my head, etc., etc. There is, one might say, hardly any room left for a feeling of similarity between these manifold experiences.

b) Compare with this the case in which it is impossible to have any difficulty in distinguishing the two objects. Supposing I say "I like to have the two kinds of flowers in this bed of similar colours to avoid a strong contrast". The experience here might be one which one may describe as an easy sliding of the glance from one to the other.

c) I listen to a variation on a theme and say "I don't see yet how this is a variation of the theme, but I see a certain similarity". What happened was that at certain points of the variation, at certain turning points of the key, I had an experience of 'knowing where I was in the theme'. And this experience might again have consisted in imagining certain figures of the theme, or in seeing them written before my mind or in actually pointing to them in the score, etc.

'But when two colours are similar, the experience of similarity should surely consist in noticing the similarity which there *is* between them'.—But is a bluish green similar to a yellowish green or not? In certain cases we should say they are similar and in others that they are most dissimilar. Would it be correct to say that in the two cases we noticed different relations between them? Suppose I observed a process in which a bluish green gradually changed into a pure green, into a yellowish green, into yellow, and into orange. I say "It only takes a short time from bluish green to yellowish green, because these colours are similar".—But mustn't you have had some experience of similarity to be able to say this?—The experience may be this, of seeing the two colours and saying that they are both green. Or it may be this, of seeing a band whose colour changes from one end to the other in the way described, and having some one of the experiences which one may call noticing how close to each other bluish green and yellowish green are, compared to bluish green and orange.

We use the word "similar" in a huge family of cases.

There is something remarkable about saying that we use the word "strain" for both mental and physical strain because there is a similarity between them. Should you say we use the word "blue" both for light blue and dark blue because there is a similarity between them? If you were asked "Why do you call this 'blue' also?", you would say "Because this *is* blue, too".

One might suggest that the explanation is that in this case you call "blue" what is *in common* between the two colours, and that, if you called "strain" what was in common between the two experiences of strain, it would have been wrong to say "I called them both 'strain' because they had a certain similarity", but that you would have had to say "I used the word 'strain' in both cases because there is a strain present in both".

Now what should we answer to the question "What do light blue and dark blue have in common?"? At first sight the answer seems obvious: "They are both shades of blue". But this is really a tautology. So let us ask "What do these colours I am pointing to have in common?" (Suppose one is light blue, the other dark blue.) The answer to this really ought to be "I don't know what game you are playing". And it depends upon this game whether I should say they had anything in common, and what I should say they had in common.

Imagine this game: A shows B different patches of colours and asks him what they have in common. B is to answer by pointing to a particular primary colour. Thus if A points to pink and orange, B is to point to pure red. If A points to two shades of greenish blue, B is to point to pure green and pure blue, etc. If in this game A showed B a light blue and a dark blue and asked what they had in common, there would be no doubt about the answer. If then he pointed to pure red and pure green, the answer would be that these have nothing in common. But I could easily imagine circumstances under which we should say that they had something in common and would not hesitate to say what it was: Imagine a use of language (a culture) in which there was a common name for green and red on the one hand, and yellow and blue on the other. Suppose, e.g., that there were two castes, one the patrician caste, wearing red and green garments, the other, the plebeian, wearing blue and yellow garments. Both yellow and blue would always be referred to as plebeian colours, green and red as patrician colours. Asked what a red patch and a green patch have in common, a man of our tribe would not hesitate to say they were both patrician.

We could also easily imagine a language (and that means again a culture) in which there existed no common expression for light blue and dark blue, in which the former, say, was called "Cambridge", the latter "Oxford". If you ask a man of this tribe what Cambridge and Oxford have in common, he'd be inclined to say "Nothing".

Compare this game with the one above: B is shown certain pictures, combinations of coloured patches. On being asked what these pictures have in common, he is to point to a sample of red, say, if there is a red patch in both, to green if there is a green patch in both, etc. This shows you in what different ways this same answer may be used.

Consider such an explanation as "I mean by 'blue' what these two colours have in common".—Now isn't it possible that someone should understand this explanation? He would, e.g., on being ordered to bring another blue object, carry out this order satisfactorily. But perhaps he will bring a red object and we shall be inclined to say: "He seems to notice some sort of similarity between samples we showed him and that red thing".

Note: Some people when asked to sing a note which we strike for them on the piano, regularly sing the fifth of that note. That makes it easy to imagine that a language might have one name only for a certain note and its fifth. On the other hand we should be embarrassed to answer the question: What do a note and its fifth have in common? For of course it is no answer to say: "They have a certain affinity".

It is one of our tasks here to give a picture of the grammar (the use) of the word "a certain".

To say that we use the word "blue" to mean 'what all these shades of colour have in common' by itself says nothing more than that we use the word "blue" in all these cases.

And the phrase "He sees what all these shades have in common", may refer to all sorts of different phenomena, i.e., all sorts of phenomena are used as criteria for 'his seeing that . . .'. Or all that happens may be that on being asked to bring another shade of blue he carries out our order satisfactorily. Or a patch of pure blue may appear before his mind's eye when we show him the different samples of blue: or he may instinctively turn his head towards some other shade of blue which we haven't shown him for sample, etc., etc.

Now should we say that a mental strain and a bodily strain were 'strains' in the same sense of the word or in different (or 'slightly different') senses of the word?—There are cases of this sort in which we should not be doubtful about the answer.

4. Consider this case: We have taught someone the use of the words "darker" and "lighter". He could, e.g., carry out such an order

as "Paint me a patch of colour darker than the one I am showing you". Suppose now I said to him: "Listen to the five vowels a, e, i, o, u and arrange them in order of their darkness". He may just look puzzled and do nothing, but he may (and some people will) now arrange the vowels in a certain order (mostly i, e, a, o, u). Now one might imagine that arranging the vowels in order of darkness pre-supposed that when a vowel was sounded a certain colour came before a man's mind, that he then arranged these colours in their order of darkness and told you the corresponding arrangement of the vowels. But this actually need not happen. A person will comply with the order: "Arrange the vowels in their order of darkness", with-out seeing any colours before his mind's eye.

Now if such a person was asked whether u was 'really' darker than e, he would almost certainly answer some such thing as "It isn't really darker, but it somehow gives me a darker impression".

But what if we asked him "What made you use the word 'darker' in this case at all?"?

Again we might be inclined to say "He must have seen something that was in common both to the relation between two colours and to the relation between two vowels". But if he isn't capable of specifying what this common element was, this leaves us just with the fact that he was prompted to use the words "darker", "lighter" in both these cases.

For, note the word "must" in "He must have seen something . . .". When you said that, you didn't mean that from past experience you conclude that he probably did see something, and that's just why this sentence adds nothing to what we know, and in fact only suggests a different form of words to describe it.

If someone said: "I do see a certain similarity, only I can't describe it", I should say: "This itself characterizes your experience".

Suppose you look at two faces and say "They are similar, but I don't know what it is that's similar about them". And suppose that after a while you said: "Now I know; their eyes have the same shape", I should say "Now your experience of their similarity is different from what it was when you saw similarity and didn't know what it consisted in". Now to the question "What made you use the word 'darker' . . .?" the answer may be "Nothing made me use the word 'darker',— that is, if you ask me for a *reason* why I use it. I just used it, and what is more, I used it with the same intonation of voice, and perhaps with the same facial expression and gesture, which I should in certain cases be inclined to use when applying the word to colours".—It is easier to see this when we speak of a *deep* sorrow, a *deep* sound, a *deep* well. Some people are able to distinguish between fat and lean days of the week. And their experience when they conceive a day as a fat one consists in applying this word together perhaps with a gesture expressive of fatness and a certain comfort.

But you may be tempted to say: This use of the word and gesture is not their primary experience. First of all they have to conceive the day as fat and then they express this conception by word or gesture.

But why do you use the expression "They have to"? Do you know of an experience in this case which you call "the conception, etc."? For if you don't, isn't it just what one might call a linguistic prejudice that made you say "He had to have a conception before . . . etc."?

Rather, you can learn from this example and from others that there are cases in which we may call a particular experience "noticing, seeing, conceiving that so and so is the case", before expressing it by word or gestures, and that there are other cases in which if we talk of an experience of conceiving at all, we have to apply this word to the experience of using certain words, gestures, etc.

When the man said "u isn't really darker than e . . . ", it was essential that he meant to say that the word "darker" was used *in different senses* when one talked of one colour being darker than another and, on the other hand, of one vowel being darker than another.

Consider this example: Suppose we had taught a man to use the words "green", "red", "blue" by pointing to patches of these colours. We had taught him to fetch us objects of a certain colour on being ordered "Bring me something red!", to sort out objects of various colours from a heap, and such like. Suppose we now show him a heap of leaves, some of which are a slightly reddish brown, others a slightly greenish yellow, and give him the order "Put the red leaves and the green leaves on separate heaps". It is quite likely that he will upon this separate the greenish yellow leaves from the reddish brown ones. Now should we say that we had here used the words "red" and "green" in the same sense as in the previous cases, or did we use them in different but similar senses? What reasons would one give for adopting the latter view? One could point out that on being asked to paint a red patch, one should certainly not have painted a slightly reddish brown one, and therefore one might say "red" means something different in the two cases. But why shouldn't I say that it had one meaning only but was, of course, used according to the circumstances?

The question is: Do we supplement our statement that the word has two meanings by a statement saying that in one case it had this, in the other that meaning? As the criterion for a word's having two meanings, we may use the fact of there being two explanations given for a word. Thus we say the word "bank" has two meanings; for in one case it means this sort of thing (pointing, say, to a river bank), in the other case that sort of thing (pointing to the Bank of England). Now what I point to here are paradigms for the use of the words. One could not say: "The word 'red' has two meanings because in one case it means this (pointing to a light red), in the other that (pointing to a dark red)", if, that is to say, there had been only one ostensive definition for the word "red" used in our game. One could, on the other hand, imagine a language game in which two words, say "red" and "reddish", were explained by two ostensive definitions, the first showing a dark red object, the second a light red one. Whether two such explanations were given or only one might depend on the natural reactions of the people using the language. We might find that a person to whom we give the ostensive definition, "This is called 'red' " (pointing to one red object) thereupon fetches any red object of whatever shade of red on being ordered: "Bring me something red!" Another person might not do so, but bring objects of a certain range of shades only in the neighbourhood of the shade pointed out to him in the explanation. We might say that this person 'does not see what is in common between all the different shades of red'. But remember please that our only criterion for that is the behaviour we have described.

Consider the following case: B has been taught a use of the words "lighter" and "darker". He has been shown objects of various colours and has been taught that one calls this a darker colour than that, trained to bring an object on being ordered "Bring something darker than this", and to describe the colour of an object by saying that it is darker or lighter than a certain sample, etc., etc. Now he is given the order to put down a series of objects, arranging them in the order of their darkness. He does this by laying out a row of books, writing down a series of names of animals, and by writing down the five vowels in the order u, o, a, e, i. We ask him why he put down that latter series, and he says, "Well, o is lighter than u, and e lighter than o". —We shall be astonished at his attitude, and at the same time admit that there is something in what he says. Perhaps we shall say: "But look, surely e isn't lighter than o in the way this look is lighter than that".—But he may shrug his shoulders and say, "I don't know, but e *is* lighter than o, isn't it?"

We may be inclined to treat this case as some kind of abnormality, and to say, "B must have a different sense, with the help of which he arranges both coloured objects and vowels". And if we tried to make this idea of ours (quite) explicit, it would come to this: The normal person registers lightness and darkness of visual objects on one instrument, and, what one might call the lightness and darkness of sounds (vowels) on another, in the sense in which one might say that we record rays of a certain wave length with the eyes, and rays of another range of wave length with our sense of temperature. B on the other hand, we wish to say, arranges both sounds and colours by the readings of one instrument (sense organ) only (in the sense in which a photographic plate might record rays of a range which we could only cover with two of our senses).

This roughly is the picture standing behind our idea that B must have 'understood' the word "darker" differently from the normal person. On the other hand let us put side by side with this picture the fact that there is in our case no evidence for 'another sense'.—And in fact the use of the word "must" when we say "B must have understood the word differently" already shows us that this sentence (really) expresses our determination to look at the phenomena we have observed after[1] the picture outlined in this sentence.

'But surely he used "lighter" in a different sense when he said e was lighter than u'.—What does this mean? Are you distinguishing between the sense in which he used the word and his usage of the word? That is, do you wish to say that if someone uses the word as B does, some other difference, say in his mind, must go along with the difference in usage? Or is all you want to say that surely the usage of "lighter" was a different one when he applied it to vowels?

Now is the fact that the usages differ anything over and above what you describe when you point out the particular differences?

What if somebody said, pointing to two patches which I had called red, "Surely you are using the word 'red' in two different ways"?— I should say "This is light red and the other dark red,—but why should I have to talk of two different usages?"—

It certainly is easy to point out differences between that part of the game in which we applied "lighter" and "darker" to coloured objects and that part in which we applied these words to vowels. In the first

[1] German "nach", i.e. "according to" or "in the light of".—*Edd.*

part there was comparison of two objects by laying them side by side and looking from one to the other, there was painting a darker or lighter shade than a certain sample given; in the second there was no comparison by the eye, no painting, etc. But when these differences are pointed out, we are still free to speak of two parts of the same game (as we have done just now) or of two different games.

'But don't I perceive that the relation between a lighter and a darker bit of material is a different one than that between the vowels e and u,— as on the other hand I perceive that the relation between u and e is the same as that between e and i?'—Under certain circumstances we shall in these cases be inclined to talk of different relations, under certain others to talk of the same relation. One might say, "It depends how one compares them".

Let us ask the question "Should we say that the arrows → and ← point in the same direction or in different directions?"—At first sight you might be inclined to say "Of course, in different directions". But look at it this way: If I look into a looking glass and see the reflection of my face, I can take this as a criterion for seeing my own head. If on the other hand I saw it in the back of a head I might say "It can't be my own head I am seeing, but a head looking in the opposite direction". Now this could lead me on to say that an arrow and the reflection of an arrow in a glass have the same direction when they point towards each other, and opposite directions when the head of the one points to the tail end of the other. Imagine the case that a man had been taught the ordinary use of the word "the same" in the cases of "the same colour", "the same shape", "the same length". He had also been taught the use of the word "to point to" in such contexts as "The arrow points to the tree". Now we show him two arrows facing each other, and two arrows one following the other, and ask him in which of these two cases he'd apply the phrase "The arrows point the same way". Isn't it easy to imagine that if certain applications were uppermost in his mind, he would be inclined to say that the arrows → ← point 'the same way'?

When we hear the diatonic scale we are inclined to say that after every seven notes the same note recurs, and, asked why we call it the same note again one might answer "Well, it's a c again". But this isn't the explanation I want, for I should ask "What made one call it a c again?" And the answer to this would seem to be "Well, don't you hear that it's the same note only an octave higher?"—Here, too, we could imagine that a man had been taught our use of the word "the same" when applied to colours, lengths, directions, etc., and that we now played the diatonic scale for him and asked him whether he'd say that he heard the same notes again and again at certain intervals, and we could easily imagine several answers, in particular for instance, this, that he heard the same note alternately after every four or three notes (he calls the tonic, the dominant, and the octave the same note).

If we had made this experiment with two people A and B, and A had applied the expression "the same note" to the octave only, B to the dominant and octave, should we have a right to say that the two hear different things when we play to them the diatonic scale?—If we say they do, let us be clear whether we wish to assert that there must be some other difference between the two cases besides the one we have observed, or whether we wish to make no such statement.

5. All the questions considered here link up with this problem: Suppose you had taught someone to write down series of numbers according to rules of the form: Always write down a number *n* greater than the preceding. (This rule is abbreviated to "Add *n*".) The numerals in this game are to be groups of dashes |, | |, | | |, etc. What I call teaching this game, of course, consisted in giving general explanations and doing examples.—These examples are taken from the range, say, between 1 and 85. We now give the pupil the order "Add 1". After some time we observe that after passing 100 he did what we should call adding 2; after passing 300 he does what we should call adding 3. We have him up for this: "Didn't I tell you always to add 1? Look what you have done before you got to 100!"—Suppose the pupil said, pointing to the numbers 102, 104, etc., "Well, didn't I do the same here? I thought this was what you wanted me to do."—You see that it would get us no further here again to say "But don't you see . . .?", pointing out to him again the rules and examples we had given to him. We might, in such a case, say that this person naturally understands (interprets) the rule (and examples) we have given as we should understand the rule (and examples) telling us: "Add 1 up to 100, then 2 up to 200, etc."

(This would be similar to the case of a man who did not naturally follow an order given by a pointing gesture by moving in the direction shoulder to hand, but in the opposite direction. And understanding here means the same as reacting.)

'I suppose what you say comes to this, that in order to follow the rule "Add 1" correctly a new insight, intuition, is needed at every step.'—

But what does it mean to follow the rule *correctly*? How and when is it to be decided which at a particular point is the correct step to take?— 'The correct step at every point is that which is in accordance with the rule as it was *meant*, intended.'—I suppose the idea is this: When you gave the rule "Add 1" and meant it, you meant him to write 101 after 100, 199 after 198, 1041 after 1040, and so on. But how did you do all these acts of meaning (I suppose an infinite number of them) when you gave him the rule? Or is this misrepresenting it? And would you say that there was only one act of meaning, from which, however, all these others, or any one of them, followed in turn? But isn't the point just: 'What does follow from the general rule?' You might say "Surely I knew when I gave him the rule that I meant him to follow up 100 by 101". But here you are misled by the grammar of the word "to know". Was knowing this some mental act by which you at the time made the transition from 100 to 101, i.e., some act like saying to yourself "I want him to write 101 after 100"? In this case ask yourself how many such acts you performed when you gave him the rule. Or do you mean by knowing some kind of disposition?— then only experience can teach us what it was a disposition for.— 'But surely if one had asked me which number he should write after 1568, I should have answered "1569".'—I dare say you would, but how can you be sure of it? Your idea really is that somehow in the mysterious act of *meaning* the rule you made the transitions without really making them. You crossed all the bridges before you were there.—This queer idea is connected with a peculiar use of the word "to mean". Suppose our man got to the number 100 and followed it up by 102. We should then say "I *meant* you to write 101". Now the past tense in the word "to mean" suggests that a particular act of meaning had been performed when the rule was given, though as a matter of fact this expression alludes to no such act. The past tense could be explained by putting the sentence into the form "Had you asked me before what I wanted you to do at this stage, I should have said . . .". But it is a hypothesis that you would have said that.

To get this clearer, think of this example: Someone says "Napoleon was crowned in 1804". I ask him "Did you mean the man who won the battle of Austerlitz?" He says "Yes, I meant him".—Does this mean that when he 'meant him', he in some way thought of Napoleon's winning the battle of Austerlitz?—

The expression "The rule meant him to follow up 100 by 101" makes it appear that this rule, as it was meant, *foreshadowed* all the transitions which were to be made according to it. But the assumption of a shadow of a transition does not get us any further, because it does not bridge the gulf between it and the real transition. If the mere words of the rule could not anticipate a future transition, no more could any mental act accompanying these words.

We meet again and again with this curious superstition, as one might be inclined to call it, that the mental act is capable of crossing a bridge before we've got to it. This trouble crops up whenever we try to think about the ideas of thinking, wishing, expecting, believing, knowing, trying to solve a mathematical problem, mathematical induction, and so forth.

It is no act of insight, intuition, which makes us use the rule as we do at the particular point of the series. It would be less confusing to call it an act of decision, though this too is misleading, for nothing like an act of decision must take place, but possibly just an act of writing or speaking. And the mistake which we here and in a thousand similar cases are inclined to make is labelled by the word "to make" as we have used it in the sentence "It is no act of insight which makes us use the rule as we do", because there is an idea that 'something must make us' do what we do. And this again joins on to the confusion between cause and reason. *We need have no reason to follow the rule as we do.* The chain of reasons has an end.

Now compare these sentences: "Surely it is using the rule 'Add 1' in a different way if after 100 you go on to 102, 104, etc." and "Surely it is using the word 'darker' in a different way if after applying it to coloured patches we apply it to the vowels".—I should say: "That depends on what you call a 'different way' ".—

But I should certainly say that *I should* call the application of "lighter" and "darker" to vowels 'another usage of the words'; and I also should carry on the series 'Add 1' in the way 101, 102, etc., but not—or not necessarily—because of some other justifying mental act.

6.   There is a kind of general disease of thinking which always looks for (and finds) what would be called a mental state from which all our acts spring as from a reservoir. Thus one says, "The fashion changes because the taste of people changes". The taste is the mental reservoir. But if a tailor to-day designs a cut of dress different from that which he designed a year ago, can't what is called his change of taste have consisted, partly or wholly, in doing just this?

And here we say "But surely designing a new shape isn't in itself changing one's taste,—and saying a word isn't meaning it,—and saying that I believe isn't believing; there must be feelings, mental acts, going along with these lines and these words".—And the reason we give for saying this is that a man certainly could design a new shape without having changed his taste, say that he believes something without believing it, etc. And this obviously is true. But it doesn't follow that what distinguishes a case of having changed one's taste from a case of not having done so isn't under certain circumstances just designing what one hasn't designed before. Nor does it follow that in cases in which designing a new shape is not the criterion for a change of taste, the criterion must be a change in some particular region of our mind.

That is to say, we don't use the word "taste" as the name of a feeling. To think that we do is to represent the practice of our language in undue simplification. This, of course, is the way in which philosophical puzzles generally arise; and our case is quite analogous to that of thinking that wherever we make a predicative statement we state that the subject has a certain ingredient (as we really do in the case, "Beer is alcoholic").

It is advantageous in treating our problem to consider parallel with the feeling or feelings characteristic for having a certain taste, changing one's taste, meaning what one says, etc., etc., the facial expression (gestures or tone of voice) characteristic for the same states or events. If someone should object, saying that feelings and facial expressions can't be compared, as the former are experiences and the latter aren't, let him consider the muscular, kinaesthetic and tactile experiences bound up with gestures and facial expressions.

7. Let us then consider the proposition "Believing something cannot merely consist in saying that you believe it, you must say it with a particular facial expression, gesture, and tone of voice". Now it cannot be doubted that we regard certain facial expressions, gestures, etc. as characteristic for the expression of belief. We speak of a 'tone of conviction'. And yet it is clear that this tone of conviction isn't always present whenever we rightly speak of conviction. "Just so", you might say, "this shows that there is something else, something behind these gestures, etc. which is the real belief as opposed to mere expressions of belief".—'Not at all", I should say, "many different criteria distinguish, under different circumstances, cases of believing what you say from those of not believing what you say". There may be

cases where the presence of a sensation other than those bound up
with gestures, tone of voice, etc. distinguishes meaning what you say
from not meaning it. But sometimes what distinguishes these two
is nothing that happens while we speak, but a variety of actions and
experiences of different kinds before and after.

To understand this family of cases it will again be helpful to consider
an analogous case drawn from facial expressions. There is a family
of friendly facial expressions. Suppose we had asked "What feature is it
that characterizes a friendly face?" At first one might think that there
are certain traits which one might call friendly traits, each of which
makes the face look friendly to a certain degree, and which when
present in a large number constitute the friendly expression. This
idea would seem to be borne out by our common speech, talking of
'friendly eyes', 'friendly mouth', etc. But it is easy to see that the
same eyes of which we say they make a face look friendly do not look
friendly, or even look unfriendly, with certain other wrinkles of the
forehead, lines round the mouth, etc. Why then do we ever say that
it is these eyes which look friendly? Isn't it wrong to say that they
characterize the face as friendly, for if we say they do so 'under certain
circumstances' (these circumstances being the other features of the
face) why did we single out the one feature from amongst the others?
The answer is that in the wide family of friendly faces there is what
one might call a main branch characterized by a certain kind of eyes,
another by a certain kind of mouth, etc.; although in the large family
of unfriendly faces we meet these same eyes when they don't mitigate
the unfriendliness of the expression.—There is further the fact that
when we notice the friendly expression of a face, our attention, our
gaze, is drawn to a particular feature in the face, the 'friendly eyes',
or the 'friendly mouth', etc., and that it does not rest on other features
although these too are responsible for the friendly expression.

'But is there no difference between saying something and meaning
it, and saying it without meaning it?'—There needn't be a difference
while he says it, and if there is, this difference may be of all sorts of
different kinds according to the surrounding circumstances. It does
not follow from the fact that there is what we call a friendly and an
unfriendly expression of the eye that there must be a difference between
the eye of a friendly and the eye of an unfriendly face.

One might be tempted to say "This trait can't be said to make the
face look friendly, as it may be belied by another trait". And this is
like saying "Saying something with the tone of conviction can't be the

characteristic of conviction, as it may be belied by experiences going along with it". But neither of these sentences is correct. It is true that other traits in this face could take away the friendly character of this eye, and yet in this face it is the eye which is the outstanding friendly feature.

It is such phrases as "He said it and meant it" which are most liable to mislead us.—Compare meaning "I shall be delighted to see you" with meaning "The train leaves at 3.30". Suppose you had said the first sentence to someone and were asked afterwards "Did you mean it?", you would then probably think of the feelings, the experiences, which you had while you said it. And accordingly you would in this case be inclined to say "Didn't you see that I meant it?" Suppose that on the other hand, after having given someone the information "The train leaves at 3.30", he asked you "Did you mean it?", you might be inclined to answer "Certainly. Why shouldn't I have meant it?"

In the first case we shall be inclined to speak about a feeling characteristic of meaning what we said, but not in the second. Compare also lying in both these cases. In the first case we should be inclined to say that lying consisted in saying what we did but without the appropriate feelings or even with the opposite feelings. If we lied in giving the information about the train, we would be likely to have different experiences while we gave it than those which we have in giving truthful information, but the difference here would not consist in the absence of a characteristic feeling, but perhaps just in the presence of a feeling of discomfort.

It is even possible while lying to have quite strong experience of what might be called the characteristic for meaning what one says— and yet under certain circumstances, and perhaps under the ordinary circumstances, one refers to just this experience in saying, "I meant what I said", because the cases in which something might give the lie to these experiences do not come into the question. In many cases therefore we are inclined to say: "Meaning what I say" means having such and such experiences while I say it.

If by "believing" we mean an activity, a process, taking place while we say that we believe, we may say that believing is something similar to or the same as expressing a belief.

8. It is interesting to consider an objection to this: What if I said "I believe it will rain" (meaning what I say) and someone wanted to

explain to a Frenchman who doesn't understand English what it was
I believed. Then, you might say, if all that happened when I believed
what I did was that I said the sentence, the Frenchman ought to know
what I believe if you tell him the exact words I used, or say "Il croit
'It will rain' ". Now it is clear that this will not tell him what I
believe and consequently, you might say, we failed to convey just
that to him which was essential, my real mental act of believing.—
But the answer is that even if my words had been accompanied by all
sorts of experiences, and if we could have transmitted these experiences
to the Frenchman, he would still not have known what I believed.
For "knowing what I believe" just doesn't mean: feeling what I do
while I say it; just as knowing what I intend with this move in our
game of chess doesn't mean knowing my exact state of mind while
I'm making the move. Though, at the same time, in certain cases,
knowing this state of mind might furnish you with very exact information about my intention.

We should say that we had told the Frenchman what I believed
if we translated my words for him into French. And it *might* be that
thereby we told him nothing—even indirectly—about what happened
'in me' when I uttered my belief. Rather, we pointed out to him
a sentence which in his language holds a similar position to my
sentence in the English language.—Again one might say that, at least
in certain cases, we could have told him much more exactly what I
believed if he had been at home in the English language, because
then, he would have known exactly what happened within me when I
spoke.

We use the words "meaning", "believing", "intending" in such a
way that they refer to certain acts, states of mind given certain circumstances; as by the expression "checkmating somebody" we refer to
the act of taking his king. If on the other hand, someone, say a child,
playing about with chessmen, placed a few of them on a chess board
and went through the motions of taking a king, we should not say
the child had checkmated anyone.—And here, too, one might think
that what distinguished this case from real checkmating was what
happened in the child's mind.

Suppose I had made a move in chess and someone asked me "Did
you intend to mate him?", I answer "I did", and he now asks me "How
could you know you did, as all you *knew* was what happened within
you when you made the move?", I might answer "Under *these* circumstances this was intending to mate him".

9.   What holds for 'meaning' holds for 'thinking'.—We very often find it impossible to think without speaking to ourselves half aloud,—and nobody asked to describe what happened in this case would ever say that something—the thinking—accompanied the speaking, were he not led into doing so by the pair of verbs "speaking"/ "thinking", and by many of our common phrases in which their uses run parallel. Consider these examples: "Think before you speak!" "He speaks without thinking", "What I said didn't quite express my thought", "He says one thing and thinks just the opposite", "I didn't mean a word of what I said", "The French language uses its words in that order in which we think them".

If anything in such a case can be said to go with the speaking, it would be something like the modulation of voice, the changes in timbre, accentuation, and the like, all of which one might call means of expressiveness. Some of these, like the tone of voice and the accent, nobody for obvious reasons would call the accompaniments of the speech; and such means of expressiveness as the play of facial expression or gestures which can be said to accompany speech, nobody would dream of calling thinking.

10.   Let us revert to our example of the use of "lighter" and "darker" for coloured objects and the vowels. A reason which we should like to give for saying that here we have two different uses and not one is this: 'We don't think that the words "darker", "lighter" actually fit the relation between the vowels, we only feel a resemblance between the relation of the sounds and the darker and lighter colours'. Now if you wish to see what sort of feeling this is, try to imagine that without previous introduction you asked someone "Say the vowels a, e, i, o, u, in the order of their darkness". If I did this, I should certainly say it in a different tone from that in which I should say "Arrange these books in the order of their darkness"; that is, I should say it haltingly, in a tone similar to that of "I wonder if you understand me", perhaps smiling slyly as I say it. And this, if anything, describes my *feeling*.

And this brings me to the following point: When someone asks me "What colour is the book over there?", and I say "Red", and then he asks "What made you call this colour 'red'?", I shall in most cases have to say: "Nothing *makes* me call it red; that is, *no reason*. I just looked at it and said 'It's red' ". One is then inclined to say: "Surely this isn't all that happened; for I could look at a colour and say a word and still not name the colour". And then one is inclined to go on to say: "The word 'red' when we pronounce it, naming the colour we look at, *comes in a particular way*". But, at the same time, asked "Can you describe the way you mean?"—one wouldn't feel prepared to give *any* description. Suppose now we asked: "Do you, at any rate, remember that the name of the colour came to you in *that particular way* whenever you named colours on former occasions?"—he would have to admit that he didn't remember a particular way in which this always happened. In fact one could easily make him see that naming a colour could go along with all sorts of different experiences. Compare such cases as these: *a*) I put an iron in the fire to heat it to light red heat. I am asking you to watch the iron and want you to tell me from time to time what stage of *heat* it has reached. You look and say: "It is beginning to get light red". *b*) We stand at a street crossing and I say: "Watch out for the green light. When it comes on, tell me and I'll run across." Ask yourself this question: If in one such case you shout "Green!" and in another "Run!", do these words come in the same way or in different ways? Can one say anything about this in a general way? *c*) I ask you: "What's the colour of the bit of material you have in your hand?" (and I can't see). You think: "Now what does one call this? Is this 'Prussian blue' or 'indigo'?"

Now it is very remarkable that when in a philosophical conversation we say: "The name of a colour comes in a particular way", we don't trouble to think of the many different cases and ways in which such a name comes.—And our chief argument is really that naming the colour is different from just pronouncing a word on some different occasion while looking at a colour. Thus one might say: "Suppose we counted some objects lying on our table, a blue one, a red one, a white one, and a black one,—looking at each in turn we say: 'One, two, three, four'. Isn't it easy to see that something different happens in this case when we pronounce the words than what would happen if we had to tell someone the colours of the objects? And couldn't we, with the same right as before, have said 'Nothing else happens when we say the numerals than just saying them while looking at the objects'? "— Now two answers can be given to this: First, undoubtedly, at least in the great majority of cases, counting the objects will be accompanied by different experiences from naming their colours. And it is easy to describe roughly what the difference will be. In counting we know a certain gesture, as it were, beating the number out with one's finger or by nodding one's head. There is, on the other hand, an experience which one might call "concentrating one's attention on the colour", getting the full impression of it. And these are the sort of things one recalls when one says "It is easy to see that something different happens when we count the objects and when we name their colours". But it is in no way necessary that certain peculiar experiences more or less characteristic for counting take place while we are counting, nor that the peculiar phenomenon of gazing at the colour takes place when we look at the object and name its colour. It is true that the processes of counting four objects and of naming their colours will, in most cases at any rate, be different taken as a whole, and *this* is what strikes us; but that doesn't mean at all that we know that something different happens every time in these two cases when we pronounce a numeral on the one hand and a name of a colour on the other.

When we philosophize about this sort of thing we almost invariably do something of this sort: We repeat to ourselves a certain experience, say, by looking fixedly at a certain object and trying to 'read off' as it were the name of its colour. And it is quite natural that doing so again and again we should be inclined to say, "Something particular happens while we say the word 'blue' ". For we are aware of going again and again through the same process. But ask yourself: Is this also the process which we usually go through when on various occasions—not philosophizing—we name the colour of an object?

11. The problem which we are concerned with we also encounter in thinking about volition, deliberate and involuntary action. Think, say, of these examples: I deliberate whether to lift a certain heavyish weight, decide to do it, I then apply my force to it and lift it. Here, you might say, you have a full-fledged case of willing and intentional action. Compare with this such a case as reaching a man a lighted match after having lit with it one's own cigarette and seeing that he wishes to light his; or again the case of moving your hand while writing a letter, or moving your mouth, larynx, etc. while speaking.— Now when I called the first example a full-fledged case of willing, I deliberately used this misleading expression. For this expression indicates that one is inclined in thinking about volition to regard this sort of example as one exhibiting most clearly the typical characteristic of willing. One takes one's ideas, and one's language, about volition from this kind of example and thinks that they must apply—if not in such an obvious way—to all cases which one can properly call cases of willing.—It is the same case that we have met over and over again:

The forms of expression of our ordinary language fit most obviously certain very special applications of the words "willing", "thinking", "meaning", "reading", etc., etc. And thus we might have called the case in which a man 'first thinks and then speaks' the full-fledged case of thinking and the case in which a man spells out the words he is reading the full-fledged case of reading. We speak of an 'act of volition' as different from the action which is willed, and in our first example there are lots of different acts clearly distinguishing this case from one in which all that happens is that the hand and the weight lift: there are the preparations of deliberation and decision, there is the effort of lifting. But where do we find the analogues to these processes in our other examples and in innumerable ones we might have given?

Now on the other hand it has been said that when a man, say, gets out of bed in the morning, all that happens may be this: he deliberates, "Is it time to get up?", he tries to make up his mind, and then suddenly *he finds himself getting up*. Describing it this way emphasizes the absence of an act of volition. Now first: where do we find the prototype of such a thing, i.e., how did we come by the idea of such an act? I think the prototype of the act of volition is the experience of muscular effort.—Now there is something in the above description which tempts us to contradict it; we say: "We don't just 'find', observe, ourselves getting up, as though we were observing someone else! It isn't like, say, watching certain reflex actions. If, e.g., I place myself sideways close to a wall, my wall-side arm hanging down outstretched, the back of the hand touching the wall, and if now keeping the arm rigid I press the back of the hand hard against the wall, doing it all by means of the deltoid muscle, if then I quickly step away from the wall, letting my arm hang down loosely, my arm without any action of mine, of its own accord begins to rise; this is the sort of case in which it would be proper to say, 'I *find* my arm rising'."

Now here again it is clear that there are many striking differences between the case of observing my arm rising in this experiment or watching someone else getting out of bed and the case of finding myself getting up. There is, e.g., in this case a perfect absence of what one might call surprise, also I don't *look* at my own movements as I might look at someone turning about in bed, e.g., saying to myself "Is he going to get up?" There is a difference between the voluntary act of getting out of bed and the involuntary rising of my arm. But there is not one common difference between so-called voluntary acts and involuntary ones, viz, the presence or absence of one element, the 'act of volition'.

The description of getting up in which a man says "I just find myself getting up" suggests that he wishes to say that he *observes* himself getting up. And we may certainly say that an attitude of observing is absent in this case. But the observing attitude again is not one continuous state of mind or otherwise which we are in the whole time while, as we should say, we are observing. Rather, there is a family of groups of activities and experiences which we call observing attitudes. Roughly speaking one might say there are observation-elements of curiosity, observant expectation, surprise, and there are, we should say, facial expressions and gestures of curiosity, of observant expectation, and of surprise; and if you agree that there is more than one facial expression characteristic for each of these cases, and that there can be these cases without any characteristic facial expression, you will admit that to each of these three words a *family* of phenomena corresponds.

12. If I had said "When I told him that the train was leaving at 3.30, believing that it did, nothing happened than that I just uttered the sentence", and if someone contradicted me, saying "Surely this couldn't have been all, as you might 'just say a sentence' without believing it",—my answer should be "I didn't wish to say that there was no difference between speaking, believing what you say, and speaking, not believing what you say; but the pair 'believing'/'not believing' refers to various differences in different cases (differences forming a family), not to one difference, that between the presence and the absence of a certain mental state."

13. Let us consider various characteristics of voluntary and involuntary acts. In the case of lifting the heavy weight, the various experiences of effort are obviously most characteristic for lifting the weight voluntarily. On the other hand, compare with this the case of writing, voluntarily, where in most of the ordinary cases there will be no effort; and even if we feel that the writing tires our hands and strains their muscles, this is not the experience of 'pulling' and 'pushing' which we would call typical voluntary actions. Further compare the lifting of your hand when you lift a weight with it with lifting your hand when, e.g., you point to some object above you. This will certainly be regarded as a voluntary act, though the element of effort will most likely be entirely absent; in fact this raising of the arm

to point at an object is very much like raising the eye to look at it, and here we can hardly conceive of an effort.—Now let us describe an act of involuntarily raising your arm. There is the case of our experiment, and this was characterized by the utter absence of muscular strain and also by our observant attitude towards the lifting of the arm. But we have just seen a case in which muscular strain was absent, and there are cases in which we should call an action voluntary although we take an observant attitude towards it. But in a large class of cases it is the peculiar impossibility of taking an observant attitude towards a certain action which characterizes it as a voluntary one. Try, e.g., to observe your hand rising when you voluntarily raise it. Of course you *see* it rising as you do, say, in the experiment; but you can't somehow follow it in the same way with your eye. This might get clearer if you compare two different cases of following lines on a piece of paper with your eye; *a*) some irregular line like this:

b) a written sentence. You will find that in *a*) the eye, as it were, alternately slips and gets stuck, whereas in reading a sentence it glides along smoothly.

Now consider a case in which we do take up an observant attitude towards a voluntary action, I mean the very instructive case of trying to draw a square with its diagonals by placing a mirror on your drawing paper and directing your hand by what you see by looking at it in the mirror. And here one is inclined to say that our real *actions*, the ones to which volition *immediately* applies, are not the movements of our hand but something further back, say, the actions of our muscles. We are inclined to compare the case with this: Imagine we had a series of levers before us, through which, by a hidden mechanism, we could direct a pencil drawing on a sheet of paper. We might then be in doubt which levers to pull in order to get the desired movement of the pencil; and we could say that *we deliberately* pulled this particular lever, although we didn't deliberately produce the wrong result that we thereby produced. But this comparison, though it easily suggests itself, is very misleading. For in the case of the levers which we saw before us, there was such a thing as deciding which one we were going to pull before pulling it. But does our volition, as it were, play on a keyboard of muscles, choosing which one it was going to use next?—For some actions which we call deliberate it is characteristic

that we, in some sense, 'know what we are going to do' before we do it.
In this sense we say that we know what object we are going to point
to, and what we might call 'the act of knowing' might consist in looking
at the object before we point to it or in describing its position by words
or pictures. Now we could describe our drawing the square through
the mirror by saying that our acts were deliberate as far as their motor
aspect is concerned, but not as far as their visual aspect is concerned.
This would, e.g., be demonstrated by our ability to repeat a movement
of the hand which had produced a wrong result, on being told to do so.
But it would obviously be absurd to say that this motor character of
voluntary motion consisted in our knowing beforehand what we were
going to do, as though we had had a picture of the kinaesthetic sensation before our mind and decided to bring about this sensation.
Remember the experiment where the subject has his fingers intertwined; if here, instead of pointing from a distance to the finger which
you order him to move, you touch that finger, he will always move it
without the slightest difficulty. And here it is tempting to say "Of
course I can move it now, because now I know which finger it is I'm
asked to move." This makes it appear as though I had now shown you
which muscle to contract in order to bring about the desired result.
The word "of course" makes it appear as though by touching your
finger I had given you an item of information telling you what to do.
(As though normally when you tell a man to move such and such a
finger he could follow your order because he knew how to bring
the movement about.)

(It is interesting here to think of the case of sucking a liquid through
a tube; if asked what part of your body you sucked with, you would
be inclined to say your mouth, although the work was done by the
muscles by which you draw your breath.)

Let us now ask ourselves what we should call "speaking involuntarily". First note that when normally you speak, voluntarily, you
could hardly describe what happened by saying that by an act of
volition you move your mouth, tongue, larynx, etc. as a means to
producing certain sounds. Whatever happens in your mouth, larynx,
etc. and whatever sensations you have in these parts while speaking
would almost seem secondary phenomena accompanying the produc-
tion of sounds, and volition, one wishes to say, operates on the sounds
themselves without intermediary mechanism. This shows how loose
our idea of this agent 'volition' is.

Now to involuntary speaking. Imagine you had to describe a

case,—what would you do? There is of course the case of speaking
in one's sleep; this is characterized by our doing it without being
aware of it and not remembering having done it. But this obviously
you wouldn't call the characteristic of an involuntary action.

A better example of involuntary speaking would, I suppose, be
that of involuntary exclamations: "Oh!", "Help!", and such like, and
these utterances are akin to shrieking with pain. (This, by the way,
could set us thinking about 'words as expressions of feelings'.) One
might say: "Surely these are good examples of involuntary speech,
because there is in these cases not only no act of volition by which
we speak, but in many cases we utter these words *against* our will".
I should say: I certainly should call this involuntary speaking; and I
agree that an act of volition preparatory to or accompanying these
words is absent,—if by "act of volition" you refer to certain acts of
intention, premeditation, or effort. But then in many cases of voluntary
speech I don't feel an effort, much that I say voluntarily is not pre-
meditated, and I don't know of any acts of intention preceding it.

Crying out with pain against our will could be compared with
raising our arm against our will when someone forces it up while
we are struggling against him. But it is important to notice that the
will—or should we say 'wish'—not to cry out is overcome in a
different way from that in which our resistance is overcome by the
strength of the opponent. When we cry out against our will, we
are as it were taken by surprise; as though someone forced up our
hands by unexpectedly sticking a gun into our ribs, commanding
"Hands up!"

14.   Consider now the following example, which is of great help
in all these considerations: In order to see what happens when one
understands a word, we play this game: You have a list of words,
partly these words are words of my native language, partly words of
foreign languages more or less familiar to me, partly words of
languages entirely unknown to me (or, which comes to the same,
nonsensical words invented for the occasion). Some of the words of
my native tongue, again, are words of ordinary everyday usage:
and some of these, like "house", "table", "man", are what we might
call primitive words, being among the first words a child learns,
and some of these again, words of baby talk like "Mamma", "Papa".
Again, there are more or less common technical terms such as "car-
burettor", "dynamo", "fuse"; etc., etc. All these words are read out

to me, and after each one I have to say "Yes" or "No" according to whether I understand the word or not. I then try to remember what happened in my mind when I understood the words I did understand, and when I didn't understand the others. And here again it will be useful to consider the particular tone of voice and facial expression with which I say "Yes" and "No", alongside of the so-called mental events.—Now it may surprise us to find that although this experiment will show us a multitude of different characteristic experiences, it will not show us any one experience which we should be inclined to call the experience of understanding. There will be such experiences as these: I hear the word "tree" and say "Yes" with the tone of voice and sensation of "Of course". Or I hear "corroboration"——I say to my-self, "Let me see", vaguely remember a case of helping, and say "Yes". I hear "gadget", I imagine the man who always used this word, and say "Yes". I hear "Mamma", this strikes me as funny and childish— "Yes". A foreign word I shall very often translate in my mind into English before answering. I hear "spinthariscope", and say to myself, "Must be some sort of scientific instrument", perhaps try to think up its meaning from its derivation and fail, and say "No". In another case I might say to myself, "Sounds like Chinese"—"No". Etc. There will, on the other hand, be a large class of cases in which I am not aware of anything happening except hearing the word and saying the answer. And there will also be cases in which I remember experiences (sensa-tions, thoughts) which, as I should say, had nothing to do with the word at all. Thus amongst the experiences which I can describe there will be a class which I might call typical experiences of under-standing and some typical experiences of not understanding. But opposed to these there will be a large class of cases in which I should have to say "I know of no particular experience at all, I just said 'Yes', or 'No' ".

Now if someone said "But surely something did happen when you understood the word 'tree', unless you were utterly absent-minded when you said 'Yes' ", I might be inclined to reflect and say to myself, "Didn't I have a sort of homely feeling when I took in the word 'tree'?" But then, do I always have this feeling which now I referred to when I hear that word used or use it myself, do I remember having had it, do I even remember a set of, say, five sensations some one of which I had on every occasion when I could be said to have understood the word? Further, isn't that 'homely feeling' I referred to an experience rather characteristic for the particular situation I'm in at present, i.e., that of philosophizing about 'understanding'?

Of course in our experiment we might call saying "Yes" or "No" characteristic experiences of understanding or not understanding, but what if we just hear a word in a sentence, where there isn't even a question of this reaction to it?—We are here in a curious difficulty: on the one hand it seems we have no reason to say that in all cases in which we understand a word one particular experience—or even one of a set—is present. On the other hand we may feel it's plainly wrong to say that in such a case all that happens may be that I hear or say the word. For that seems to be saying that part of the time we act as mere automatons. And the answer is that in a sense we do and in a sense we don't.

If someone talked to me with a kindly play of facial expressions, is it necessary that in any short interval his face should have looked such that seeing it under any other circumstances I should have called its expression distinctly kindly? And if not, does this mean that his 'kindly play of expression' was interrupted by periods of inexpressiveness?—We certainly should not say this under the circumstances which I am assuming, and we don't feel that the look at this moment interrupts the expressiveness, although taken alone we should call it inexpressive.

Just in this way we refer by the phrase "understanding a word" not necessarily to that which happens while we are saying or hearing it, but to the whole environment of the event of saying it. And this also applies to our saying that someone speaks like an automaton or like a parrot. Speaking with understanding certainly differs from speaking like an automaton, but this doesn't mean that the speaking in the first case is all the time accompanied by something which is lacking in the second case. Just as when we say that two people move in different circles this doesn't mean that they mayn't walk the street in identical surroundings.

Thus also, acting voluntarily (or involuntarily) is, in many cases, characterized as such by a multitude of circumstances under which the action takes place rather than by an experience which we should call characteristic of voluntary action. And in this sense it is true to say that what happened when I got out of bed—when I should certainly not call it involuntary—was that I found myself getting up. Or rather, this is a possible case; for of course every day something different happens.

15. The troubles which we have been turning over since §7 were all closely connected with the use of the word "particular". We have been inclined to say that seeing familiar objects we have a particular feeling, that the word "red" came in a particular way when we recognized the colour as red, that we had a particular experience when we acted voluntarily.

Now the use of the word "particular" is apt to produce a kind of delusion and roughly speaking this delusion is produced by the double usage of this word. On the one hand, we may say, it is used preliminary to a specification, description, comparison; on the other hand, as what one might describe as an emphasis. The first usage I shall call the transitive one, the second the intransitive one. Thus, on the one hand I say "This face gives me a particular impression which I can't describe". The latter sentence may mean something like: "This face gives me a strong impression". These examples would perhaps be more striking if we substituted the word "peculiar" for "particular", for the same comments apply to "peculiar". If I say "This soap has a peculiar smell: it is the kind we used as children", the word "peculiar" may be used merely as an introduction to the comparison which follows it, as though I said "I'll tell you what this soap smells like: . . .". If, on the other hand, I say "This soap has a *peculiar* smell!" or "It has a most peculiar smell", "peculiar" here stands for some such expression as "out of the ordinary", "uncommon", "striking".

We might ask "Did you say it had a peculiar smell, as opposed to no peculiar smell, or that it had this smell, as opposed to some other smell, or did you wish to say both the first and the second?"—Now what was it like when, philosophizing, I said that the word "red" came in a particular way when I described something I saw as red? Was it that I was going to describe the way in which the word "red" came, like saying "It always comes quicker than the word 'two' when I'm counting coloured objects", or "It always comes with a shock", etc.?—Or was it that I wished to say that "red" comes in a striking way?—Not exactly that either. But certainly rather the second than the first. To see this more clearly, consider another example: You are, of course, constantly changing the position of your body throughout the day; arrest yourself in any such attitude (while writing, reading, talking, etc., etc.) and say to yourself in the way in which you say " 'Red' comes in a particular way . . .", "I am now in a particular attitude". You will find that you can quite naturally say this. But aren't you always in a particular attitude? And of course you didn't mean that you were just then in a particularly striking attitude. What was it that happened? You concentrated on, as it were stared at, your sensations. And this is exactly what you did when you said that "red" came in a particular way.

"But didn't I mean that 'red' came in a different way from 'two'?"— You may have meant this, but the phrase, "They come in different ways", is itself liable to cause confusion. Suppose I said "Smith and Jones always enter my room in different ways": I might go on and say "Smith enters quickly, Jones slowly", I am specifying the ways. I might on the other hand say "I don't know what the difference is", intimating that I'm *trying* to specify the difference, and perhaps later on I shall say "Now I know what it is; it is . . .".—I could on the other hand tell you that they came in different ways, and you wouldn't know what to make of this statement, and perhaps answer "Of course they come in different ways; they just *are* different".—We could describe our trouble by saying that we feel as though we could give an experience a name without at the same time committing ourselves about its use, and in fact without any intention to use it at all. Thus when I say "red" comes in a particular way . . . , I feel that I might now give this way a name if it hasn't already got one, say "A". But at the same time I am not at all prepared to say that I recognize this to be the way "red" has always come on such occasions, nor even to say that there are, say, four ways, A, B, C, D, in one of which it always comes. You might say that the two ways in which "red" and "two" come can be identified by, say, exchanging the meaning of the two words, using "red" as the second cardinal numeral, "two" as the name of a colour. Thus, on being asked how many eyes I had, I should answer "red", and to the question "What is the colour of blood?", "two". But the question now arises whether you can identify the 'way in which these words come' independently of the ways in which they are used,—I mean the ways just described. Did you wish to say that as a matter of experience, the word when used in *this* way always comes in the way A, but may, the next time, come in the way "two" usually comes? You will see then that you meant nothing of the sort.

What is *particular* about the way "red" comes is that it comes while you're philosophizing about it, as what is particular about the position of your body when you concentrated on it was concentration. We appear to ourselves to be on the verge of describing the way, whereas we aren't really opposing it to any other way. We are emphasizing, not comparing, but we express ourselves as though this emphasis was really a comparison of the object with itself; there seems to be a reflexive comparison. Let me explain myself in this way: suppose I speak of the way in which A enters the room, I may say "I have noticed the way in which A enters the room", and on being asked "What is it?", I may answer "He always sticks his head into the room before coming in". Here I'm referring to a definite feature, and I could say that B had the same way, or that A no longer had it. Consider on the other hand the statement "I've now been observing the way A sits and smokes". I want to draw him like this. In this case I needn't be ready to give any description of a particular feature of his attitude, and my statement may just mean "I've been observing A as he sat and smoked".—'The way' can't in this case be separated from him. Now if I wished to draw him as he sat there, and was contemplating, studying, his attitude, I should while doing so be inclined to say and repeat to myself "He has a particular way of sitting". But the answer to the question "What way?" would be "Well, *this* way", and perhaps one would give it by drawing the characteristic outlines of his attitude. On the other hand, my phrase "He has a particular way . . .", might just have to be translated into "I'm contemplating his attitude". Putting it in this form we have, as it were, straightened out the proposition; whereas in its first form its meaning seems to describe a loop, that is to say, the word "particular" here seems to be used transitively and, more particularly, reflexively, i.e., we are regarding its use as a special case of the transitive use. We are inclined to answer the question "What way do you mean?" by "*This* way", instead of answering: "I didn't refer to any particular feature; I was just contemplating his position". My expression made it appear as though I was pointing out something *about* his way of sitting, or, in our previous case, about the way the word "red" came, whereas what makes me use the word "particular" here is that by my attitude towards the phenomenon I am laying an emphasis on it: I am concentrating on it, or retracing it in my mind, or drawing it, etc.

Now this is a characteristic situation to find ourselves in when thinking about philosophical problems. There are many troubles which arise in this way, that a word has a transitive and an intransitive use, and that we regard the latter as a particular case of the former, explaining the word when it is used intransitively by a reflexive construction.

Thus we say, "By 'kilogram' I mean the weight of one litre of water", "By 'A' I mean 'B', where B is an explanation of A".

But there is also the intransitive use: "I said that I was sick of it and meant it". Here again, meaning what you said could be called "retracing it", "laying an emphasis on it". But using the word "meaning" in this sentence makes it appear that it must have sense to ask "*What* did you mean?" and to answer "By what I said I meant what I said," treating the case of "I mean what I say" as a special case of "By saying 'A' I mean 'B' ". In fact one uses the expression "I mean what I mean" to say, "I have no explanation for it". The question, "What does this sentence *p* mean?", if it doesn't ask for a translation of *p* into other symbols, has no more sense than "What sentence is formed by this sequence of words?"

Suppose to the question, "What's a kilogram?" I answered, "It is what a litre of water weighs", and someone asked, "Well, what does a litre of water weigh?"—

We often use the reflexive form of speech as a means of emphasizing something. And in all such cases our reflexive expressions can be 'straightened out'. Thus we use the expression "If I can't, I can't", "I am as I am", "It is just what it is", also "That's that". This latter phrase means as much as "That's settled", but why should we express "That's settled" by "That's that"? The answer can be given by laying before ourselves a series of interpretations which make a transition between the two expressions. Thus for "That's settled", I will say "The matter is closed". And this expression, as it were, files the matter and shelves it. And filing it is like drawing a line around it, as one sometimes draws a line around the results of a calculation, thereby marking it as final. But this also makes it stand out; it is a way of emphasizing it. And what the expression "That's that" does is to emphasize the 'that'.

Another expression akin to those we have just considered is this: "Here it is; take it or leave it!" And this again is akin to a kind of introductory statement which we sometimes make before remarking on certain alternatives, as when we say: "It either rains or it doesn't rain; if it rains we'll stay in my room, if it doesn't . . .". The first part of this sentence is no piece of information (just as "Take it or leave it" is no order). Instead of, "It either rains or it doesn't rain" we could have said, "Consider the two cases . . .". Our expression underlines these cases, presents them to your attention.

It is closely connected with this that in describing a case like 30)[1] we are tempted to use the phrase, "There is, *of course*, a number beyond

[1] Language game no. 30 in Part I of the *Brown Book*.

which no one of the tribe has ever counted; let this number be . . .".
Straightened out this reads: "Let the number beyond which no one
of the tribe has ever counted be . . .". Why we tend to prefer the first
expression to the one straightened out is that it more strongly directs
our attention to the upper end of the range of numerals used by our
tribe in their actual practice.

16. Let us now consider a very instructive case of that use of the
word "particular" in which it does not point to a comparison and yet
seems most strongly to do so,—the case when we contemplate the
expression of a face primitively drawn in this way:

                                                    Let this face produce
an impression on you. You may then feel inclined to say: "Surely I
don't see mere dashes. I see a face with a *particular* expression".
But you don't mean that it has an outstanding expression nor is it
said as an introduction to a description of the expression, though
we might give such a description and say, e.g., "It looks like a com-
placent business man, stupidly supercilious, who though fat, imagines
he's a lady killer". But this would only be meant as an approximate
description of the expression. "Words can't exactly describe it", one
sometimes says. And yet one feels that what one calls the expression
of the face is something that can be detached from the drawing of
the face. It is as though we could say: "This face has a particular
expression: namely this" (pointing to something). But if I had to point
to anything in this place it would have to be the drawing I am looking
at. (We are, as it were, under an optical delusion which by some sort
of reflection makes us think that there are two objects where there is
only one. The delusion is assisted by our using the verb "to have",
saying "The face *has* a particular expression". Things look different
when, instead of this, we say: "This *is* a peculiar face". What a thing *is*,
we mean, is bound up with it; what it has can be separated from it.)

'This face has a particular expression.'—I am inclined to say this
when I am trying to let it make its full impression upon me.

What goes on here is an act, as it were, of digesting it, getting hold
of it, and the phrase "getting hold of the expression of this face"
suggests that we are getting hold of a thing which is *in* the face and
different from it. It seems we are looking for something, but we don't

do so in the sense of looking for a model of the expression outside the face we see, but in the sense of sounding the thing without attention. It is, when I let the face make an impression on me, as though there existed a double of its expression, as though the double was the prototype of the expression and as though seeing the expression of the face was finding the prototype to which it corresponded—as though in our mind there had been a mould and the picture we see had fallen into that mould, fitting it. But it is rather that we let the picture sink into our mind and make a mould there.

When we say, "This is a *face*, and not mere strokes", we are, of course, distinguishing such a drawing

from such a one

And it is true: If you ask anyone: "What is this?" (pointing to the first drawing) he will certainly say: "It's a face", and he will be able straight away to reply to such questions as, "Is it male or female?", "Smiling or sad?", etc. If on the other hand you ask him: "What is this?" (pointing to the second drawing), he will most likely say, "This is nothing at all", or "These are just dashes". Now think of looking for a man in a picture puzzle; there it often happens that what at first sight appears as 'mere dashes' later appears as a face. We say in such cases: "Now I see it is a face". It must be quite clear to you that this doesn't mean that we recognize it as the face of a friend or that we are under the delusion of seeing a 'real' face: rather, this 'seeing it *as a face*' must be compared with seeing this drawing

either as a cube or as a plane figure consisting of a square and two rhombuses; or with seeing this 'as a square with diagonals', or 'as a swastika', that is, as a limiting case of this;

or again with seeing these four dots . . . . as two pairs of dots side by side with each other, or as two interlocking pairs, or as one pair inside the other, etc.

The case of 'seeing

as a swastika' is of special interest because this expression might mean being, somehow, under the optical delusion that the square is not quite closed, that there are the gaps which distinguish the swastika from our drawing. On the other hand it is quite clear that this was not what we meant by "seeing our drawing as a swastika". We saw it in a way which suggested the description, "I see it as a swastika". One might suggest that we ought to have said "I see it as a closed swastika";—but then, what is the difference between a closed swastika and a square with diagonals? I think that in this case it is easy to recognize 'what happens when we see our figure as a swastika'. I believe it is that we retrace the figure with our eyes in a particular way, viz., by staring at the centre, looking along a radius, and along a side adjacent to it, starting at the centre again, taking the next radius and the next side, say in a right-handed sense of rotation, etc. But this *explanation* of the phenomenon of seeing the figure as a swastika is of no fundamental interest to us. It is of interest to us only in so far as it helps one to see that the expression "seeing the figure as a swastika" did not mean seeing *this* or *that*, seeing one thing as something else, when, essentially, *two* visual objects entered the process of doing so.—Thus also seeing the first figure as a cube did not mean 'taking it to be a cube'. (For we might never have seen a cube and still have this experience of 'seeing it as a cube'.)

And in this way 'seeing dashes as a face' does not involve a comparison between a group of dashes and a real human face; and, on the other hand, this form of expression most strongly suggests that we are alluding to a comparison.

Consider also this example: Look at W once as a capital double-U, and another time as a capital M upside down. Observe what doing the one and doing the other consists in.

We distinguish seeing a drawing as a face and seeing it as something else or as 'mere dashes'. And we also distinguish between superficially glancing at a drawing (seeing it as a face), and letting the face make its full impression on us. But it would be queer to say: "I am letting the face make *a particular* impression on me" (except in such cases in which you can say that you can let the same face make different impressions on you). And in letting the face impress itself on me and contemplating its 'particular impression', no two things of the multiplicity of a face are compared with each other; there is only *one* which is laden with emphasis. Absorbing its expression, I don't find a prototype of this expression in my mind; rather, I, as it were, cut a seal from the impression.

And this also describes what happens when in 15)[1] we say to ourselves "The word 'red' comes in a particular way . . .". The reply could be: "I see, you're repeating to yourself some experience and again and again gazing at it."

17. We may shed light on all these considerations if we compare what happens when we remember the face of someone who enters our room, when we recognize him as Mr. So and So,—when we compare what really happens in such cases with the representation we are sometimes inclined to make of the events. For here we are often obsessed by a primitive conception, viz., that we are comparing the man we see with a memory image in our mind and we find the two to agree. I.e., we are representing 'recognizing someone' as a process of identification by means of a picture (as a criminal is identified by his photo). I needn't say that in most cases in which we recognize someone no comparison between him and a mental picture takes place. We are, of course, tempted to give this description by the fact that there are memory images. Very often, for instance, such an image comes before our mind immediately *after* having recognized someone. I see him as he stood when we last saw each other ten years ago.

I will here again describe the *kind* of thing that happens in your mind and otherwise when you recognize a person coming into your room by means of what you might *say* when you recognize him. Now this may just be: "Hello!" And thus we may say that one kind of event of recognizing a thing we see consists in saying "Hello!" to it in words,

[1] § 15, *Brown Book*, Part II.

gestures, facial expressions, etc.—And thus also we may think that when we look at our drawing and see it as a face, we compare it with some paradigm, and it agrees with it, or it fits into a mould ready for it in our mind. But no such mould or comparison enters into our experience, there is only this shape, not any other to compare it with, and as it were, say "Of course" to. As when in putting together a jig-saw puzzle, somewhere a small space is left unfilled and I see a piece obviously fitting it and put it in the place saying to myself "Of course". But here we say, "Of course" *because* the piece fits the mould, whereas in our case of seeing the drawing as a face, we have the same attitude for *no* reason.

The same strange illusion which we are under when we seem to seek the something which a face expresses whereas, in reality, we are giving ourselves up to the features before us—that same illusion possesses us even more strongly if repeating a tune to ourselves and letting it make its full impression on us, we say "This tune says *something*", and it is as though I had to find *what* it says. And yet I know that it doesn't say anything such that I might express in words or pictures what it says. And if, recognizing this, I resign myself to saying "It just expresses a musical thought", this would mean no more than saying "It expresses itself".—"But surely when you play it you don't play it *anyhow*, you play it in this particular way, making a crescendo here, a diminuendo there, a caesura in this place, etc."—Precisely, and that's all I can say about it, or may be all that I can say about it. For in certain cases I can justify, explain the particular expression with which I play it by a comparison, as when I say "At this point of the theme, there is, as it were, a colon", or "This is, as it were, the answer to what came before", etc. (This, by the way, shows what a 'justification' and an 'explanation' in aesthetics is like.) It is true I may hear a tune played and say "This is not how it ought to be played, it goes like this"; and I whistle it in a different tempo. Here one is inclined to ask "What is it like to know the tempo in which a piece of music should be played?" And the idea suggests itself that there *must* be a paradigm somewhere in our mind, and that we have adjusted the tempo to conform to that paradigm. But in most cases if someone asked me "How do you think this melody should be played?", I will, as an answer, just whistle it in a particular way, and nothing will have been present to my mind but the tune *actually whistled* (not an image of *that*).

This doesn't mean that suddenly understanding a musical theme may not consist in finding a form of verbal expression which I conceive as the verbal counterpoint of the theme. And in the same way I may say "Now I understand the expression of this face", and what happened when the understanding came was that I found the word which seemed to sum it up.

Consider also this expression: "Tell yourself that it's a *waltz*, and you will play it correctly".

What we call "understanding a sentence" has, in many cases, a much greater similarity to understanding a musical theme than we might be inclined to think. But I don't mean that understanding a musical theme is more like the picture which one tends to make oneself of understanding a sentence; but rather that this picture is wrong, and that understanding a sentence is much more like what really happens when we understand a tune than at first sight appears. For understanding a sentence, we say, points to a reality outside the sentence. Whereas one might say "Understanding a sentence means getting hold of its content; and the content of the sentence is *in* the sentence."

18. We may now return to the ideas of 'recognizing' and 'familiarity', and in fact to that example of recognition and familiarity which started our reflections on the use of these terms and of a multitude of terms connected with them. I mean the example of reading, say, a written sentence in a well-known language.—I read such a sentence to see what the experience of reading is like, what 'really happens' when one reads, and I get a particular experience which I take to be the experience of reading. And, it seems, this doesn't simply consist in seeing and pronouncing the words, but, besides, in an experience of an intimate character, as I should like to say. (I am as it were on an intimate footing with the word 'I read'.)

In reading the spoken words come in a particular way, I am inclined to say; and the written words themselves which I read don't just look to me like any kind of scribbles. At the same time I am unable to point to, or get a grasp on, that 'particular way'.

The phenomenon of seeing and speaking the words seems enshrouded by a particular atmosphere. But I don't recognize this atmosphere as one which always characterized the situation of reading. Rather, I notice it when I read a line, trying to see what reading is like.

When noticing this atmosphere I am in the situation of a man who is working in his room, reading, writing, speaking, etc., and who suddenly concentrates his attention on some soft uniform noise, such as one can almost always hear, particularly in a town (the dim noise resulting from all the various noises of the street, the sounds of wind, rain, workshops, etc.). We could imagine that this man might think that a particular noise was a common element of all the experiences he had in this room. We should then draw his attention to the fact that most of the time he hadn't noticed any noises going on outside, and secondly, that the noise he could hear wasn't always the same (there was sometimes wind, sometimes not, etc.).

Now we have used a misleading expression when we said that besides the experiences of seeing and speaking in reading there was another experience, etc. This is saying that to certain experiences another experience is added.—Now take the experience of seeing a sad face, say in a drawing,—we can say that to see the drawing as a sad face is not 'just' to see it as some complex of strokes (think of a puzzle picture). But the word 'just' here seems to intimate that in seeing the drawing as a face some experience is added to the experience of seeing it as mere strokes; as though I had to say that seeing the drawing as a face consisted of two experiences, elements.

You should now notice the difference between the various cases in which we say that an experience consists of several elements or that it is a *compound* experience. We might say to the doctor, "I don't have one pain; I have two: toothache and headache". And one might express this by saying, "My experience of pain is not simple, but compound, I have toothache and headache". Compare with this case that in which I say, "I have got both pains in my stomach and a general feeling of sickness". Here I don't separate the constituent experiences by pointing to two localities of pain. Or consider this statement: "When I drink sweet tea, my taste experience is a compound of the taste of sugar and the taste of tea". Or again: "If I hear the C Major chord my experience is composed of hearing C, E, and G". And, on the other hand, "I hear a piano playing and some noise in the street". A most instructive example is this: In a song words are sung to certain notes. In what sense is the experience of hearing the vowel *a* sung to the note C a composite one? Ask yourself in each of these cases: What is it like to single out the constituent experiences in the compound experience?

Now although the expression that seeing a drawing as a face is not merely seeing strokes seems to point to some kind of addition of experiences, we certainly should not say that when we see the drawing as a face we also have the experience of seeing it as mere strokes and some other experience *besides*. And this becomes still clearer when we imagine that someone said that seeing the drawing

as a cube consisted in seeing it as a plane figure plus having an experience of depth.

Now when I felt that though while reading a certain constant experience went on and on, I could not in a sense lay hold of that experience, my difficulty arose through wrongly comparing this case with one in which one part of my experience can be said to be an accompaniment of another. Thus we are sometimes tempted to ask: "If I feel this constant hum going on while I read, *where* is it?" I wish to make a pointing gesture, and there is nothing to point to. And the words "lay hold of" express the same misleading analogy.

Instead of asking the question "Where is this constant experience which seems to go on all through my reading?", we should ask "What is it in saying 'A particular atmosphere enshrouds the words which I am reading', that I am contrasting this case with?"

I will try to elucidate this by an analogous case: We are inclined to be puzzled by the three-dimensional appearance of the drawing

in a way expressed by the question "What does seeing it three-dimensionally consist in?" And this question really asks 'What is it that is added to simply seeing the drawing when we see it three-dimensionally?' And yet what answer can we expect to this question? It is the form of this question which produces the puzzlement. As Hertz says: "Aber offenbar irrt die Frage in Bezug auf die Antwort, welche sie erwartet" (p. 9, Einleitung, *Die Prinzipien der Mechanik*). The question itself keeps the mind pressing against a blank wall, thereby preventing it from ever finding the outlet. To show a man how to get out you have first of all to free him from the misleading influence of the question.

Look at a written word, say "read",—"It isn't just a scribble, it's 'read' ", I should like to say, "it has one definite physiognomy". But what is it that I am really saying about it? What is this statement, straightened out? "The word falls", one is tempted to explain, "into a mould of my mind *long* prepared for it". But as I don't perceive both the word and a mould, the metaphor of the word's fitting a mould can't allude to an experience of comparing the hollow and the solid shape before they are fitted together, but rather to an experience of seeing the solid shape accentuated by a particular background.

i) would be the picture of the hollow and the solid shape before they are fitted together. We here see two circles and can compare them. *ii*) is the picture of the solid in the hollow. There is only one circle, and what we call the mould only accentuates, or as we sometimes said, emphasizes it.

I am tempted to say, "This isn't just a scribble, but it's *this* particular face".—But I can't say, "I see *this* as *this* face", but ought to say "I see this as *a* face". But I feel I want to say, "I don't see this as *a* face, I see it as *this* face". But in the second half of this sentence the word "face" is redundant, and it should have run, "I don't see this as a face, I see it like *this*".

Suppose I said "I see this scribble like *this*", and while saying "this scribble" I look at it as a mere scribble, and while saying "like *this*", I see the face,—this would come to something like saying "What at one time appears to me like this, at another appears to me like that", and here the "this" and the "that" would be accompanied by the two different ways of seeing.—But we must ask ourselves in what game is this sentence with the processes accompanying it to be used. E.g., whom am I telling this? Suppose the answer is "I'm saying it to my-self". But that is not enough. We are here in the grave danger of believing that we know what to do with a sentence if it looks more or less like one of the common sentences of our language. But here in order not to be deluded we have to ask ourselves: What is the use, say, of the words "this" and "that"?—or rather, What are the different uses which we make of them? What we call their meaning is not anything which they have got in them or which is fastened to them irrespective of what use we make of them. Thus it is one use of the word "this" to go along with a gesture pointing to something: We say "I am seeing the square with the diagonals like this", pointing to a swastika. And referring to the square with diagonals I might have said, "What at one time appears to me like this

at another time appears to me like that

".

And this is certainly not the use we made of the sentence in the above case.—One might think the whole difference between the two cases is this, that in the first the pictures are mental, in the second, real drawings. We should here ask ourselves in what sense we can call mental images pictures, for in some ways they are comparable to drawn or painted pictures, and in others not. It is, e.g., one of the essential points about the use of a 'material' picture that we say that it remains the same not only on the ground that it seems to us to be the same, that we remember that it looked before as it looks now. In fact we shall say under certain circumstances that the picture hasn't changed although it seems to have changed; and we say it hasn't changed because it has been kept in a certain way, certain influences have been kept out. Therefore the expression "The picture hasn't changed" is used in a different way when we talk of a material picture on the one hand, and of a mental one on the other. Just as the statement "These ticks follow at equal intervals" has got one grammar if the ticks are the tick of a pendulum and the criterion for their regularity is the result of measurements which we have made on our apparatus, and another grammar if the ticks are ticks which we imagine. I might for instance ask the question: When I said to myself "What at one time appears to me like this, at another . . .", did I recognize the two aspects, this and that, as the same which I got on previous occasions? Or were they new to me and I tried to remember them for future occasions? Or was all that I meant to say "I can change the aspect of this figure"?

19. The danger of delusion which we are in becomes most clear if we propose to ourselves to give the aspects 'this' and 'that' names,

say A and B. For we are most strongly tempted to imagine that giving a name consists in correlating in a peculiar and rather mysterious way a sound (or other sign) with something. How we make use of this peculiar correlation then seems to be almost a secondary matter. (One could almost imagine that naming was done by a peculiar sacramental act, and that this produced some magic relation between the name and the thing.)

But let us look at an example; consider this language game: A sends B to various houses in their town to fetch goods of various sorts from various people. A gives B various lists. On top of every list he puts a scribble, and B is trained to go to that house on the door of which he finds the same scribble, this is the name of the house. In the first column of every list he then finds one or more scribbles which he has been taught to read out. When he enters the house he calls out these words, and every inhabitant of the house has been trained to run up to him when a certain one of these sounds is called out, these sounds are the names of the people. He then addresses himself to each one of them in turn and shows to each two consecutive scribbles which stand on the list against his name. The first of these two, people of that town have been trained to associate with some particular kind of object, say, apples. The second is one of a series of scribbles which each man carries about him on a slip of paper. The person thus addressed fetches say, five apples. The first scribble was the generic name of the objects required, the second, the name of their number.

What now is the relation between a name and the object named, say, the house and its name? I suppose we could give either of two answers. The one is that the relation consists in certain strokes having been painted on the door of the house. The second answer I meant is that the relation we are concerned with is established, not just by painting these strokes on the door, but by the particular role which they play in the practice of our language as we have been sketching it.—Again, the relation of the name of a person to the person here consists in the person having been trained to run up to someone who calls out the name; or again, we might say that it consists in this and the whole of the usage of the name in the language game.

Look into this language game and see if you can find the mysterious relation of the object and its name.—The relation of name and object we may say, consists in a scribble being written on an object (or some other such very trivial relation), and that's all there is to it. But we are not satisfied with that, for we feel that a scribble written on an object in itself is of no importance to us, and interests us in no way. And this is true; the whole importance lies in the particular use we make of the scribble written on the object, and we, in a sense, simplify matters by saying that the name has a peculiar relation to its object, a relation other than that, say, of being written on the object, or of being spoken by a person pointing to an object with his finger. A primitive philosophy condenses the whole usage of the name into the idea of a relation, which thereby becomes a mysterious relation. (Compare the ideas of mental activities, wishing, believing, thinking, etc., which for the same reason have something mysterious and inexplicable about them.)

Now we might use the expression "The relation of name and object does not merely consist in this kind of trivial, 'purely external', connection", meaning that what we call the relation of name and object is characterized by the entire usage of the name; but then it is clear that there is no one relation of name to object, but as many as there are uses of sounds or scribbles which we call names.

We can therefore say that if naming something is to be more than just uttering a sound while pointing to something, there must also be, in some form or other, the knowledge of how in the particular case the sound or scratch is to be used.

Now when we proposed to give the aspects of a drawing names, we made it appear that by seeing the drawing in two different ways, and each time saying something, we had done more than performing just this uninteresting action; whereas we now see that it is the usage of the 'name' and in fact the detail of this usage which gives the naming its peculiar significance.

It is therefore not an unimportant question, but a question about the essence of the matter; "Are 'A' and 'B' to remind me of these aspects; can I carry out such an order as 'See this drawing in the aspect A'; are there, in some way, pictures of these aspects correlated with the names 'A' and 'B' (like

and);

are 'A' and 'B' used in communicating with other people, and what exactly is the game played with them?"

When I say "I don't see mere dashes (a mere scribble) but a face (or word) with this particular physiognomy", I don't wish to assert any general characteristic of what I see, but to assert that I see that particular physiognomy which I do see. And it is obvious that here my expression is moving in a circle. But this is so because really the particular physiognomy which I saw ought to have entered my proposition.—When I find that "In reading a sentence, a peculiar experience goes on all the while", I have actually to read over a fairly long stretch to get the peculiar impression which makes one say this.

I might then have said "I find that the same experience goes on all the time", but I wished to say: "I don't just notice that it's the same experience throughout, I notice a particular experience". Looking at a uniformly coloured wall I might say, "I don't just see that it has the same colour all over, but I see a particular colour". But in saying this I am mistaking the function of a sentence.—It seems that you wish to specify the colour you see, but not by saying anything about it, nor by comparing it with a sample,—but by pointing to it; using it at the same time as the sample and that which the sample is compared with.

Consider this example: You tell me to write a few lines, and while I am doing so you ask "Do you feel something in your hand while you are writing?" I say, "Yes, I have a peculiar feeling".—Can't I say to myself when I write, "I have *this* feeling"? Of course I can say it, and while saying "this feeling", I concentrate on the feeling.—But what do I do with this sentence? What use is it to me? It seems that I am pointing out to myself what I am feeling,—as though my act of concentration was an 'inward' act of pointing, one which no one else but me is aware of, this however is unimportant. But I don't point to the feeling by attending to it. Rather, attending to the feeling means producing or modifying it. (On the other hand, observing a chair does not mean producing or modifying the chair.)

Our sentence "I have *this* feeling while I'm writing" is of the kind of the sentence "I see this". I don't mean the sentence when it is used to inform someone that I am looking at the object which I am pointing to, nor when it is used, as above, to convey to someone that I see a certain drawing in the way A and not in the way B. I mean the sentence, "I see this", as it is sometimes contemplated by us when we are brooding over certain philosophical problems. We are then, say, holding on to a particular visual impression by staring at some object, and we feel it is most natural to say to ourselves "I see this", though we know of no further use we can make of this sentence.

20. 'Surely it makes sense to say what I see, and how better could
I do this than by letting what I see speak for itself!'

But the words "I see" in our sentence are redundant. I don't wish to
tell myself that it is *I* who see this, nor that I *see* it. Or, as I might put
it, it is impossible that I should not see *this*. This comes to the same
as saying that I can't point out to myself by a visual hand what I am
seeing; as this hand does not point to what I see but is part of what
I see.

It is as though the sentence was singling out the particular colour I
saw; as if it presented it to me.

It seems as though the colour which I see was its own description.

For the pointing with my finger was ineffectual. (And the looking
is no pointing, it does not, for me, indicate a direction, which would
mean contrasting a direction with other directions.)

What I see, or feel, enters my sentence as a sample does; but no
use is made of this sample; the words of my sentence don't seem to
matter, they only serve to present the sample to me.

I don't really speak *about* what I see, but *to* it.

I am in fact going through the acts of attending which could
accompany the use of a sample. And this is what makes it seem as
though I was making use of a sample. This error is akin to that of
believing that an ostensive definition says something about the object
to which it directs our attention.

When I said "I am mistaking the function of a sentence" it was
because by its help I seemed to be pointing out to myself which
colour it is I see, whereas I was just contemplating a sample of a
colour. It seemed to me that the sample was the description of its own
colour.

21. Suppose I said to someone: "Observe the particular lighting
of this room".—Under certain circumstances the sense of this order
will be quite clear, e.g., if the walls of the room were red with the
setting sun. But suppose at any other time when there is nothing
striking about the lighting I said "Observe the particular lighting of
this room":—Well, isn't there a particular lighting? So what is the
difficulty about observing it? But the person who was told to observe
the lighting when there was nothing striking about it would probably
look about the room and say "Well, what about it?" Now I might go
on and say "It is exactly the same lighting as yesterday at this hour",

or "It is just this slightly dim light which you see in this picture of the room".

In the first case, when the room was lit a striking red, you could have pointed out the peculiarity which you were meant, though not explicitly told, to observe. You could, e.g., have used a sample of the particular colour in order to do so. We shall in this case be inclined to say that a peculiarity was added to the normal appearance of the room.

In the second case, when the room was just ordinarily lighted and there was nothing striking about its appearance, you didn't know exactly what to do when you were told to observe the lighting of the room. All you could do was to look about you waiting for something further to be said which would give the first order its full sense.

But wasn't the room, in both cases, lit in a particular way? Well, this question, as it stands, is senseless, and so is the answer "It was ...". The order "Observe the particular lighting of this room", does not imply any statement about the appearance of this room. It seemed to say: "This room has a particular lighting, which I need not name; observe it!" The lighting referred to, it seems, is given by a sample, and you are to make use of the sample; as you would be doing in copying the precise shade of a colour sample on a palette. Whereas the order is similar to this: "Get hold of this sample!"

Imagine yourself saying "There is a particular lighting which I'm to observe". You could imagine yourself in this case staring about you in vain, that is, without seeing the lighting.

You could have been given a sample, e.g., a piece of colour material, and been asked: "Observe the colour of this patch".—And we can draw a distinction between observing, attending to, the shape of the sample and attending to its colour. But, attending to the colour can't be described as looking at a thing which is connected with the sample, rather, as looking at the sample in a peculiar way.

When we obey the order, "Observe the colour ...", what we do is to open our eyes to colour. "Observe the colour ..." doesn't mean "See the colour you see". The order, "Look at so and so", is of the kind, "Turn your head in this direction"; what you will see when you do so does not enter this order. By attending, looking, you produce the impression; you can't look at the impression.

Suppose someone answered to our order: "All right, I am now observing the particular lighting this room has",—this would sound as though he could point out to us which lighting it was. The order, that is to say, may seem to have told you to do something with this particular lighting, as opposed to another one (like "Paint this light-ing, not that"). Whereas you obey the order by taking in *lighting*, as opposed to dimensions, shapes, etc.

(Compare, "Get hold of the colour of this sample" with "Get hold of this pencil", i.e., there it is, take hold of it.)

I return to our sentence: "this face has a particular expression". In this case too I did not compare or contrast my impression with anything, I did not make use of the sample before me. The sentence was an utterance[1] of a state of attention.

What has to be explained is this: Why do we talk to our impression?— You read, put yourself into a state of attention and say: "Something peculiar happens undoubtedly". You are inclined to go on: "There is a certain smoothness about it"; but you feel that this is only an inade-quate description and that the experience can only stand for itself. "Something peculiar happens undoubtedly" is like saying, "I have had an experience". But you don't wish to make a general statement independent of the particular experience you have had, but rather a statement into which this experience enters.

You are under an impression. This makes you say "I am under a *particular* impression", and this sentence seems to say, to yourself at least, under what impression you are. As though you were referring to a picture ready in your mind, and said "This is what my impression is like". Whereas you have only pointed to your impression. In our case (p. 174), saying "I notice the particular colour of this wall" is like drawing, say, a black rectangle enclosing a small patch of the wall and thereby designating that patch as a sample for further use.

When you read, as it were attending closely to what happened in reading, you seemed to be observing reading as under a magnifying glass and to see the reading process. (But the case is more like that of observing something through a coloured glass.) You think you have noticed the process of reading, the particular way in which signs are translated into spoken words.

22. I have read a line with a peculiar attention; I am impressed by the reading, and this makes me say that I have observed something besides the mere seeing of the written signs and the speaking of words. I have also expressed it by saying that I have noticed a par-ticular atmosphere round the seeing and speaking. How such a metaphor as that embodied in the last sentence can come to suggest

---

[1] *I.e.* Äußerung. See *Philosophical Investigations*, § 256.—*Edd.*

itself to me may be seen more clearly by looking at this example: If you heard sentences spoken in a monotone, you might be tempted to say that the words were all enshrouded in a particular atmosphere. But wouldn't it be using a peculiar way of representation to say that speaking the sentence in a monotone was adding something to the mere saying of it? Couldn't we even conceive speaking in a monotone as the result of *taking away* from the sentence its inflexion? Different circumstances would make us adopt different ways of representation. If, e.g., certain words had to be read out in a monotone, this being indicated by a staff and a sustained note beneath the written words, this notation would very strongly suggest the idea that something had been added to the mere speaking of the sentence.

I am impressed by the reading of a sentence, and I say the sentence has shown me something, that I have noticed something in it. This made me think of the following example: A friend and I once looked at beds of pansies. Each bed showed a different kind. We were impressed by each in turn. Speaking about them my friend said "What a variety of colour patterns, and each says something". And this was just what I myself wished to say.

Compare such a statement with this: "Every one of these men says something".—

If one had asked what the colour pattern of the pansy said, the right answer would have seemed to be that it said itself. Hence we could have used an intransitive form of expression, say "Each of these colour patterns impresses one".

It has sometimes been said that what music conveys to us are feelings of joyfulness, melancholy, triumph, etc., etc. and what repels us in this account is that it seems to say that music is an instrument for producing in us sequences of feelings. And from this one might gather that any other means of producing such feelings would do for us instead of music.—To such an account we are tempted to reply "Music conveys to us *itself*!"

It is similar with such expressions as "Each of these colour patterns impresses one". We feel we wish to guard against the idea that a colour pattern is a means to producing in us a certain impression— the colour pattern being like a drug and we interested merely in the effect this drug produces.—We wish to avoid any form of expression which would seem to refer to an effect produced by an object on a subject. (Here we are bordering on the problem of idealism and realism and on the problem whether statements of aesthetics are subjective or objective.) Saying, "I see this and am impressed" is apt to make it seem as though the impression was some feeling accompanying the seeing, and that the sentence said something like "I see this and feel a pressure".

I could have used the expression "Each of these colour patterns has meaning"; but I didn't say "has meaning", for this would provoke the question, "What meaning?", which in the case we are considering is senseless. We are distinguishing between meaningless patterns and patterns which have meaning; but there is no such expression in our game as "This pattern has the meaning so and so". Nor even the expression "These two patterns have different meanings", unless this is to say: "These are two different patterns and both have meaning".

It is easy to understand though why we should be inclined to use the transitive form of expression. For let us see what use we make of such an expression as "This face says something", that is, what the situations are in which we use this expression, what sentences would precede or follow it (what kind of conversation it is a part of). We should perhaps follow up such a remark by saying, "Look at the line of these eyebrows" or "The *dark* eyes and the *pale* face!", these expressions would draw attention to certain features. We should in the same connection use comparisons, as for instance, "The nose is like a beak",—but also such expressions as "The whole face expresses bewilderment", and here we have used "expressing" transitively.

23. We can now consider sentences which, as one might say, give an analysis of the impression we get, say, from a face. Take such a statement as, "The particular impression of this face is due to its small eyes and low forehead". Here the words "the particular impression" may stand for a certain specification, e.g., "the stupid expression". Or, on the other hand, they may mean 'what makes this expression a striking one' (i.e., an extraordinary one); or, 'what strikes one about this face' (i.e., 'what draws one's attention'). Or again, our sentence may mean "If you change *these* features in the slightest the expression will change entirely (whereas you might change other features without changing the expression nearly so much)". The form of this statement, however, mustn't mislead us into thinking that there is in every case a supplementing statement of the form "First the expression was *this*, after the change it's *that*". We can, of course, say "Smith frowned, and his expression changed from this to that", pointing, say, at two draw-

ings of his face.—(Compare with this the two statements: "He said these words", and "His words said something".)

When, trying to see what reading consisted in, I read a written sentence, let the reading of it impress itself upon me, and said that I had a particular impression, one could have asked me such a question as whether my impression was not due to the particular handwriting. This would be asking me whether my impression would not be a different one if the writing had been a different one, or say, if each word of the sentence were written in a different handwriting. In this sense we could also ask whether that impression wasn't due after all to the *sense* of the particular sentence which I read. One might suggest: Read a different sentence (or the same one in a different handwriting) and see if you would still say that you had the same impression. And the answer might be: "Yes, the impression I had was really due to the handwriting".—But this would *not* imply that when I first said the sentence gave me a particular impression I had contrasted one impression with another, or that my statement had not been of the kind "This sentence has *its own character*". This will get clearer by considering the following example: Suppose we have three faces drawn side by side:

I contemplate the first one, saying to myself "This face has a peculiar expression". Then I am shown the second one and asked whether it has the same expression. I answer "Yes". Then the third one is shown to me and I say "It has a different expression". In my two answers I might be said to have distinguished the face and its expression: for b) is different from a) and still I say they have the same expression, whereas the difference between c) and a) corresponds to a difference of expression; and this may make us think that also in my first utterance I distinguished between the face and its expression.

24.   Let us now go back to the idea of a feeling of familiarity, which arises when I see familiar objects. Pondering about the question whether there is such a feeling or not, we are likely to gaze at some object and say, "Don't I have a particular feeling when I look at my old coat and hat?" But to this we now answer: What feeling do you compare this with, or oppose it to? Should you say that your old coat gives you the same feeling as your old friend A with whose

appearance too you are well acquainted, or that *whenever* you happened to look at your coat you get that feeling, say of intimacy and warmth?

'But is there no such thing as a feeling of familiarity?'—I should say that there are a great many different experiences, some of them feelings, which we might call "experiences (feelings) of familiarity".

Different experiences of familiarity: *a*) Someone enters my room, I haven't seen him for a long time, and didn't expect him. I look at him, say or feel "Oh, it's you".—Why did I in giving this example say that I hadn't seen the man for a long time? Wasn't I setting out to describe *experiences of* familiarity? And whatever the experience was I alluded to, couldn't I have had it even if I had seen the man half an hour ago? I mean, I gave the circumstances of recognizing the man as a means to the end of describing the precise situation of the recognition. One might object to this way of describing the *experience*, saying that it brought in irrelevant things, and in fact wasn't a *description* of the feeling at all. In saying this one takes as the prototype of a description, say, the description of a table, which tells you the exact shape, dimensions, the material which it is made of, and its colour. Such a description one might say pieces the table together. There is on the other hand a different kind of description of a table, such as you might find in a novel, e.g., "It was a small rickety table decorated in Moorish style, the sort that is used for smoker's requisites". Such a description might be called an indirect one; but if the purpose of it is to bring a vivid image of the table before your mind in a flash, it might serve this purpose incomparably better than a detailed 'direct' description.—Now if I am to give the description of a feeling of familiarity or recognition,—what do you expect me to do? Can I piece the feeling together? In a sense of course I could, giving you many different stages and the way my feelings changed. Such detailed descriptions you can find in some of the great novels. Now if you think of descriptions of pieces of furniture as you might find them in a novel, you see that to this kind of description you can oppose another making use of drawings, measures such as one should give to a cabinet maker. This latter kind one is inclined to call the only direct and complete description (though this way of expressing ourselves shows that we forget that there are certain purposes which the 'real' description does not fulfil). These considerations should warn you not to think that there is one real and direct description of, say, the feeling of recognition as opposed to the 'indirect' one which I have given.

182 THE BROWN BOOK

b) The same as *a*), but the face is not familiar to me immediately. After a little, recognition 'dawns upon me'. I say, "Oh, it's you", but with totally different inflexion than in *a*). (Consider tone of voice, inflexion, gestures, as *essential* parts of our experience, not as inessential accompaniments or mere means of communication. (Compare pp. 144–6.)) *c*) There is an experience directed towards people or things which we see every day when suddenly we feel them to be 'old acquaintances' or 'good old friends'; one might also describe the feeling as one of warmth or of being at home with them. *d*) My room with all the objects in it is thoroughly familiar to me. When I enter it in the morning do I greet the familiar chairs, tables, etc., with a feeling of "Oh, hello!"? or have such a feeling as described in *c*)? But isn't the way I walk about in it, take something out of a drawer, sit down, etc., different from my behaviour in a room I don't know? And why shouldn't I say therefore, that I had experiences of familiarity whenever I lived amongst these familiar objects? *e*) Isn't it an experience of familiarity when on being asked "Who is this man?" I answer straight away (or after some reflection) "It is so and so"? Compare with this experience, *f*), that of looking at the written word "feeling" and saying "This is A's handwriting" and on the other hand *g*) the experience of reading the word, which also is an experience of familiarity.

To *e*) one might object, saying that the experience of saying the man's name was not the experience of familiarity, that he had to be familiar to us in order that we might know his name, and that we had to *know his name* in order that we might say it. Or, we might say "Saying his name is not enough, for surely we might say the name without knowing that it was his name". And this remark is certainly true if only we realize that it does not imply that knowing the name is a process accompanying or preceding saying the name.

25. Consider this example: What is the difference between a memory image, an image that comes with expectation, and, say, an image of a daydream. You may be inclined to answer, "There is an intrinsic difference between the images".—Did you notice that difference, or did you only say there was one because you think there must be one?

But surely I recognize a memory image as a memory image, an image of a daydream as an image of a daydream, etc.!—Remember that you are sometimes doubtful whether you actually saw a certain event happening or whether you dreamt it, or just had heard of it and imagined it vividly. But apart from that, what do you mean by "recognizing an image as a memory image"? I agree that (at least in most cases) while an image is before your mind's eye you are not in a state of doubt as to whether it is a memory image, etc. Also, if asked whether your image was a memory image, you would (in most cases) answer the question without hesitation. Now what if I asked you *"When* do you know what sort of an image it is?" Do you call knowing what sort of image it is not being in a state of doubt, not wondering about it? Does introspection make you see a state or activity of mind which you would call knowing that the image was a memory image, and which takes place while the image is before your mind?—Further, if you answer the question what sort of image it was you had, do you do so by, as it were, looking at the image and discovering a certain characteristic in it (as though you had been asked by whom a picture was painted, looked at it, recognized the style, and said it was a Rembrandt)?

It is easy, on the other hand, to point out experiences characteristic of remembering, expecting, etc., accompanying the images, and further differences in the immediate or more remote surrounding of them. Thus we certainly *say* different things in the different cases, e.g., "I remember his coming into my room", "I expect his coming into my room", "I imagine his coming into my room".—"But surely this can't be all the difference there is!" It isn't all: There are the three different games played with these three words surrounding these statements.

When challenged: do we *understand* the word "remember", etc.? is there really a difference between the cases besides the mere verbal one? our thoughts move in the immediate surroundings of the image we had or the expression we used. I have an image of dining in Hall with T. If asked whether this is a memory image, I say "Of course", and my thoughts begin to move on paths starting from this image. I remember who sat next to us, what the conversation was about, what I thought about it, what happened to T later on, etc., etc.

Imagine two different games both played with chess men on a chess board. The initial positions of both are alike. One of the games is always played with red and green pieces, the other with black and white. Two people are beginning to play, they have the chess board between them with the green and red pieces in position. Someone asks them "Do you know what game you're intending to play?" A player answers "Of course; we are playing no. 2". "What is the

difference now between playing no. 2 and no. 1?"—"Well, there are
red and green pieces on the board and not black and white ones,
also we say that we are playing no. 2".—"But this couldn't be the only
difference; don't you *understand* what 'no. 2' means and what game the
red and green pieces stand for?" Here we are inclined to say "Certainly
I do", and to prove this to ourselves we actually begin to move the
pieces according to the rules of game no. 2. This is what I should call
moving in the immediate surrounding of our initial position.

But isn't there also a peculiar feeling of pastness characteristic of
images as memory images? There certainly are experiences which I
should be inclined to call feelings of pastness, although not always
when I remember something is one of these feelings present.—To
get clear about the nature of these feelings it is again very useful
to remember that there are gestures of pastness and inflexions of
pastness which we can regard as representing the experiences of
pastness.

I will examine one particular case, that of a feeling which I shall
roughly describe by saying it is the feeling of 'long, long ago'. These
words and the tone in which they are said are a gesture of pastness.
But I will specify the experience which I mean still further by saying
that it is that corresponding to a certain tune (Davids Bündler Tänze—
"Wie aus weiter Ferne"). I'm imagining this tune played with the right
expression and thus recorded, say, for a gramophone. Then this is
the most elaborate and exact expression of a feeling of pastness which
I can imagine.

Now should I say that hearing this tune played with this expression
is in itself that particular experience of pastness, or should I say that
hearing the tune causes the feeling of pastness to arise and that this
feeling accompanies the tune? I.e., can I separate what I call this
experience of pastness from the experience of hearing the tune?
Or, can I separate an experience of pastness expressed by a gesture
from the experience of making this gesture? Can I discover something,
the essential feeling of pastness, which remains after abstracting all
those experiences which we might call the experiences of expressing
the feeling?

I am inclined to suggest to you to put the expression of our
experience in place of the experience. 'But these two aren't the same'.
This is certainly true, at least in the sense in which it is true to say that
a railway train and a railway accident aren't the same thing. And yet
there is a justification for talking as though the expression "the gesture

'long, long ago' ", and the expression "the feeling 'long, long ago' " had the same meaning. Thus I could give the rules of chess in the following way: I have a chess board before me with a set of chess men on it. I give rules for moving these particular chess men (these particular pieces of wood) on this particular board. Can these rules be the rules of the game of chess? They can be converted into them by the usage of a single operator, such as the word "any". Or, the rules for my particular set may stand as they are and be made into rules of the game of chess by changing our standpoint towards them.

There is the idea that the feeling, say, of pastness, is an amorphous something in a place, the mind, and that this something is the cause or effect of what we call the expression of feeling. The expression of feeling then is an indirect way of transmitting the feeling. And people have often talked of a direct transmission of feeling which would obviate the external medium of communication.

Imagine that I tell you to mix a certain colour and I describe the colour by saying that it is that which you get if you let sulphuric acid react on copper. This might be called an indirect way of communicating the colour I meant. It is conceivable that the reaction of sulphuric acid on copper under certain circumstances does not produce the colour I wished you to mix, and that on seeing the colour you had got I should have to say "No, it's not this", and to give you a sample.

Now can we say that the communication of feelings by gestures is in this sense indirect? Does it make sense to talk of a direct communication as opposed to that indirect one? Does it make sense to say "I can't feel his toothache, but if I could I'd know what he feels like"?

If I speak of communicating a feeling to someone else, mustn't I in order to understand what I say know what I shall call the criterion of having succeeded in communicating?

We are inclined to say that when we communicate a feeling to someone, something which we can never know happens at the other end. All that we can receive from him is again an expression. This is closely analogous to saying that we can never know when in Fizeau's experiment the ray of light reaches the mirror.

Revised December, 1967

harper ☨ torchbooks

HUMANITIES AND SOCIAL SCIENCES

American Studies: General

LOUIS D. BRANDEIS: Other People's Money, *and How the Bankers Use It.* ‡ *Ed. with an Intro. by Richard M. Abrams* TB/3081
THOMAS C. COCHRAN: The Inner Revolution. *Essays on the Social Sciences in History* TB/1140
HENRY STEELE COMMAGER, Ed.: The Struggle for Racial Equality TB/1300
EDWARD S. CORWIN: American Constitutional History. *Essays edited by Alpheus T. Mason and Gerald Garvey* △ TB/1136
CARL N. DEGLER, Ed.: Pivotal Interpretations of American History Vol. I TB/1240; Vol. II TB/1241
A. HUNTER DUPREE: Science in the Federal Government: *A History of Policies and Activities to 1940* TB/573
A. S. EISENSTADT, Ed.: The Craft of American History: *Recent Essays in American Historical Writing* Vol. I TB/1255; Vol. II TB/1256
CHARLOTTE P. GILMAN: Women and Economics: *A Study of the Economic Relation between Men and Women as a Factor in Social Evolution.* ‡ *Ed. with an Introduction by Carl N. Degler* TB/3073
OSCAR HANDLIN, Ed.: This Was America: *As Recorded by European Travelers in the Eighteenth, Nineteenth and Twentieth Centuries. Illus.* TB/1119
MARCUS LEE HANSEN: The Atlantic Migration: 1607-1860. *Edited by Arthur M. Schlesinger* TB/1052
MARCUS LEE HANSEN: The Immigrant in American History. TB/1120
JOHN HIGHAM, Ed.: The Reconstruction of American History △ TB/1068
ROBERT H. JACKSON: The Supreme Court in the American System of Government TB/1106
JOHN F. KENNEDY: A Nation of Immigrants. △ *Illus.* TB/1118
LEONARD W. LEVY, Ed.: American Constitutional Law: *Historical Essays* TB/1285
LEONARD W. LEVY, Ed.: Judicial Review and the Supreme Court TB/1296
LEONARD W. LEVY: The Law of the Commonwealth and Chief Justice Shaw TB/1309
HENRY F. MAY: Protestant Churches and Industrial America. *New Intro. by the Author* TB/1334
RALPH BARTON PERRY: Puritanism and Democracy TB/1138
ARNOLD ROSE: The Negro in America TB/3048
MAURICE R. STEIN: The Eclipse of Community. *An Interpretation of American Studies* TB/1128
W. LLOYD WARNER and Associates: Democracy in Jonesville: *A Study in Quality and Inequality* ¶ TB/1129
W. LLOYD WARNER: Social Class in America: *The Evaluation of Status* TB/1013

American Studies: Colonial

BERNARD BAILYN, Ed.: Apologia of Robert Keayne: *Self-Portrait of a Puritan Merchant* TB/1201
BERNARD BAILYN: The New England Merchants in the Seventeenth Century TB/1149
JOSEPH CHARLES: The Origins of the American Party System TB/1049
HENRY STEELE COMMAGER & ELMO GIORDANETTI, Eds.: Was America a Mistake? *An Eighteenth Century Controversy* TB/1329
CHARLES GIBSON: Spain in America † TB/3077
LAWRENCE HENRY GIPSON: The Coming of the Revolution: 1763-1775. † *Illus.* TB/3007
LEONARD W. LEVY: Freedom of Speech and Press in Early American History: *Legacy of Suppression* TB/1109
PERRY MILLER: Errand Into the Wilderness TB/1139
PERRY MILLER & T. H. JOHNSON, Eds.: The Puritans: *A Sourcebook of Their Writings* Vol. I TB/1093; Vol. II TB/1094
EDMUND S. MORGAN, Ed.: The Diary of Michael Wigglesworth, 1653-1657: *The Conscience of a Puritan* TB/1228
EDMUND S. MORGAN: The Puritan Family: *Religion and Domestic Relations in Seventeenth-Century New England* TB/1227
RICHARD B. MORRIS: Government and Labor in Early America TB/1244
KENNETH B. MURDOCK: Literature and Theology in Colonial New England TB/99
WALLACE NOTESTEIN: The English People on the Eve of Colonization: 1603-1630. † *Illus.* TB/3006
JOHN P. ROCHE: Origins of American Political Thought: *Selected Readings* TB/1301
JOHN SMITH: Captain John Smith's America: *Selections from His Writings. Ed. with Intro. by John Lankford* TB/3078
LOUIS B. WRIGHT: The Cultural Life of the American Colonies: 1607-1763. † *Illus.* TB/3005

American Studies: From the Revolution to 1860

JOHN R. ALDEN: The American Revolution: 1775-1783. † *Illus.* TB/3011
MAX BELOFF, Ed.: The Debate on the American Revolution, 1761-1783: *A Sourcebook* △ TB/1225
RAY A. BILLINGTON: The Far Western Frontier: 1830-1860. † *Illus.* TB/3012
EDMUND BURKE: On the American Revolution: *Selected Speeches and Letters.* ‡ *Edited by Elliott Robert Barkan* TB/3068
WHITNEY R. CROSS: The Burned-Over District: *The Social and Intellectual History of Enthusiastic Religion in Western New York, 1800-1850* △ TB/1242
GEORGE DANGERFIELD: The Awakening of American Nationalism: 1815-1828. † *Illus.* TB/3061

† The New American Nation Series, edited by Henry Steele Commager and Richard B. Morris.
‡ American Perspectives series, edited by Bernard Wishy and William E. Leuchtenburg.
* The Rise of Modern Europe series, edited by William L. Langer.
** History of Europe series, edited by J. H. Plumb.
¶ Researches in the Social, Cultural and Behavioral Sciences, edited by Benjamin Nelson.
§ The Library of Religion and Culture, edited by Benjamin Nelson.
Σ Harper Modern Science Series, edited by James R. Newman.
° Not for sale in Canada.
△ Not for sale in the U. K.

1

CLEMENT EATON: The Freedom-of-Thought Struggle in the Old South. *Revised and Enlarged. Illus.* TB/1150
CLEMENT EATON: The Growth of Southern Civilization: 1790-1860. † *Illus.* TB/3040
LOUIS FILLER: The Crusade Against Slavery: 1830-1860. † *Illus.* TB/3029
DIXON RYAN FOX: The Decline of Aristocracy in the Politics of New York: 1801-1840. ‡ *Edited by Robert V. Remini* TB/3064
WILLIAM W. FREEHLING, Ed.: The Nullification Era: *A Documentary Record* ‡ TB/3079
FELIX GILBERT: The Beginnings of American Foreign Policy: *To the Farewell Address* TB/1200
FRANCIS GRIERSON: The Valley of Shadows: *The Coming of the Civil War in Lincoln's Midwest: A Contemporary Account* TB/1246
FRANCIS J. GRUND: Aristocracy in America: *Social Class in the Formative Years of the New Nation* TB/1001
ALEXANDER HAMILTON: The Reports of Alexander Hamilton. ‡ *Edited by Jacob E. Cooke* TB/3060
THOMAS JEFFERSON: Notes on the State of Virginia. ‡ *Edited by Thomas P. Abernethy* TB/3052
JAMES MADISON: The Forging of American Federalism: *Selected Writings of James Madison. Edited by Saul K. Padover* TB/1226
BERNARD MAYO: Myths and Men: *Patrick Henry, George Washington, Thomas Jefferson* TB/1108
JOHN C. MILLER: Alexander Hamilton and the Growth of the New Nation TB/3057
RICHARD B. MORRIS, Ed.: The Era of the American Revolution TB/1180
R. B. NYE: The Cultural Life of the New Nation: 1776-1801. † *Illus.* TB/3026
JAMES PARTON: The Presidency of Andrew Jackson. *From Vol. III of the Life of Andrew Jackson. ‡ Ed. with an Intro. by Robert V. Remini* TB/3080
FRANCIS S. PHILBRICK: The Rise of the West, 1754-1830. † *Illus.* TB/3067
TIMOTHY L. SMITH: Revivalism and Social Reform: *American Protestantism on the Eve of the Civil War* TB/1229
ALBION W. TOURGÉE: A Fool's Errand. ‡ *Ed. by George Fredrickson* TB/3074
A. F. TYLER: Freedom's Ferment: *Phases of American Social History from the Revolution to the Outbreak of the Civil War. 31 illus.* TB/1074
GLYNDON G. VAN DEUSEN: The Jacksonian Era: 1828-1848. † *Illus.* TB/3028
LOUIS B. WRIGHT: Culture on the Moving Frontier TB/1053

American Studies: The Civil War to 1900

W. R. BROCK: An American Crisis: Congress and Reconstruction, 1865-67 º △ TB/1283
THOMAS C. COCHRAN & WILLIAM MILLER: The Age of Enterprise: *A Social History of Industrial America* TB/1054
W. A. DUNNING: Essays on the Civil War and Reconstruction. *Introduction by David Donald* TB/1181
W. A. DUNNING: Reconstruction, Political and Economic: 1865-1877 TB/1073
HAROLD U. FAULKNER: Politics, Reform and Expansion: 1890-1900. † *Illus.* TB/3020
HELEN HUNT JACKSON: A Century of Dishonor: *The Early Crusade for Indian Reform. ‡ Edited by Andrew F. Rolle* TB/3063
ALBERT D. KIRWAN: Revolt of the Rednecks: *Mississippi Politics, 1876-1925* TB/1199
ROBERT GREEN MC CLOSKEY: American Conservatism in the Age of Enterprise: 1865-1910 TB/1137
ARTHUR MANN: Yankee Reformers in the Urban Age: *Social Reform in Boston, 1880-1900* TB/1247
WHITELAW REID: After the War: *A Tour of the Southern States, 1865-1866. ‡ Edited by C. Vann Woodward* TB/3066

CHARLES H. SHINN: Mining Camps: *A Study in American Frontier Government. ‡ Edited by Rodman W. Paul* TB/3062
VERNON LANE WHARTON: The Negro in Mississippi: 1865-1890 TB/1178

American Studies: 1900 to the Present

RAY STANNARD BAKER: Following the Color Line: *American Negro Citizenship in Progressive Era. ‡ Illus. Edited by Dewey W. Grantham, Jr.* TB/3053
RANDOLPH S. BOURNE: War and the Intellectuals: *Collected Essays, 1915-1919. ‡ Edited by Carl Resek* TB/3043
A. RUSSELL BUCHANAN: The United States and World War II. † *Illus.* Vol. I TB/3044; Vol. II TB/3045
ABRAHAM CAHAN: The Rise of David Levinsky: *a documentary novel of social mobility in early twentieth century America. Intro. by John Higham* TB/1028
THOMAS C. COCHRAN: The American Business System: *A Historical Perspective, 1900-1955* TB/1080
FOSTER RHEA DULLES: America's Rise to World Power: 1898-1954. † *Illus.* TB/3021
JOHN D. HICKS: Republican Ascendancy: 1921-1933. † *Illus.* TB/3041
SIDNEY HOOK: Reason, Social Myths, and Democracy TB/1237
ROBERT HUNTER: Poverty: *Social Conscience in the Progressive Era. ‡ Edited by Peter d'A. Jones* TB/3065
WILLIAM L. LANGER & S. EVERETT GLEASON: The Challenge to Isolation: *The World Crisis of 1937-1940 and American Foreign Policy* Vol. I TB/3054; Vol. II TB/3055
WILLIAM E. LEUCHTENBURG: Franklin D. Roosevelt and the New Deal: 1932-1940. † *Illus.* TB/3025
ARTHUR S. LINK: Woodrow Wilson and the Progressive Era: 1910-1917. † *Illus.* TB/3023
GEORGE E. MOWRY: The Era of Theodore Roosevelt and the Birth of Modern America: 1900-1912. † *Illus.* TB/3022
RUSSEL B. NYE: Midwestern Progressive Politics: *A Historical Study of Its Origins and Development, 1870-1958* TB/1202
WILLIAM PRESTON, JR.: Aliens and Dissenters: *Federal Suppression of Radicals, 1903-1933* TB/1287
WALTER RAUSCHENBUSCH: Christianity and the Social Crisis. ‡ *Edited by Robert D. Cross* TB/3059
JACOB RIIS: The Making of an American. ‡ *Edited by Roy Lubove* TB/3070
PHILIP SELZNICK: TVA and the Grass Roots: *A Study in the Sociology of Formal Organization* TB/1230
IDA M. TARBELL: The History of the Standard Oil Company: *Briefer Version. ‡ Edited by David M. Chalmers* TB/3071
GEORGE B. TINDALL, Ed.: A Populist Reader ‡ TB/3069
TWELVE SOUTHERNERS: I'll Take My Stand: *The South and the Agrarian Tradition. Intro. by Louis D. Rubin, Jr., Biographical Essays by Virginia Rock* TB/1072

Anthropology

JACQUES BARZUN: Race: *A Study in Superstition. Revised Edition* TB/1172
JOSEPH B. CASAGRANDE, Ed.: In the Company of Man: *Twenty Portraits of Anthropological Informants. Illus.* TB/3047
W. E. LE GROS CLARK: The Antecedents of Man: *Intro. to Evolution of the Primates.* º △ *Illus.* TB/559
CORA DU BOIS: The People of Alor. *New Preface by the author. Illus.* Vol. I TB/1042; Vol. II TB/1043
RAYMOND FIRTH, Ed.: Man and Culture: *An Evaluation of the Work of Bronislaw Malinowski* ¶ º △ TB/1133
DAVID LANDY: Tropical Childhood: *Cultural Transmission and Learning in a Puerto Rican Village* ¶ TB/1235

L. S. B. LEAKEY: Adam's Ancestors: *The Evolution of Man and His Culture.* △ *Illus.* TB/1019

EDWARD BURNETT TYLOR: Religion in Primitive Culture. *Part II of "Primitive Culture."* § *Intro. by Paul Radin* TB/34

W. LLOYD WARNER: A Black Civilization: *A Study of an Australian Tribe.* ¶ *Illus.* TB/3056

Art and Art History

WALTER LOWRIE: Art in the Early Church. *Revised Edition. 452 illus.* TB/124

EMILE MÂLE: The Gothic Image: *Religious Art in France of the Thirteenth Century.* § △ *190 illus.* TB/44

MILLARD MEISS: Painting in Florence and Siena after the Black Death: *The Arts, Religion and Society in the Mid-Fourteenth Century. 169 illus.* TB/1148

ERICH NEUMANN: The Archetypal World of Henry Moore. △ *107 illus.* TB/2020

DORA & ERWIN PANOFSKY: Pandora's Box: *The Changing Aspects of a Mythical Symbol. Revised Edition. Illus.* TB/2021

ERWIN PANOFSKY: Studies in Iconology: *Humanistic Themes in the Art of the Renaissance.* △ *180 illustrations* TB/1077

ALEXANDRE PIANKOFF: The Shrines of Tut-Ankh-Amon. *Edited by N. Rambova. 117 illus.* TB/2011

JEAN SEZNEC: The Survival of the Pagan Gods: *The Mythological Tradition and Its Place in Renaissance Humanism and Art. 108 illustrations* TB/2004

OTTO VON SIMSON: The Gothic Cathedral: *Origins of Gothic Architecture and the Medieval Concept of Order.* △ *58 illus.* TB/2018

HEINRICH ZIMMER: Myth and Symbols in Indian Art and Civilization. *70 illustrations* TB/2005

Business, Economics & Economic History

REINHARD BENDIX: Work and Authority in Industry: *Ideologies of Management in the Course of Industrialization* TB/3035

GILBERT BURCK & EDITORS OF FORTUNE: The Computer Age: *And Its Potential for Management* TB/1179

THOMAS C. COCHRAN: The American Business System: *A Historical Perspective, 1900-1955* TB/1080

THOMAS C. COCHRAN: The Inner Revolution: *Essays on the Social Sciences in History* △ TB/1140

THOMAS C. COCHRAN & WILLIAM MILLER: The Age of Enterprise: *A Social History of Industrial America* TB/1054

ROBERT DAHL & CHARLES E. LINDBLOM: Politics, Economics, and Welfare: *Planning and Politico-Economic Systems Resolved into Basic Social Processes* TB/3037

PETER F. DRUCKER: The New Society: *The Anatomy of Industrial Order* △ TB/1082

EDITORS OF FORTUNE: America in the Sixties: *The Economy and the Society* TB/1015

ROBERT L. HEILBRONER: The Great Ascent: *The Struggle for Economic Development in Our Time* TB/3030

ROBERT L. HEILBRONER: The Limits of American Capitalism TB/1305

FRANK H. KNIGHT: The Economic Organization TB/1214

FRANK H. KNIGHT: Risk, Uncertainty and Profit TB/1215

ABBA P. LERNER: Everybody's Business: *Current Assumptions in Economics and Public Policy* TB/3051

ROBERT GREEN MC CLOSKEY: American Conservatism in the Age of Enterprise, 1865-1910 △ TB/1137

PAUL MANTOUX: The Industrial Revolution in the Eighteenth Century: *The Beginnings of the Modern Factory System in England* ○ △ TB/1079

WILLIAM MILLER, Ed.: Men in Business: *Essays on the Historical Role of the Entrepreneur* TB/1081

RICHARD B. MORRIS: Government and Labor in Early America △ TB/1244

HERBERT SIMON: The Shape of Automation: *For Men and Management* TB/1245

PERRIN STRYKER: The Character of the Executive: *Eleven Studies in Managerial Qualities* TB/1041

Education

JACQUES BARZUN: The House of Intellect △ TB/1051

RICHARD M. JONES, Ed.: Contemporary Educational Psychology: *Selected Readings* TB/1292

CLARK KERR: The Uses of the University TB/1264

JOHN U. NEF: Cultural Foundations of Industrial Civilization △ TB/1024

Historiography & Philosophy of History

JACOB BURCKHARDT: On History and Historians. △ *Introduction by H. R. Trevor-Roper* TB/1216

WILHELM DILTHEY: Pattern and Meaning in History: *Thoughts on History and Society.* ○ △ *Edited with an Introduction by H. P. Rickman* TB/1075

J. H. HEXTER: Reappraisals in History: *New Views on History & Society in Early Modern Europe* △ TB/1100

H. STUART HUGHES: History as Art and as Science: *Twin Vistas on the Past* TB/1207

RAYMOND KLIBANSKY & H. J. PATON, Eds.: Philosophy and History: *The Ernst Cassirer Festschrift. Illus.* TB/1115

ARNALDO MOMIGLIANO: Studies in Historiography ○ △ TB/1283

GEORGE H. NADEL, Ed.: Studies in the Philosophy of History: *Selected Essays from History and Theory* TB/1208

JOSE ORTEGA Y GASSET: The Modern Theme. *Introduction by Jose Ferrater Mora* TB/1038

KARL R. POPPER: The Open Society and Its Enemies △ *Vol. I: The Spell of Plato* TB/1101 *Vol. II: The High Tide of Prophecy: Hegel, Marx and the Aftermath* TB/1102

KARL R. POPPER: The Poverty of Historicism ○ △ TB/1126

G. J. RENIER: History: Its Purpose and Method △ TB/1209

W. H. WALSH: Philosophy of History: *An Introduction* △ TB/1020

History: General

WOLFGANG FRANKE: China and the West. *Trans by R. A. Wilson* TB/1326

L. CARRINGTON GOODRICH: A Short History of the Chinese People. △ *Illus.* TB/3015

DAN N. JACOBS & HANS H. BAERWALD: Chinese Communism: *Selected Documents* TB/3031

BERNARD LEWIS: The Arabs in History △ TB/1029

BERNARD LEWIS: The Middle East and the West ○ △ TB/1274

History: Ancient

A. ANDREWES: The Greek Tyrants △ TB/1103

ADOLF ERMAN, Ed. The Ancient Egyptians: *A Sourcebook of Their Writings. New material and Introduction by William Kelly Simpson* TB/1233

MICHAEL GRANT: Ancient History ○ △ TB/1190

SAMUEL NOAH KRAMER: Sumerian Mythology △ TB/1055

NAPHTALI LEWIS & MEYER REINHOLD, Eds.: Roman Civilization. *Sourcebook I: The Republic* TB/1231

NAPHTALI LEWIS & MEYER REINHOLD, Eds.: Roman Civilization. *Sourcebook II: The Empire* TB/1232

History: Medieval

P. BOISSONNADE: Life and Work in Medieval Europe: *The Evolution of the Medieval Economy, the 5th to the 15th Century.* ○ △ *Preface by Lynn White, Jr.* TB/1141

HELEN CAM: England before Elizabeth △ TB/1026

NORMAN COHN: The Pursuit of the Millennium: *Revolutionary Messianism in Medieval and Reformation Europe* △ TB/1037

G. G. COULTON: Medieval Village, Manor, and Monastery
TB/1022

CHRISTOPHER DAWSON, Ed.: Mission to Asia: *Narratives and Letters of the Franciscan Missionaries in Mongolia and China in the 13th and 14th Centuries* △
TB/315

HEINRICH FICHTENAU: The Carolingian Empire: *The Age of Charlemagne* △
TB/1142

GALBERT OF BRUGES: The Murder of Charles the Good. *Trans. with Intro. by James Bruce Ross*
TB/1311

F. L. GANSHOF: Feudalism △
TB/1058

DENO GEANAKOPLOS: Byzantine East and Latin West: *Two Worlds of Christendom in the Middle Ages and Renaissance*
TB/1265

EDWARD GIBBON: The Triumph of Christendom in the Roman Empire *(Chaps. XV-XX of "Decline and Fall," J. B. Bury edition).* § △ *Illus.*
TB/46

W. O. HASSALL, Ed.: Medieval England: *As Viewed by Contemporaries* △
TB/1205

DENYS HAY: Europe: The Emergence of an Idea △
TB/1275

DENYS HAY: The Medieval Centuries ○ △
TB/1192

J. M. HUSSEY: The Byzantine World △
TB/1057

ROBERT LATOUCHE: The Birth of Western Economy: *Economic Aspects of the Dark Ages.* ○ △ *Intro. by Philip Grierson*
TB/1290

FERDINAND LOT: The End of the Ancient World and the Beginnings of the Middle Ages. *Introduction by Glanville Downey*
TB/1044

ACHILLE LUCHAIRE: Social France at the Time of Philip Augustus. *New Intro. by John W. Baldwin*
TB/1314

MARSILIUS OF PADUA: The Defender of the Peace. *Trans. with Intro. by Alan Gewirth*
TB/1310

G. MOLLAT: The Popes at Avignon: 1305-1378 △
TB/308

CHARLES PETIT-DUTAILLIS: The Feudal Monarchy in France and England: *From the Tenth to the Thirteenth Century* ○ △
TB/1165

HENRI PIRENNE: Early Democracies in the Low Countries: *Urban Society and Political Conflict in the Middle Ages and the Renaissance. Introduction by John H. Mundy*
TB/1110

STEVEN RUNCIMAN: A History of the Crusades. △
Volume I: *The First Crusade and the Foundation of the Kingdom of Jerusalem. Illus.*
TB/1143
Volume II: *The Kingdom of Jerusalem and the Frankish East, 1100-1187. Illus.*
TB/1243
Volume III: *The Kingdom of Acre and the Later Crusades*
TB/1298

SULPICIUS SEVERUS et al.: The Western Fathers: *Being the Lives of Martin of Tours, Ambrose, Augustine of Hippo, Honoratus of Arles and Germanus of Auxerre.* △ *Edited and trans. by F. O. Hoare*
TB/309

J. M. WALLACE-HADRILL: The Barbarian West: *The Early Middle Ages, A.D. 400-1000* △
TB/1061

History: Renaissance & Reformation

JACOB BURCKHARDT: The Civilization of the Renaissance in Italy. △ *Intro. by Benjamin Nelson & Charles Trinkaus. Illus.* Vol. I TB/40; Vol. II TB/41

JOHN CALVIN & JACOPO SADOLETO: A Reformation Debate. *Edited by John C. Olin*
TB/1239

ERNST CASSIRER: The Individual and the Cosmos in Renaissance Philosophy. △ *Translated with an Introduction by Mario Domandi*
TB/1097

FEDERICO CHABOD: Machiavelli and the Renaissance △
TB/1193

EDWARD P. CHEYNEY: The Dawn of a New Era, 1250-1453. * *Illus.*
TB/3002

G. CONSTANT: The Reformation in England: *The English Schism, Henry VIII, 1509-1547* §
TB/314

R. TREVOR DAVIES: The Golden Century of Spain, 1501-1621 ○ △
TB/1194

G. R. ELTON: Reformation Europe, 1517-1559 ** ○ △
TB/1270

DESIDERIUS ERASMUS: Christian Humanism and the Reformation: *Selected Writings. Edited and translated by John C. Olin*
TB/1166

WALLACE K. FERGUSON et al.: Facets of the Renaissance
TB/1098

WALLACE K. FERGUSON et al.: The Renaissance: *Six Essays. Illus.*
TB/1084

JOHN NEVILLE FIGGIS: The Divine Right of Kings. *Introduction by G. R. Elton*
TB/1191

JOHN NEVILLE FIGGIS: Political Thought from Gerson to Grotius: 1414-1625: *Seven Studies. Introduction by Garrett Mattingly*
TB/1032

MYRON P. GILMORE: The World of Humanism, 1453-1517. * *Illus.*
TB/3003

FRANCESCO GUICCIARDINI: Maxims and Reflections of a Renaissance Statesman *(Ricordi). Trans. by Mario Domandi. Intro. by Nicolai Rubinstein*
TB/1160

J. H. HEXTER: More's Utopia: *The Biography of an Idea. New Epilogue by the Author*
TB/1195

HAJO HOLBORN: Ulrich von Hutten and the German Reformation
TB/1238

JOHAN HUIZINGA: Erasmus and the Age of Reformation. △ *Illus.*
TB/19

JOEL HURSTFIELD: The Elizabethan Nation △
TB/1312

JOEL HURSTFIELD, Ed.: The Reformation Crisis △
TB/1267

ULRICH VON HUTTEN et al.: On the Eve of the Reformation: *"Letters of Obscure Men." Introduction by Hajo Holborn*
TB/1124

PAUL O. KRISTELLER: Renaissance Thought: *The Classic, Scholastic, and Humanist Strains*
TB/1048

PAUL O. KRISTELLER: Renaissance Thought II: *Papers on Humanism and the Arts*
TB/1163

NICCOLÒ MACHIAVELLI: History of Florence and of the Affairs of Italy: *from the earliest times to the death of Lorenzo the Magnificent.* △ *Introduction by Felix Gilbert*
TB/1027

ALFRED VON MARTIN: Sociology of the Renaissance. *Introduction by Wallace K. Ferguson*
TB/1099

GARRETT MATTINGLY et al.: Renaissance Profiles. △ *Edited by J. H. Plumb*
TB/1162

MILLARD MEISS: Painting in Florence and Siena after the Black Death: *The Arts, Religion and Society in the Mid-Fourteenth Century.* △ *169 illus.*
TB/1148

J. E. NEALE: The Age of Catherine de Medici ○ △
TB/1085

ERWIN PANOFSKY: Studies in Iconology: *Humanistic Themes in the Art of the Renaissance.* △ *180 illustrations*
TB/1077

J. H. PARRY: The Establishment of the European Hegemony: 1415-1715: *Trade and Exploration in the Age of the Renaissance* △
TB/1045

BUONACCORSO PITTI & GREGORIO DATI: Two Memoirs of Renaissance Florence: *The Diaries of Buonaccorso Pitti and Gregorio Dati. Ed. with an Intro. by Gene Brucker. Trans. by Julia Martines*
TB/1333

J. H. PLUMB: The Italian Renaissance: *A Concise Survey of Its History and Culture* △
TB/1161

A. F. POLLARD: Henry VIII. ○ △ *Introduction by A. G. Dickens*
TB/1249

A. F. POLLARD: Wolsey. ○ △ *Introduction by A. G. Dickens*
TB/1248

CECIL ROTH: The Jews in the Renaissance. *Illus.* TB/834

A. L. ROWSE: The Expansion of Elizabethan England. ○ △ *Illus.*
TB/1220

GORDON RUPP: Luther's Progress to the Diet of Worms ○ △
TB/120

FERDINAND SCHEVILL: The Medici. *Illus.*
TB/1010

FERDINAND SCHEVILL: Medieval and Renaissance Florence. *Illus.* Volume I: *Medieval Florence* TB/1090
Volume II: *The Coming of Humanism and the Age of the Medici*
TB/1091

R. H. TAWNEY: The Agrarian Problem in the Sixteenth Century. *New Intro. by Lawrence Stone*
TB/1315

G. M. TREVELYAN: England in the Age of Wycliffe, 1368-1520 ○ △
TB/1112

VESPASIANO: Renaissance Princes, Popes, and Prelates: *The Vespasiano Memoirs: Lives of Illustrious Men of the XVth Century. Intro. by Myron P. Gilmore*
TB/1111

History: Modern European

FREDERICK B. ARTZ: Reaction and Revolution, 1815-1832. * *Illus.* TB/3034
MAX BELOFF: The Age of Absolutism, 1660-1815 △ TB/1062
ROBERT C. BINKLEY: Realism and Nationalism, 1852-1871. * *Illus.* TB/3038
EUGENE C. BLACK, Ed.: European Political History, 1815-1870: *Aspects of Liberalism* TB/1331
ASA BRIGGS: The Making of Modern England, 1784-1867: *The Age of Improvement* o △ TB/1203
CRANE BRINTON: A Decade of Revolution, 1789-1799. * *Illus.* TB/3018
D. W. BROGAN: The Development of Modern France. o △ Volume I: *From the Fall of the Empire to the Dreyfus Affair* TB/1184
Volume II: *The Shadow of War, World War I, Between the Two Wars. New Introduction by the Author* TB/1185
J. BRONOWSKI & BRUCE MAZLISH: The Western Intellectual Tradition: *From Leonardo to Hegel* △ TB/3001
GEOFFREY BRUUN: Europe and the French Imperium, 1799-1814. * *Illus.* TB/3033
ALAN BULLOCK: Hitler, A Study in Tyranny. o △ *Illus.* TB/1123
E. H. CARR: German-Soviet Relations Between the Two World Wars, 1919-1939 TB/1278
E. H. CARR: International Relations Between the Two World Wars, 1919-1939 o △ TB/1279
E. H. CARR: The Twenty Years' Crisis, 1919-1939: *An Introduction to the Study of International Relations* o △ TB/1122
GORDON A. CRAIG: From Bismarck to Adenauer: *Aspects of German Statecraft. Revised Edition* TB/1171
DENIS DIDEROT: The Encyclopedia: *Selections. Ed. and trans. by Stephen Gendzier* TB/1299
WALTER L. DORN: Competition for Empire, 1740-1763. * *Illus.* TB/3032
FRANKLIN L. FORD: Robe and Sword: *The Regrouping of the French Aristocracy after Louis XIV* TB/1217
CARL J. FRIEDRICH: The Age of the Baroque, 1610-1660. * *Illus.* TB/3004
RENÉ FUELOEP-MILLER: The Mind and Face of Bolshevism: *An Examination of Cultural Life in Soviet Russia. New Epilogue by the Author* TB/1188
M. DOROTHY GEORGE: London Life in the Eighteenth Century △ TB/1182
LEO GERSHOY: From Despotism to Revolution, 1763-1789. * *Illus.* TB/3017
C. C. GILLISPIE: Genesis and Geology: *The Decades before Darwin* § TB/51
ALBERT GOODWIN, Ed.: The European Nobility in the Eighteenth Century △ TB/1313
ALBERT GOODWIN: The French Revolution △ TB/1064
ALBERT GUÉRARD: France in the Classical Age: *The Life and Death of an Ideal* △ TB/1183
CARLTON J. H. HAYES: A Generation of Materialism, 1871-1900. * *Illus.* TB/3039
J. H. HEXTER: Reappraisals in History: *New Views on History and Society in Early Modern Europe* △ TB/1100
STANLEY HOFFMANN et al.: In Search of France: *The Economy, Society and Political System in the Twentieth Century* TB/1219
A. R. HUMPHREYS: The Augustan World: *Society, Thought, & Letters in 18th Century England* o △ TB/1105
DAN N. JACOBS, Ed.: The New Communist Manifesto *and Related Documents. Third edition, revised* TB/1078

LIONEL KOCHAN: The Struggle for Germany: *1914-45* TB/1304
HANS KOHN: The Mind of Germany: *The Education of a Nation* △ TB/1204
HANS KOHN, Ed.: The Mind of Modern Russia: *Historical and Political Thought of Russia's Great Age* TB/1065
WALTER LAQUEUR & GEORGE L. MOSSE, Eds.: Education and Social Structure in the 20th Century. o △ *Vol. 6 of the Journal of Contemporary History* TB/1339
WALTER LAQUEUR & GEORGE L. MOSSE, Eds.: International Fascism, 1920-1945. o △ *Volume 1* of Journal of Contemporary History TB/1276
WALTER LAQUEUR & GEORGE L. MOSSE, Eds.: The Left-Wing Intellectuals between the Wars 1919-1939. o △ *Volume 2* of Journal of Contemporary History TB/1286
WALTER LAQUEUR & GEORGE L. MOSSE, Eds.: Literature and Politics in the 20th Century. o △ *Vol. 5 of the Journal of Contemporary History* TB/1328
WALTER LAQUEUR & GEORGE L. MOSSE, Eds.: The New History: *Trends in Historical Research and Writing since World War II.* o △ *Vol. 4 of the Journal of Conporary History* TB/1327
WALTER LAQUEUR & GEORGE L. MOSSE, Eds.: 1914: *The Coming of the First World War.* o △ *Volume 3 of Journal of Contemporary History* TB/1306
FRANK E. MANUEL: The Prophets of Paris: *Turgot, Condorcet, Saint-Simon, Fourier, and Comte* TB/1218
KINGSLEY MARTIN: French Liberal Thought in the Eighteenth Century: *A Study of Political Ideas from Bayle to Condorcet* TB/1114
ROBERT K. MERTON: Science, Technology and Society in Seventeenth Century England ¶ *New Intro. by the Author* TB/1324
L. B. NAMIER: Facing East: *Essays on Germany, the Balkans, and Russia in the 20th Century* △ TB/1280
L. B. NAMIER: Personalities and Powers: *Selected Essays* △ TB/1186
L. B. NAMIER: Vanished Supremacies: *Essays on European History, 1812-1918* o TB/1088
NAPOLEON III: Napoleonic Ideas: *Des Idées Napoléoniennes, par le Prince Napoléon-Louis Bonaparte. Ed. by Brison D. Gooch* TB/1336
FRANZ NEUMANN: Behemoth: *The Structure and Practice of National Socialism, 1933-1944* TB/1289
FREDERICK L. NUSSBAUM: The Triumph of Science and Reason, 1660-1685. * *Illus.* TB/3009
DAVID OGG: Europe of the Ancien Régime, 1715-1783 ** o △ TB/1271
JOHN PLAMENATZ: German Marxism and Russian Communism. o △ *New Preface by the Author* TB/1189
RAYMOND W. POSTGATE, Ed.: Revolution from 1789 to 1906: *Selected Documents* TB/1063
PENFIELD ROBERTS: The Quest for Security, 1715-1740. * *Illus.* TB/3016
PRISCILLA ROBERTSON: Revolutions of 1848: *A Social History* TB/1025
GEORGE RUDÉ: Revolutionary Europe, 1783-1815 ** o △ TB/1272
LOUIS, DUC DE SAINT-SIMON: Versailles, The Court, and Louis XIV. o △ *Introductory Note by Peter Gay* TB/1250
HUGH SETON-WATSON: Eastern Europe Between the Wars, 1918-1941 TB/1330
ALBERT SOREL: Europe Under the Old Regime. *Translated by Francis H. Herrick* TB/1121
N. N. SUKHANOV: The Russian Revolution, 1917: *Eyewitness Account.* △ *Edited by Joel Carmichael* Vol. I TB/1066; Vol. II TB/1067
A. J. P. TAYLOR: From Napoleon to Lenin: *Historical Essays* o △ TB/1268
A. J. P. TAYLOR: The Habsburg Monarchy, 1809-1918: *A History of the Austrian Empire and Austria-Hungary* o △ TB/1187
G. M. TREVELYAN: British History in the Nineteenth Century and After: *1782-1919.* o △ *Second Edition* TB/1251

5

H. R. TREVOR-ROPER: Historical Essays ° △   TB/1269
ELIZABETH WISKEMANN: Europe of the Dictators, 1919-
1945 ** ° △   TB/1273
JOHN B. WOLF: The Emergence of the Great Powers,
1685-1715. * Illus.   TB/3010
JOHN B. WOLF: France: 1814-1919: The Rise of a Liberal-
Democratic Society   TB/3019

Intellectual History & History of Ideas

HERSCHEL BAKER: The Image of Man: A Study of the
Idea of Human Dignity in Classical Antiquity, the
Middle Ages, and the Renaissance   TB/1047
R. R. BOLGAR: The Classical Heritage and Its Benefici-
aries: From the Carolingian Age to the End of the
Renaissance △   TB/1125
RANDOLPH S. BOURNE: War and the Intellectuals: Col-
lected Essays, 1915-1919. △ ‡ Edited by Carl Resek
          TB/3043
J. BRONOWSKI & BRUCE MAZLISH: The Western Intellectual
Tradition: From Leonardo to Hegel △   TB/3001
ERNST CASSIRER: The Individual and the Cosmos in
Renaissance Philosophy. △ Translated with an Intro-
duction by Mario Domandi   TB/1097
NORMAN COHN: The Pursuit of the Millennium: Revo-
lutionary Messianism in Medieval and Reformation
Europe △   TB/1037
C. C. GILLISPIE: Genesis and Geology: The Decades be-
fore Darwin §   TB/51
G. RACHEL LEVY: Religious Conceptions of the Stone Age
and Their Influence upon European Thought. △ Illus.
Introduction by Henri Frankfort   TB/106
ARTHUR O. LOVEJOY: The Great Chain of Being: A Study
of the History of an Idea   TB/1009
FRANK E. MANUEL: The Prophets of Paris: Turgot, Con-
dorcet, Saint-Simon, Fourier, and Comte △   TB/1218
PERRY MILLER & T. H. JOHNSON, Editors: The Puritans: A
Sourcebook of Their Writings
          Vol. I TB/1093; Vol. II TB/1094
RALPH BARTON PERRY: The Thought and Character of
William James: Briefer Version   TB/1156
GEORG SIMMEL et al.: Essays on Sociology, Philosophy,
and Aesthetics. ¶ Edited by Kurt H. Wolff   TB/1234
BRUNO SNELL: The Discovery of the Mind: The Greek
Origins of European Thought △   TB/1018
PAGET TOYNBEE: Dante Alighieri: His Life and Works.
Edited with Intro. by Charles S. Singleton △ TB/1206
W. WARREN WAGAR, Ed.: European Intellectual History
since Darwin and Marx   TB/1297
PHILIP P. WIENER: Evolution and the Founders of Prag-
matism. △ Foreword by John Dewey   TB/1212
BASIL WILLEY: Nineteenth Century Studies: Coleridge to
Matthew Arnold ° △   TB/1261
BASIL WILLEY: More Nineteenth Century Studies: A
Group of Honest Doubters ° △   TB/1262

Law

EDWARD S. CORWIN: American Constitutional History:
Essays edited by Alpheus T. Mason & Gerald Garvey
          TB/1136
ROBERT H. JACKSON: The Supreme Court in the Ameri-
can System of Government   TB/1106
LEONARD W. LEVY, Ed.: American Constitutional Law:
Historical Essays   TB/1285
LEONARD W. LEVY: Freedom of Speech and Press in Early
American History: Legacy of Suppression   TB/1109
LEONARD W. LEVY, Ed.: Judicial Review and the Supreme
Court   TB/1296
LEONARD W. LEVY: The Law of the Commonwealth and
Chief Justice Shaw   TB/1309
RICHARD B. MORRIS: Fair Trial: Fourteen Who Stood Ac-
cused, from Anne Hutchinson to Alger Hiss. New
Preface by the Author.   TB/1335

Literature, Poetry, The Novel & Criticism

JAMES BAIRD: Ishmael: The Art of Melville in the Con-
texts of International Primitivism   TB/1023
JACQUES BARZUN: The House of Intellect △   TB/1051
W. J. BATE: From Classic to Romantic: Premises of Taste
in Eighteenth Century England   TB/1036
RACHEL BESPALOFF: On the Iliad   TB/2006
JAMES BOSWELL: The Life of Dr. Johnson & The Journal
of a Tour to the Hebrides with Samuel Johnson
LL.D.: Selections. ° △ Edited by F. V. Morley. Illus. by
Ernest Shepard   TB/1254
ERNST R. CURTIUS: European Literature and the Latin
Middle Ages △   TB/2015
ADOLF ERMAN, Ed.: The Ancient Egyptians: A Source-
book of Their Writings. New Material and Introduc-
tion by William Kelly Simpson   TB/1233
ALFRED HARBAGE: As They Liked It: A Study of Shakes-
peare's Moral Artistry   TB/1035
STANLEY R. HOPPER, Ed : Spiritual Problems in Con-
temporary Literature §   TB/21
A. R. HUMPHREYS: The Augustan World: Society,
Thought and Letters in 18th Century England ° △
          TB/1105
ARNOLD KETTLE: An Introduction to the English Novel. △
Volume I: Defoe to George Eliot   TB/1011
Volume II: Henry James to the Present   TB/1012
RICHMOND LATTIMORE: The Poetry of Greek Tragedy △
          TB/1257
J. B. LEISHMAN: The Monarch of Wit: An Analytical and
Comparative Study of the Poetry of John Donne ° △
          TB/1258
J. B. LEISHMAN: Themes and Variations in Shakespeare's
Sonnets ° △   TB/1259
ROGER SHERMAN LOOMIS: The Development of Arthurian
Romance △   TB/1167
JOHN STUART MILL: On Bentham and Coleridge. △ Intro-
duction by F. R. Leavis   TB/1070
KENNETH B. MURDOCK: Literature and Theology in
Colonial New England   TB/99
SAMUEL PEPYS: The Diary of Samuel Pepys. ° Edited by
O. F. Morshead. Illus. by Ernest Shepard   TB/1007
ST.-JOHN PERSE: Seamarks   TB/2002
V. DE S. PINTO: Crisis in English Poetry, 1880-1940 °
          TB/1260
ROBERT PREYER, Ed.: Victorian Literature   TB/1302
GEORGE SANTAYANA: Interpretations of Poetry and Re-
ligion §   TB/9
C. K. STEAD: The New Poetic: Yeats to Eliot △   TB/1263
HEINRICH STRAUMANN: American Literature in the
Twentieth Century. △ Third Edition, Revised TB/1168
PAGET TOYNBEE: Dante Alighieri: His Life and Works.
Edited with Intro. by Charles S. Singleton △ TB/1206
DOROTHY VAN GHENT: The English Novel: Form and
Function   TB/1050
BASIL WILLEY: Nineteenth Century Studies: Coleridge to
Matthew Arnold △   TB/1261
BASIL WILLEY: More Nineteenth Century Studies: A
Group of Honest Doubters ° △   TB/1262
RAYMOND WILLIAMS: Culture and Society, 1780-1950 ° △
          TB/1252
RAYMOND WILLIAMS: The Long Revolution. ° △ Revised
Edition   TB/1253
MORTON DAUWEN ZABEL, Editor: Literary Opinion in
America   Vol. I TB/3013; Vol. II TB/3014

Myth, Symbol & Folklore

MIRCEA ELIADE: Cosmos and History: The Myth of the
Eternal Return § △   TB/2050
MIRCEA ELIADE: Rites and Symbols of Initiation: The
Mysteries of Birth and Rebirth § △   TB/1236
THEODOR H. GASTER: Thespis: Ritual, Myth and Drama
in the Ancient Near East △   TB/1281

C. G. JUNG & C. KERÉNYI: Essays on a Science of Mythology: *The Myths of the Divine Child and the Divine Maiden* TB/2014

DORA & ERWIN PANOFSKY : Pandora's Box: *The Changing Aspects of a Mythical Symbol.* △ *Revised edition. Illus.* TB/2021

ERWIN PANOFSKY: Studies in Iconology: *Humanistic Themes in the Art of the Renaissance.* △ *180 illustrations* TB/1077

JEAN SEZNEC: The Survival of the Pagan Gods: *The Mythological Tradition and its Place in Renaissance Humanism and Art.* △ *108 illustrations* TB/2004

HELLMUT WILHELM: Change: *Eight Lectures on the I Ching* △ TB/2019

HEINRICH ZIMMER: Myths and Symbols in Indian Art and Civilization. △ *70 illustrations* TB/2005

Philosophy

G. E. M. ANSCOMBE: An Introduction to Wittgenstein's Tractatus. ° △ *Second Edition, Revised* TB/1210

HENRI BERGSON: Time and Free Will: *An Essay on the Immediate Data of Consciousness* ° △ TB/1021

H. J. BLACKHAM: Six Existentialist Thinkers: *Kierkegaard, Nietzsche, Jaspers, Marcel, Heidegger, Sartre* ° △ TB/1002

CRANE BRINTON: Nietzsche. *New Preface, Bibliography and Epilogue by the Author* TB/1197

MARTIN BUBER: The Knowledge of Man. △ *Ed. with an Intro. by Maurice Friedman. Trans. by Maurice Friedman and Ronald Gregor Smith* TB/135

ERNST CASSIRER: The Individual and the Cosmos in Renaissance Philosophy. △ *Translated with an Introduction by Mario Domandi* TB/1097

ERNST CASSIRER: Rousseau, Kant and Goethe. *Introduction by Peter Gay* TB/1092

FREDERICK COPLESTON: Medieval Philosophy ° △ TB/376

F. M. CORNFORD: Principium Sapientiae: *A Study of the Origins of Greek Philosophical Thought. Edited by W. K. C. Guthrie* TB/1213

F. M. CORNFORD: From Religion to Philosophy: *A Study in the Origins of Western Speculation* § TB/20

WILFRID DESAN: The Tragic Finale: *An Essay on the Philosophy of Jean-Paul Sartre* TB/1030

A. P. D'ENTRÈVES: Natural Law: *An Historical Survey* △ TB/1223

MARVIN FARBER: The Aims of Phenomenology: *The Motives, Methods, and Impact of Husserl's Thought* TB/1291

MARVIN FARBER: Phenomenology and Existence: *Towards a Philosophy within Nature* TB/1295

HERBERT FINGARETTE: The Self in Transformation: *Psychoanalysis, Philosophy and the Life of the Spirit* ¶ TB/1177

PAUL FRIEDLÄNDER: Plato: *An Introduction* △ TB/2017

J. GLENN GRAY: The Warriors: *Reflections on Men in Battle. Intro. by Hannah Arendt* TB/1294

WILLIAM CHASE GREENE: Moira: *Fate, Good, and Evil in Greek Thought* TB/1104

W. K. C. GUTHRIE: The Greek Philosophers: *From Thales to Aristotle* ° △ TB/1008

G. W. F. HEGEL: The Phenomenology of Mind ° △ TB/1303

F. H. HEINEMANN: Existentialism and the Modern Predicament △ TB/28

ISAAC HUSIK: A History of Medieval Jewish Philosophy JP/3

EDMUND HUSSERL: Phenomenology and the Crisis of Philosophy. *Translated with an Introduction by Quentin Lauer* TB/1170

IMMANUEL KANT: The Doctrine of Virtue, *being Part II of the Metaphysic of Morals. Trans. with Notes & Intro. by Mary J. Gregor. Foreword by H. J. Paton* TB/110

IMMANUEL KANT: Groundwork of the Metaphysic of Morals. *Trans. & analyzed by H. J. Paton* TB/1159

IMMANUEL KANT: Lectures on Ethics. § △ *Introduction by Lewis W. Beck* TB/105

IMMANUEL KANT: Religion Within the Limits of Reason Alone. § *Intro. by T. M. Greene & J. Silber* TB/67

QUENTIN LAUER: Phenomenology: *Its Genesis and Prospect* TB/1169

MAURICE MANDELBAUM: The Problem of Historical Knowledge: *An Answer to Relativism. New Preface by the Author* TB/1338

GABRIEL MARCEL: Being and Having: *An Existential Diary.* △ *Intro. by James Collins* TB/310

GEORGE A. MORGAN: What Nietzsche Means TB/1198

H. J. PATON: The Categorical Imperative: *A Study in Kant's Moral Philosophy* △ TB/1325

PHILO, SAADYA GAON, & JEHUDA HALEVI: Three Jewish Philosophers. *Ed. by Hans Lewy, Alexander Altmann, &Isaak Heinemann* TB/813

MICHAEL POLANYI: Personal Knowledge: *Towards a Post-Critical Philosophy* △ TB/1158

WILLARD VAN ORMAN QUINE: Elementary Logic: *Revised Edition* TB/577

WILLARD VAN ORMAN QUINE: From a Logical Point of View: *Logico-Philosophical Essays* TB/566

BERTRAND RUSSELL et al.: The Philosophy of Bertrand Russell. *Edited by Paul Arthur Schilpp*
Vol. I TB/1095; Vol. II TB/1096

L. S. STEBBING: A Modern Introduction to Logic △ TB/538

ALFRED NORTH WHITEHEAD: Process and Reality: *An Essay in Cosmology* △ TB/1033

PHILIP P. WIENER: Evolution and the Founders of Pragmatism. *Foreword by John Dewey* TB/1212

WILHELM WINDELBAND: A History of Philosophy
Vol. I: *Greek, Roman, Medieval* TB/38
Vol. II: *Renaissance, Enlightenment, Modern* TB/39

LUDWIG WITTGENSTEIN: The Blue and Brown Books ° TB/1211

Political Science & Government

JEREMY BENTHAM: The Handbook of Political Fallacies: *Introduction by Crane Brinton* TB/1069

C. E. BLACK: The Dynamics of Modernization: *A Study in Comparative History* TB/1321

KENNETH E. BOULDING: Conflict and Defense: *A General Theory* TB/3024

CRANE BRINTON: English Political Thought in the Nineteenth Century TB/1071

ROBERT CONQUEST: Power and Policy in the USSR: *The Study of Soviet Dynastics* △ TB/1307

EDWARD S. CORWIN: American Constitutional History: *Essays edited by Alpheus T. Mason and Gerald Garvey* TB/1136

ROBERT DAHL & CHARLES E. LINDBLOM: Politics, Economics, and Welfare: *Planning and Politico-Economic Systems Resolved into Basic Social Processes* TB/3037

JOHN NEVILLE FIGGIS: The Divine Right of Kings. *Introduction by G. R. Elton* TB/1191

JOHN NEVILLE FIGGIS: Political Thought from Gerson to Grotius: 1414-1625: *Seven Studies. Introduction by Garrett Mattingly* TB/1032

F. L. GANSHOF: Feudalism △ TB/1058

G. P. GOOCH: English Democratic Ideas in the Seventeenth Century TB/1006

J. H. HEXTER: More's Utopia: *The Biography of an Idea. New Epilogue by the Author* TB/1195

SIDNEY HOOK: Reason, Social Myths and Democracy △ TB/1237

ROBERT H. JACKSON: The Supreme Court in the American System of Government △ TB/1106

DAN N. JACOBS, Ed.: The New Communist Manifesto *and Related Documents. Third Edition, Revised* TB/1078

DAN N. JACOBS & HANS BAERWALD, Eds.: Chinese Communism: *Selected Documents* TB/3031

7

HANS KOHN: Political Ideologies of the 20th Century
TB/1277

ROY C. MACRIDIS, Ed.: Political Parties: *Contemporary Trends and Ideas* TB/1322

ROBERT GREEN MC CLOSKEY: American Conservatism in the Age of Enterprise, 1865-1910 TB/1137

KINGSLEY MARTIN: French Liberal Thought in the Eighteenth Century: *Political Ideas from Bayle to Condorcet* △ TB/1114

ROBERTO MICHELS: First Lectures in Political Sociology. *Edited by Alfred de Grazia* ¶ ° TB/1224

JOHN STUART MILL: On Bentham and Coleridge. △ *Introduction by F. R. Leavis* TB/1070

BARRINGTON MOORE, JR.: Political Power and Social Theory: *Seven Studies* ¶ TB/1221

BARRINGTON MOORE, JR.: Soviet Politics—The Dilemma of Power: *The Role of Ideas in Social Change* ¶
TB/1222

BARRINGTON MOORE, JR.: Terror and Progress—USSR: *Some Sources of Change and Stability in the Soviet Dictatorship* ¶ TB/1266

JOHN B. MORRALL: Political Thought in Medieval Times △ TB/1076

JOHN PLAMENATZ: German Marxism and Russian Communism. ° △ *New Preface by the Author* TB/1189

KARL R. POPPER: The Open Society and Its Enemies △
Vol. I: *The Spell of Plato* TB/1101
Vol. II: *The High Tide of Prophecy: Hegel, Marx and the Aftermath* TB/1102

JOHN P. ROCHE, Ed.: American Political Thought: *From Jefferson to Progressivism* TB/1332

HENRI DE SAINT-SIMON: Social Organization, The Science of Man, and Other Writings. *Edited and Translated by Felix Markham* TB/1152

CHARLES I. SCHOTTLAND, Ed.: The Welfare State TB/1323

JOSEPH A. SCHUMPETER: Capitalism, Socialism and Democracy △ TB/3008

BENJAMIN I. SCHWARTZ: Chinese Communism and the Rise of Mao TB/1308

CHARLES H. SHINN: Mining Camps: *A Study in American Frontier Government.* ‡ *Edited by Rodman W. Paul*
TB/3062

PETER WOLL, Ed.: Public Administration and Policy: *Selected Essays* TB/1284

Psychology

ALFRED ADLER: The Individual Psychology of Alfred Adler. △ *Edited by Heinz L. and Rowena R. Ansbacher*
TB/1154

ALFRED ADLER: Problems of Neurosis. *Introduction by Heinz L. Ansbacher* TB/1145

ARTHUR BURTON & ROBERT E. HARRIS, Eds.: Clinical Studies of Personality
Vol. I TB/3075; Vol. II TB/3076

HADLEY CANTRIL: The Invasion from Mars: *A Study in the Psychology of Panic* ¶ TB/1282

HERBERT FINGARETTE: The Self in Transformation: *Psychoanalysis, Philosophy and the Life of the Spirit* ¶
TB/1177

SIGMUND FREUD: On Creativity and the Unconscious: *Papers on the Psychology of Art, Literature, Love, Religion.* § △ *Intro. by Benjamin Nelson* TB/45

C. JUDSON HERRICK: The Evolution of Human Nature
TB/545

WILLIAM JAMES: Psychology: *The Briefer Course. Edited with an Intro. by Gordon Allport* TB/1034

C. G. JUNG: Psychological Reflections △ TB/2001

C. G. JUNG: Symbols of Transformation: *An Analysis of the Prelude to a Case of Schizophrenia.* △ *Illus.*
Vol. I TB/2009; Vol. II TB/2010

C. G. JUNG & C. KERÉNYI: Essays on a Science of Mythology: *The Myths of the Divine Child and the Divine Maiden* TB/2014

KARL MENNINGER: Theory of Psychoanalytic Technique
TB/1144

ERICH NEUMANN: Amor and Psyche: *The Psychic Development of the Feminine* △ TB/2012

ERICH NEUMANN: The Archetypal World of Henry Moore. △ *107 illus.* TB/2020

ERICH NEUMANN: The Origins and History of Consciousness △ Vol. I *Illus.* TB/2007; Vol. II TB/2008

RALPH BARTON PERRY: The Thought and Character of William James: *Briefer Version* TB/1156

JOHN H. SCHAAR: Escape from Authority: *The Perspectives of Erich Fromm* TB/1155

MUZAFER SHERIF: The Psychology of Social Norms
TB/3072

Sociology

JACQUES BARZUN: Race: *A Study in Superstition. Revised Edition* TB/1172

BERNARD BERELSON, Ed.: The Behavioral Sciences Today
TB/1127

ABRAHAM CAHAN: The Rise of David Levinsky: *A documentary novel of social mobility in early twentieth century America. Intro. by John Higham* TB/1028

KENNETH B. CLARK: Dark Ghetto: *Dilemmas of Social Power. Foreword by Gunnar Myrdal* TB/1317

LEWIS A. COSER, Ed.: Political Sociology TB/1293

ALLISON DAVIS & JOHN DOLLARD: Children of Bondage: *The Personality Development of Negro Youth in the Urban South* ¶ TB/3049

ST. CLAIR DRAKE & HORACE R. CAYTON: Black Metropolis: *A Study of Negro Life in a Northern City.* △ *Revised and Enlarged. Intro. by Everett C. Hughes*
Vol. I TB/1086; Vol. II TB/1087

EMILE DURKHEIM et al.: Essays on Sociology and Philosophy: *With Analyses of Durkheim's Life and Work.* ¶ *Edited by Kurt H. Wolff* TB/1151

LEON FESTINGER, HENRY W. RIECKEN & STANLEY SCHACHTER: When Prophecy Fails: *A Social and Psychological Account of a Modern Group that Predicted the Destruction of the World* ¶ TB/1132

ALVIN W. GOULDNER: Wildcat Strike: *A Study in Worker-Management Relationships* ¶ TB/1176

CÉSAR GRAÑA: Modernity and Its Discontents: *French Society and the French Man of Letters in the Nineteenth Century* ¶ TB/1318

FRANCIS J. GRUND: Aristocracy in America: *Social Class in the Formative Years of the New Nation* △ TB/1001

KURT LEWIN: Field Theory in Social Science: *Selected Theoretical Papers.* ¶ △ *Edited with a Foreword by Dorwin Cartwright* TB/1135

R. M. MAC IVER: Social Causation TB/1153

ROBERT K. MERTON, LEONARD BROOM, LEONARD S. COTTRELL, JR., Editors: Sociology Today: *Problems and Prospects* ¶ Vol. I TB/1173; Vol. II TB/1174

ROBERTO MICHELS: First Lectures in Political Sociology. *Edited by Alfred de Grazia* ¶ ° TB/1224

BARRINGTON MOORE, JR.: Political Power and Social Theory: *Seven Studies* ¶ TB/1221

BARRINGTON MOORE, JR.: Soviet Politics—The Dilemma of Power: *The Role of Ideas in Social Change* ¶
TB/1222

TALCOTT PARSONS & EDWARD A. SHILS, Editors: Toward a General Theory of Action: *Theoretical Foundations for the Social Sciences* TB/1083

ARNOLD ROSE: The Negro in America: *The Condensed Version of Gunnar Myrdal's An American Dilemma*
TB/3048

GEORGE ROSEN: Madness in Society: *Chapters in the Historical Sociology of Mental Illness.* ¶ *Preface by Benjamin Nelson* TB/1337

KURT SAMUELSSON: Religion and Economic Action: *A Critique of Max Weber's The Protestant Ethic and the Spirit of Capitalism.* ¶ ° *Trans. by E. G. French. Ed. with Intro. by D. C. Coleman* TB/1131

PHILIP SELZNICK: TVA and the Grass Roots: *A Study in the Sociology of Formal Organization*   TB/1230
GEORG SIMMEL et al.: Essays on Sociology, Philosophy, and Aesthetics. ¶ *Edited by Kurt H. Wolff*   TB/1234
HERBERT SIMON: The Shape of Automation: *For Men and Management* △   TB/1245
PITIRIM A. SOROKIN: Contemporary Sociological Theories. *Through the First Quarter of the 20th Century* TB/3046
MAURICE R. STEIN: The Eclipse of Community: *An Interpretation of American Studies*   TB/1128
WILLIAM I. THOMAS: The Unadjusted Girl: *With Cases and Standpoint for Behavior Analysis.* ¶ *New Intro. by Michael Parenti*   TB/1319
EDWARD A. TIRYAKIAN, Ed.: Sociological Theory, Values and Sociocultural Change: *Essays in Honor of Pitirim A. Sorokin* ¶ △ ○   TB/1316
FERDINAND TÖNNIES: Community and Society: *Gemeinschaft und Gesellschaft. Translated and edited by Charles P. Loomis*   TB/1116
W. LLOYD WARNER & Associates: Democracy in Jonesville: *A Study in Quality and Inequality*   TB/1129
W. LLOYD WARNER: Social Class in America: *The Evaluation of Status*   TB/1013

RELIGION

Ancient & Classical

J. H. BREASTED: Development of Religion and Thought in Ancient Egypt. *Intro. by John A. Wilson*   TB/57
HENRI FRANKFORT: Ancient Egyptian Religion: *An Interpretation*   TB/77
G. RACHEL LEVY: Religious Conceptions of the Stone Age and their Influence upon European Thought. △ *Illus. Introduction by Henri Frankfort*   TB/106
MARTIN P. NILSSON: Greek Folk Religion. *Foreword by Arthur Darby Nock*   TB/78
ALEXANDRE PIANKOFF: The Shrines of Tut-Ankh-Amon. △ *Edited by N. Rambova. 117 illus.*   TB/2011
ERWIN ROHDE: Psyche: *The Cult of Souls and Belief in Immortality Among the Greeks.* △ *Intro. by W. K. C. Guthrie*   Vol. I TB/140; Vol. II TB/141
H. J. ROSE: Religion in Greece and Rome △   TB/55

Biblical Thought & Literature

W. F. ALBRIGHT: The Biblical Period from Abraham to Ezra   TB/102
C. K. BARRETT, Ed.: The New Testament Background: *Selected Documents* △   TB/86
C. H. DODD: The Authority of the Bible △   TB/43
M. S. ENSLIN: Christian Beginnings △   TB/5
M. S. ENSLIN: The Literature of the Christian Movement △   TB/6
JOHN GRAY: Archaeology and the Old Testament World. △ *Illus.*   TB/127
JAMES MUILENBURG: The Way of Israel: *Biblical Faith and Ethics* △   TB/133
H. H. ROWLEY: The Growth of the Old Testament △   TB/107
GEORGE ADAM SMITH: The Historical Geography of the Holy Land. ○ △ *Revised and reset*   TB/138
D. WINTON THOMAS, Ed.: Documents from Old Testament Times △   TB/85
WALTHER ZIMMERLI: The Law and the Prophets: *A Study of the Meaning of the Old Testament* △   TB/144

The Judaic Tradition

LEO BAECK: Judaism and Christianity. *Trans. with Intro. by Walter Kaufmann*   TB/823
SALO W. BARON: Modern Nationalism and Religion   TB/818
MARTIN BUBER: Eclipse of God: *Studies in the Relation Between Religion and Philosophy* △   TB/12

MARTIN BUBER: For the Sake of Heaven   TB/801
MARTIN BUBER: Hasidism and Modern Man. △ *Ed. and Trans. by Maurice Friedman*   TB/839
MARTIN BUBER: The Knowledge of Man. △ *Edited with an Introduction by Maurice Friedman. Translated by Maurice Friedman and Ronald Gregor Smith*   TB/135
MARTIN BUBER: Moses: *The Revelation and the Covenant* △   TB/837
MARTIN BUBER: The Origin and Meaning of Hasidism △   TB/835
MARTIN BUBER: Pointing the Way. △ *Introduction by Maurice S. Friedman*   TB/103
MARTIN BUBER: The Prophetic Faith   TB/73
MARTIN BUBER: Two Types of Faith: *the interpenetration of Judaism and Christianity* ○ △   TB/75
ERNST LUDWIG EHRLICH: A Concise History of Israel: *From the Earliest Times to the Destruction of the Temple in A.D. 70* ○ △   TB/128
MAURICE S. FRIEDMAN: Martin Buber: *The Life of Dialogue* △   TB/64
GENESIS: The NJV Translation   TB/836
SOLOMON GRAYZEL: A History of the Contemporary Jews   TB/816
WILL HERBERG: Judaism and Modern Man   TB/810
ARTHUR HERTZBERG: The Zionist Idea   TB/817
ABRAHAM J. HESCHEL: God in Search of Man: *A Philosophy of Judaism*   TB/807
ISAAC HUSIK: A History of Medieval Jewish Philosophy   TB/803
JACOB R. MARCUS: The Jew in the Medieval World TB/814
MAX L. MARGOLIS & ALEXANDER MARX: A History of the Jewish People   TB/806
T. J. MEEK: Hebrew Origins   TB/69
JAMES PARKES: The Conflict of the Church and the Synagogue: *The Jews and Early Christianity*   TB/821
PHILO, SAADYA GAON, & JEHUDA HALEVI: Three Jewish Philosophers. *Ed. by Hans Lewey, Alexander Altmann, & Isaak Heinemann*   TB/813
CECIL ROTH: A History of the Marranos   TB/812
CECIL ROTH: The Jews in the Renaissance. *Illus.*   TB/834
HERMAN L. STRACK: Introduction to the Talmud and Midrash   TB/808
JOSHUA TRACHTENBERG: The Devil and the Jews: *The Medieval Conception of the Jew and its Relation to Modern Anti-Semitism*   TB/822

Christianity: General

ROLAND H. BAINTON: Christendom: *A Short History of Christianity and its Impact on Western Civilization.* △ *Illus.*   Vol. I TB/131; Vol. II TB/132

Christianity: Origins & Early Development

AUGUSTINE: An Augustine Synthesis. △ *Edited by Erich Przywara*   TB/335
W. D. DAVIES: Paul and Rabbinic Judaism: *Some Rabbinic Elements in Pauline Theology. New Intro. by the Author* △ ○   TB/146
ADOLF DEISSMANN: Paul: *A Study in Social and Religious History*   TB/15
EDWARD GIBBON: The Triumph of Christendom in the Roman Empire *(Chaps. XV-XX of "Decline and Fall," J. B. Bury edition).* § △ *Illus.*   TB/46
EDGAR J. GOODSPEED: A Life of Jesus   TB/1
ROBERT M. GRANT: Gnosticism and Early Christianity. △ *Revised Edition*   TB/136
ADOLF HARNACK: The Mission and Expansion of Christianity in the First Three Centuries. *Introduction by Jaroslav Pelikan*   TB/92
R. K. HARRISON: The Dead Sea Scrolls : *An Introduction* ○ △   TB/84
EDWIN HATCH: The Influence of Greek Ideas on Christianity. § △ *Introduction and Bibliography by Frederick C. Grant*   TB/18

9

GERHART B. LADNER: The Idea of Reform: *Its Impact on Christian Thought and Action in the Age of the Fathers*   TB/149
ARTHUR DARBY NOCK: Early Gentile Christianity and Its Hellenistic Background   TB/111
ARTHUR DARBY NOCK: St. Paul ○ △   TB/104
ORIGEN: On First Principles. △ Edited by G. W. Butterworth. *Introduction by Henri de Lubac*   TB/311
JAMES PARKES: The Conflict of the Church and the Synagogue: *The Jews and Early Christianity*   TB/821
SULPICIUS SEVERUS et al.: The Western Fathers: *Being the Lives of Martin of Tours, Ambrose, Augustine of Hippo, Honoratus of Arles and Germanus of Auxerre.* △ *Edited and translated by F. R. Hoare*   TB/309
JOHANNES WEISS: Earliest Christianity: *A History of the Period A.D. 30-150. Introduction and Bibliography by Frederick C. Grant*   Volume I TB/53
                                                                       Volume II TB/54

Christianity: The Middle Ages and The Reformation

ANSELM OF CANTERBURY: Truth, Freedom and Evil: *Three Philosophical Dialogues. Ed., trans., and Intro. by Jasper Hopkins & Herbert Richardson*   TB/317
JOHN CALVIN & JACOPO SADOLETO: A Reformation Debate. *Edited by John C. Olin*   TB/1239
G. CONSTANT: The Reformation in England: *The English Schism, Henry VIII, 1509-1547* △   TB/314
CHRISTOPHER DAWSON, Ed.: Mission to Asia: *Narratives and Letters of the Franciscan Missionaries in Mongolia and China in the 13th and 14th Centuries* △
                                                                                       TB/315
JOHANNES ECKHART: Meister Eckhart: *A Modern Translation by R. B. Blakney*   TB/8
DESIDERIUS ERASMUS: Christian Humanism and the Reformation: *Selected Writings. Edited and translated by John C. Olin*   TB/1166
ÉTIENNE GILSON: Dante and Philosophy △   TB/1089
WILLIAM HALLER: The Rise of Puritanism △   TB/22
HAJO HOLBORN: Ulrich von Hutten and the German Reformation   TB/1238
JOHAN HUIZINGA: Erasmus and the Age of Reformation. △ *Illus.*   TB/19
A. C. MC GIFFERT: Protestant Thought Before Kant △ *Preface by Jaroslav Pelikan*   TB/93
JOHN T. MC NEILL: Makers of the Christian Tradition: *From Alfred the Great to Schleiermacher* △   TB/121
G. MOLLAT: The Popes at Avignon, 1305-1378 △   TB/308
GORDON RUPP: Luther's Progress to the Diet of Worms ○ △   TB/120

Christianity: The Protestant Tradition

KARL BARTH: Church Dogmatics: *A Selection* △   TB/95
KARL BARTH: Dogmatics in Outline △   TB/56
KARL BARTH: The Word of God and the Word of Man
                                                                                        TB/13
RUDOLF BULTMANN et al: Translating Theology into the Modern Age: *Historical, Systematic and Pastoral Reflections on Theology and the Church in the Contemporary Situation. Volume 2 of Journal for Theology and the Church, edited by Robert W. Funk in association with Gerhard Ebeling*   TB/252
WHITNEY R. CROSS: The Burned-Over District: *The Social and Intellectual History of Enthusiastic Religion in Western New York, 1800-1850* △   TB/1242
NELS F. S. FERRÉ: Swedish Contributions to Modern Theology. *New Preface by the Author. Additional chapter by William A. Johnson*   TB/147
ERNST KÄSEMANN, et al.: Distinctive Protestant and Catholic Themes Reconsidered. *Volume 3 of Journal for Theology and the Church, edited by Robert W. Funk in association with Gerhard Ebeling*   TB/253

SOREN KIERKEGAARD: On Authority and Revelation: *The Book on Adler. Translated by Walter Lowrie. Intro. by Frederick Sontag*   TB/139
SOREN KIERKEGAARD: Crisis in the Life of an Actress *and Other Essays on Drama.* △ *Trans. with Intro. by Stephen D. Crites*   TB/145
SOREN KIERKEGAARD: Edifying Discourses. *Edited with an Introduction by Paul Holmer*   TB/32
SOREN KIERKEGAARD: The Journals of Kierkegaard. ○ △ *Ed. with Intro. by Alexander Dru*   TB/52
SOREN KIERKEGAARD: The Point of View for My Work as an Author: *A Report to History.* § *Preface by Benjamin Nelson*   TB/88
SOREN KIERKEGAARD: The Present Age. § △ *Translated and edited by Alexander Dru. Introduction by Walter Kaufmann*   TB/94
SOREN KIERKEGAARD: Purity of Heart △   TB/4
SOREN KIERKEGAARD: Repetition: *An Essay in Experimental Psychology.* △ *Translated with Introduction & Notes by Walter Lowrie*   TB/117
SOREN KIERKEGAARD: Works of Love: *Some Christian Reflections in the Form of Discourses* △   TB/122
WALTER LOWRIE: Kierkegaard: *A Life*   Vol. I TB/89
                                                                    Vol. II TB/90
JOHN MACQUARRIE: The Scope of Demythologizing: *Bultmann and His Critics* △   TB/134
PERRY MILLER & T. H. JOHNSON, Editors: The Puritans: *A Sourcebook of Their Writings*   Vol. I TB/1093
                                                                     Vol. II TB/1094
WOLFHART PANNENBERG, et al.: History and Hermeneutic. *Volume 4 of Journal for Theology and the Church, edited by Robert W. Funk in association with Gerhard Ebeling*   TB/254
JAMES M. ROBINSON et al.: The Bultmann School of Biblical Interpretation: New Directions? *Volume 1 of Journal for Theology and the Church, edited by Robert W. Funk in association with Gerhard Ebeling*
                                                                                       TB/251
F. SCHLEIERMACHER: The Christian Faith. △ *Introduction by Richard R. Niebuhr*   Vol. I TB/108
                                                                    Vol. II TB/109
F. SCHLEIERMACHER: On Religion: *Speeches to Its Cultured Despisers. Intro. by Rudolf Otto*   TB/36
TIMOTHY L. SMITH: Revivalism and Social Reform: *American Protestantism on the Eve of the Civil War*
                                                                                       TB/1229
PAUL TILLICH: Dynamics of Faith △   TB/42
PAUL TILLICH: Morality and Beyond   TB/142
EVELYN UNDERHILL: Worship △   TB/10

Christianity: The Roman and Eastern Traditions

DOM CUTHBERT BUTLER: Western Mysticism: *The Teaching of Augustine, Gregory and Bernard on Contemplation and the Contemplative Life* § ○ △   TB/312
A. ROBERT CAPONIGRI, Ed.: Modern Catholic Thinkers I: *God and Man* △   TB/306
A. ROBERT CAPONIGRI, Ed.: Modern Catholic Thinkers II: *The Church and the Political Order*△   TB/307
THOMAS CORBISHLEY, S.J.: Roman Catholicism △   TB/112
CHRISTOPHER DAWSON: The Historic Reality of Christian Culture   TB/305
G. P. FEDOTOV: The Russian Religious Mind: *Kievan Christianity, the 10th to the 13th centuries* △   TB/370
ÉTIENNE GILSON: The Spirit of Thomism   TB/313
GABRIEL MARCEL: Being and Having: *An Existential Diary.* △ *Introduction by James Collins*   TB/310
GABRIEL MARCEL: Homo Viator: *Introduction to a Metaphysic of Hope* △   TB/397
FRANCIS DE SALES: Introduction to the Devout Life. *Trans. by John K. Ryan*   TB/316
GUSTAVE WEIGEL, S. J.: Catholic Theology in Dialogue
                                                                                       TB/301

Oriental Religions: Far Eastern, Near Eastern

TOR ANDRAE: Mohammed: The Man and His Faith △
TB/62
EDWARD CONZE: Buddhism: Its Essence and Development. ° △ Foreword by Arthur Waley TB/58
EDWARD CONZE et al., Editors: Buddhist Texts Through the Ages △ TB/113
ANANDA COOMARASWAMY: Buddha and the Gospel of Buddhism. △ Illus. TB/119
H. G. CREEL: Confucius and the Chinese Way TB/63
FRANKLIN EDGERTON, Trans. & Ed.: The Bhagavad Gita
TB/115
SWAMI NIKHILANANDA, Trans. & Ed.: The Upanishads: A One-Volume Abridgment △ TB/114
HELLMUT WILHELM: Change: Eight Lectures on the I Ching △ TB/2019

Philosophy of Religion

NICOLAS BERDYAEV: The Beginning and the End § △ TB/14
NICOLAS BERDYAEV: Christian Existentialism: A Berdyaev Synthesis. △ Ed. by Donald A. Lowrie TB/130
NICOLAS BERDYAEV: The Destiny of Man △ TB/61
RUDOLF BULTMANN: History and Eschatology: The Presence of Eternity ° TB/91
RUDOLF BULTMANN AND FIVE CRITICS: Kerygma and Myth: A Theological Debate △ TB/80
RUDOLF BULTMANN and KARL KUNDSIN: Form Criticism: Two Essays on New Testament Research. △ Translated by Frederick C. Grant TB/96
MIRCEA ELIADE: Myths, Dreams, and Mysteries: The Encounter between Contemporary Faiths and Archaic Realities § △ ° TB/1320
MIRCEA ELIADE: The Sacred and the Profane TB/81
LUDWIG FEUERBACH: The Essence of Christianity. § Introduction by Karl Barth. Foreword by H. Richard Niebuhr TB/11
ÉTIENNE GILSON: The Spirit of Thomism TB/313
ADOLF HARNACK: What is Christianity? § △ Introduction by Rudolf Bultmann TB/17
FRIEDRICH HEGEL: On Christianity: Early Theological Writings. Ed. by R. Kroner and T. M. Knox TB/79
KARL HEIM: Christian Faith and Natural Science △ TB/16
IMMANUEL KANT: Religion Within the Limits of Reason Alone. § Intro. by T. M. Greene & J. Silber TB/67
K. E. KIRK: The Vision of God: The Christian Doctrine of the Summum Bonum § △ TB/137
JOHN MACQUARRIE: An Existentialist Theology: A Comparison of Heidegger and Bultmann. ° △ Preface by Rudolf Bultmann TB/125
PAUL RAMSEY, Ed.: Faith and Ethics: The Theology of H. Richard Niebuhr TB/129
EUGEN ROSENSTOCK-HUESSY: The Christian Future or the Modern Mind Outrun. Intro. by Harold Stahmer
TB/143
PIERRE TEILHARD DE CHARDIN: The Divine Milieu ° △
TB/384
PIERRE TEILHARD DE CHARDIN: The Phenomenon of Man ° △ TB/383

Religion, Culture & Society

JOSEPH L. BLAU, Ed.: Cornerstones of Religious Freedom in America: Selected Basic Documents, Court Decisions and Public Statements. Revised and Enlarged Edition TB/118
WILLIAM A. CLEBSCH & CHARLES R. JAEKLE: Pastoral Care in Historical Perspective: An Essay with Exhibits. New Preface by the Authors TB/148
C. C. GILLISPIE: Genesis and Geology: The Decades before Darwin § TB/51
KYLE HASELDEN: The Racial Problem in Christian Perspective TB/116

WALTER KAUFMANN, Ed.: Religion from Tolstoy to Camus: Basic Writings on Religious Truth and Morals. Enlarged Edition TB/123
KENNETH B. MURDOCK: Literature and Theology in Colonial New England TB/99
H. RICHARD NIEBUHR: Christ and Culture △ TB/3
H. RICHARD NIEBUHR: The Kingdom of God in America
TB/49
R. B. PERRY: Puritanism and Democracy TB/1138
PAUL PFUETZE: Self, Society, Existence: Human Nature and Dialogue in the Thought of George Herbert Mead and Martin Buber TB/1059
WALTER RAUSCHENBUSCH: Christianity and the Social Crisis. ‡ Edited by Robert D. Cross TB/3059
KURT SAMUELSSON: Religion and Economic Action: A Critique of Max Weber's The Protestant Ethic and the Spirit of Capitalism ¶ ° △ Trans. by E. G. French. Ed. with Intro. by D. C. Coleman TB/1131
TIMOTHY L. SMITH: Revivalism and Social Reform: American Protestantism on the Eve of the Civil War △
TB/1229

NATURAL SCIENCES AND MATHEMATICS

Biological Sciences

CHARLOTTE AUERBACH: The Science of Genetics Σ △
TB/568
JOHN TYLER BONNER: The Ideas of Biology. Σ △ Illus.
TB/570
A. J. CAIN: Animal Species and their Evolution. △ Illus.
TB/519
W. E. LE GROS CLARK: The Antecedents of Man: An Introduction to Evolution of the Primates. ° △ Illus. TB/559
W. H. DOWDESWELL: Animal Ecology. △ Illus. TB/543
W. H. DOWDESWELL: The Mechanism of Evolution. △ Illus. TB/527
R. W. GERARD: Unresting Cells. Illus. TB/541
J. E. MORTON: Molluscs: An Introduction to Their Form and Functions. Illus. TB/529
P. M. SHEPPARD: Natural Selection and Heredity. △ Illus.
TB/528
EDMUND W. SINNOTT: Cell and Psyche: The Biology of Purpose TB/546
C. H. WADDINGTON: The Nature of Life: The Main Problems and Trends in Modern Biology △ TB/580

Chemistry

J. R. PARTINGTON: A Short History of Chemistry. △ Illus.
TB/522

Communication Theory

J. R. PIERCE: Symbols, Signals and Noise: The Nature and Process of Communication △ TB/574

Geography

R. E. COKER: This Great and Wide Sea: An Introduction to Oceanography and Marine Biology. Illus. TB/551
F. K. HARE: The Restless Atmosphere △ TB/560

History of Science

MARIE BOAS: The Scientific Renaissance, 1450-1630 ° △
TB/583
W. DAMPIER, Ed.: Readings in the Literature of Science. Illus. TB/512
A. HUNTER DUPREE: Science in the Federal Government: A History of Policies and Activities to 1940 △ TB/573
ALEXANDRE KOYRÉ: From the Closed World to the Infinite Universe: Copernicus, Kepler, Galileo, Newton, etc. △
TB/31

A. G. VAN MELSEN: From Atomos to Atom: *A History of the Concept* Atom TB/517

STEPHEN TOULMIN & JUNE GOODFIELD: The Architecture of Matter: *Physics, Chemistry & Physiology of Matter, Both Animate & Inanimate, As it Evolved Since the Beginning of Science* ᵒ △ TB/584

STEPHEN TOULMIN & JUNE GOODFIELD: The Discovery of Time ᵒ △ TB/585

Mathematics

E. W. BETH: The Foundations of Mathematics: *A Study in the Philosophy of Science* △ TB/581

S. KÖRNER: The Philosophy of Mathematics: *An Introduction* △ TB/547

GEORGE E. OWEN: Fundamentals of Scientific Mathematics TB/569

WILLARD VAN ORMAN QUINE: Mathematical Logic TB/558

FREDERICK WAISMANN: Introduction to Mathematical Thinking. *Foreword by Karl Menger* TB/511

Philosophy of Science

R. B. BRAITHWAITE: Scientific Explanation TB/515

J. BRONOWSKI: Science and Human Values. △ *Revised and Enlarged Edition* TB/505

ALBERT EINSTEIN et al.: Albert Einstein: Philosopher-Scientist. *Edited by Paul A. Schilpp* Vol. I TB/502 Vol. II TB/503

WERNER HEISENBERG: Physics and Philosophy: *The Revolution in Modern Science* △ TB/549

KARL R. POPPER: Logic of Scientific Discovery △ TB/576

STEPHEN TOULMIN: Foresight and Understanding: *An Enquiry into the Aims of Science.* △ *Foreword by Jacques Barzun* TB/564

STEPHEN TOULMIN: The Philosophy of Science: *An Introduction* △ TB/513

Physics and Cosmology

JOHN E. ALLEN: Aerodynamics: *A Space Age Survey* △ TB/582

P. W. BRIDGMAN: Nature of Thermodynamics TB/537

C. V. DURELL: Readable Relativity. △ *Foreword by Freeman J. Dyson* TB/530

ARTHUR EDDINGTON: Space, Time and Gravitation: *An Outline of the General Relativity Theory* TB/510

GEORGE GAMOW: Biography of Physics Σ △ TB/567

STEPHEN TOULMIN & JUNE GOODFIELD: The Fabric of the Heavens: *The Development of Astronomy and Dynamics.* △ *Illus.* TB/579